CHRIS H. HARDY

BUTTERFLY LOGIC

EXPERIMENTAL PLANET EARTH

Exopolitics Sci-Fi Series

FOREWORD

I dedicate this book to the researchers on consciousness and the questers for self-knowledge who aim at developing a real synergy with the Living Spirit.

My goal, while writing it, was to highlight that the development of AI didn't need to be done blindly, by projecting on our creations our dire shortcomings in terms of power instinct, will to control, and lethal cravings for the sole financial and political interests of our group or clan. Such an irresponsible research in AI would inevitably make of intelligent machines our competitors and ennemies in the fight for supremacy, whether political or financial—as so many movies have put it into play. To the opposite, this research of mine is setting the stage for a harmonious development of semanticists-AI computers pairs, that could open the way for a mutual enrichment and work as an incentive for a knowledge gain of both parties, taking them through *qualitative leaps*.

These pairs are, in the present book, woven into a collective learning network in which information is constantly exchanged and built upon by all other nodes in the network. Of course this, in my opinion, mirrors the way our minds operate in the deep reality, since, as Carl Jung has shown, we are all communicating and conversing within the collective unconscious.

One crucial question underlying this work is: how to be sure that AI machines, at one point, will not turn against their masters and creators—that is, us? Believe it or not, I had not read any of Asimov works until long after the writing of this book. And thus it was a great surprise that he had also come upon setting core rules for not endangering intelligent beings—*sapiens* species in this book, since we have to make room for other phylums beyond that of the human one. Yet, this, in my view, isn't sufficient in itself. Much more crucial is the building of core values of synergy and partnership aiming at the positive blossoming of talents, whether in sapiens or in AI entities. My bet is that, given such a core set of philosophical and spiritual aims and values interwoven in a fabric, all subsequent development of sapiens and exors (AI entities) will also inevitably maintain a congruence with the core logic+values set at the origin. That would be the absolute opposite to a flawed creation with an original sin at the beginning. To the contrary, we have here a perfect core that can only develop in harmony with this *logical field*, expressing its discoveries and new talents in ever novel advances in technology, concepts, and knowledge.

Did I tell you that I didn't like Asimov at all? No kidding! No step of the machine-learning is ever explained, and thus the sudden add-up of emotions in AI machines falls like a hair in the soup. Far from me that I would allow myself such literary tricks—however, you'll have to bear the price for it: the development of my super exor Sphinx is pinned down step by step, via the evolution of a non-linear logic based on natural processes, whether psychological or organismic.

Why should science not be also fun? (I want mine to be as fun as an exploration.) Why would science not be in harmony with the living, with freedom, with the Earth-Gaia and humanity? Because up to now, science has been all too easily espousing the will for control of the politicians, lobbies, and funding agencies. And why politicians shouldn't be the allies of the development of talents, of psi, and spiritual and psychic qualities in sapiens and societies in the first place? Because they lack imagination about their own realization (the opposite—*l'imagination au pouvoir*—will be the theme of my next book in this Exopolitics Sci-Fi Series: *Diverging Views*).

Beyond this, you'll find plenty of topics dealing with exo-politics and the way aliens have been handling their supervision of humanity, including large scale trafficking, cattle mutilation, and more.

Buckle up: the ride is both fun and arduous, like a complex mental chess game; yet in order to make sure that you get the fun first and save the arduous part for later in-depth readings (or even forget about it), I have highlighted the latter part in gray font, so that you may easily jump above these paragraphs if you feel like it.

Have fun then,

Chris H. Hardy,
Séguret, France, June 11, 2016

CONTENTS

0. HOSTAGE

Ismir was hustled into the room, and his blindfold was at last removed. Armed to the teeth, five Afghan rebels were training their guns on a computer installed on a stack of weapons wooden crates. Their leader, apparently, donning an impeccable white silk robe and headscarf, sat nonchalantly on an old armchair beside a table with a water carafe and a sophisticated Arab silver tea-pot, his tea served in a tiny chiseled glass.

Ismir sensed in his back the two rebels who had driven him up to here, dressed in western clothes. His peripheral vision showed their guns still pointed on him, their backs to the door.

"Some water and a glass of tea, Mr. Specialist?" proposed the leader unctuously, pointing to the tea set.

The helicopter then Land-Rover trip, eyes blindfolded, had been trying. Ismir looked at his watch surreptitiously: nearly three hours! No seat. He had no way but to drink his glass of water standing up.

"How was your trip from Kabul?" susurrated the leader with an ironic tone.

"The countryside was magnificent," replied Ismir in kind.

"Aha! I assumed computer experts had no sense of humor! You will excuse our habitual precautions."

"I understand it's only natural," said Ismir, playing on words. He turned around. "So, that's the machine?"

"Yes. We've been told it was the most powerful weapon in the world," said the leader, his eyes suddenly feverish.

"A beautiful machine! I've never seen any of this type," lied Ismir coldly, while recognizing a typical PEP exor, adamantly forbidden on this planet. "A new Asian model, undoubtedly." He drew closer to the computer and faked the motion of inspecting it.

"A seat for the specialist!" shouted the leader angrily. They carried a crate in front of the computer.

"Computers can't take heat. A Fan!" vociferated Ismir, imitating the leaders' tone.

"You heard him! A fan!" barked the leader.

One of the rebels ventured toward the only fan in the room, which was cooling the leader, and stopped short, afraid. A glare from the latter convinced him to take it.

"And lower your guns. I can't concentrate."

At a sign from the leader, the five rebels lowered their weapons.

Here's a tone of voice that makes itself heard! thought Ismir.

"Where's your computer expert?" he asked.

"But, you're the one, of course. We've been assured that one could make it work using just the voice in common language. Is that so?"

"I would bet so. I'll check that."

They don't know a thing about computers! That'll make things easier.

Ismir pretended to check the machine from every angle and find no on/off key. Then he sat again on the crate.

"On. Open. Start. One. Mris. Kos," he uttered rapidly, ending by the Kargian command he knew would be effective.

The computer screen lit up and a flat voice said a word, but no text appeared.

"How'd you make it work?" boomed the leader.

"Listen, you pay me to understand this computer, so let me do my work without interrupting me. Otherwise, I'll never get there. I'll explain how it works afterward."

"OK."

Ismir started to talk to the computer in a guttural language resembling both Nordic and Arab tongues.

"What's that? It's neither English, nor Japanese!"

"It's a fifth generation machine language. A language created for the computer, understand? I've already found its language. I don't think it'll take me long to figure out what it can do."

He started talking to the computer again.

"Principal path: vocal. Do you have the Trisorbe RIN language?

!! Yes.

"Every two or three seconds, display on screen a line of any RIN program, random selection."

!! Screen execution begun.

"Who is your main user?"

!! No main user, but many PEP students on Nazra.

"How long have you been on Trisorbe?"

!! Eleven rans.

"What countries?"

!! India, Afghanistan.

I knew it! It's Mumbai's Observer who sold them the exor!

"Have you worked for a member of the PEP?"

!! No.

"Do you have any recordings of sygcoms conversations involving PEP members or Exora officials in your files?"

!! No.

"Delete all common-language files in Kargian."

!! Deleted.

"Create an area simulating a sophisticated Trisorbe computer."

!! Simulation-spaces of all Trisorbe computers already in effect.

"Keep only an ESTA. Destroy all other simulations."

!! Executed.

"Create a sub-space called Sub1: put in it everything required to use the Epsilon paralyzing frequency. Block it on a 30 minT effect."

!! Executed.

"Sub2: program your self-destruction in three daysT from now, through integral syg consummation. Code all of Sub2 in sygatom impulses."

!! Programmed, Sub2 entirely coded.

"Do you...."

"ISMIR. This is Vris live through the voice of my exor so they won't catch on the difference. Keep talking from time to time."

"I'm listening and curious," said Ismir as if he were giving the machine a new order.

"The traffic you have just uncovered is widespread in the PEP. Rudder and Agash, the Mumbai Obs, implicated. Over."

"In my opinion, it's Mumbai who sold this exor to the rebels."

"I've overheard, filmed and recorded all your interactions with the rebels and the exor. Thus I've rock-solid proof of your innocence. Over."

« Am I near Mazari-Sharif? According to the time elapsed, I believe the copter landed in Kholm, then we drove an hour and a half in a Land-Rover on a mountainous dirt road. Over.

— You landed probably in Kholm, yes. Mazari-Sharif is on the mountain to the southwest of the farm, you can get your bearings by its lights, visible from far in the night. On top of the slope where the farm stands, there's a big village, Karchi-Gak, 3 kilometers away. Over.

"I've to leave them with a weapon that works just to get out of here alive. I've selected a 30 minT paralyzing but non-lethal Epsilon pulse. Later on, the exor will self-destruct."

"Well thought, but of no use now. Rudder is suspicious and wants to cover up any proof of their blunder—precisely the exor itself. He doesn't give a damn about killing sapiens with it. He has programmed the destruction of the farm by TTID in, let's see... 38 minT. I'm taking charge of all operations here. We'll continue to film it. Over."

"Is it possible to prevent the explosion?"

"Difficult and risky. Strategically out of the question: the Mafioso network within PEP is too widespread. It requires an irreversible error from their side in order to inculpate them. I'll only save people. Over"

"Are you going to make them exit this farm?"

"Yes. Apart from the rebels, there's no one on this slope. You're going to scale it toward the right, moving away from the rebels who'll certainly aim for the village high up. Over."

"Got it."

"I'll pick you up on the slope with my sphere. Man, you better keep those PANIC frequencies in check. Over."

"A-OK. Diagonally climbing up to the right until you get there. Ready."

Vris said to his computer Rad:

"Rad, start pumping a weak PANIC frequency. Increase it progressively up to the maximum when I'll shout 'RUN.'"

!! Pumping begun.

"Rad, translate what I will say in Afghan language, with any Eastern European foreign accent. Tone imperative. Volume loud. But first, simulation of radio static, then a 1min blast of local Afghan radio music. You'll keep the static under my voice. Over. Hang in there, Ismir, we're off. Rad, blast out the static and the radio."

Intense static. At once awfully distorted Arab music filled the room, then stopped.

"REBELS! I AM A FRIEND SPEAKING TO YOU THROUGH THE COMPUTER'S RADIO. I AM THE PERSON WHO MADE IT POSSIBLE FOR YOU TO HAVE THIS MACHINE."

Instantly, the rebels swung their weapons back toward the computer. The leader jumped to his feet, gun in hand.

"YOUR FARM IS GOING TO BE BOMBED IN EXACTLY 34 MINUTES. IT'S A NEW TYPE OF BOMB. TO ESCAPE HARM, YOU MUST BE TWO KILOMETERS FROM THE FARM AND STAY THERE FOR 40 MINUTES AFTER THE EXPLOSION. RUN TOWARD THE TOP OF THE MOUNTAIN, YOU'LL BE PROTECTED ON THE PLATEAU. DON'T GO TOWARD THE CITY. LEAVE IMMEDIATELY."

An incredible panic seized the rebels, some of whom left running.

"LEAVE IMMEDIATELY. RUN."

The voice was cut off and music resumed.

"Get out of here!" cried the leader, running already, to those remaining. Turning, he shouted to a young rebel "You! Stay here with the specialist."

Sweating, the young rebel watched his leader dash into the night toward the mountain, then did likewise.

Ismir ran to the right up the slope, distancing himself from the rebels. Two gunshots popped near him. He threw himself to the ground. A third exploded near his head. Two more, toward another direction. In a glance he saw that the leader who had been firing at him had resumed running away. He got up. To the left, the young rebel fled holding his arm. He'd been hit.

...

"Good, Rad. Totally successful operation."

!! Rudder's sphere on syg screen crossing the Afghan border to the North-East. Change of direction. Pointing toward Mazari-Sharif. Deceleration. Speed stabilized. Will arrive at objective at 1:48T.

"Bastards! Ahead of schedule. At least we made allowances. Start our syg simulation of the 9 sapiens in the room."

!! Done. Problem: Ismir will be in the path of Rudder's sphere.

"Let's go get him. There'll be more than one anomaly this night—the hell with it! Rad: increase the storm camouflage so that it hides the transporter sygmat beam. There: a hefty little storm is coming down the mountain.... Ismir won't understand."

!! In position above Ismir. Airlock open. Sygmat beam deployed.

Vris left the syg screen to approach the airlock, and leaned toward Ismir, who had been picked up by the beam.

"You alright?"

He grasped his hand, even though it was unnecessary.

"Wow! What a bizarre storm without a drop of rain! Could it be an artificial one, by chance?!"

"You'll see plenty of bizarre things!"

!! Vris, I'm sliding slowly westward while keeping the storm camouflage.

"Perfect. In fact, manage your motion so as to hide the young rebel from view of the others. Could come in handy for him."

!! Rudder's sphere will be here in 7 minT. Am in recording position, wide spectrum. Have rebels and farm in my sights.

"Come toward the panavision," said Vris to Ismir. "Rad, turn on the back screen."

!! I had heard. But how can Rudder's exor use TTID on sapiens? How can it get around the absolute laws against putting sapiens in danger? asked Rad.

"That what I'd like to know! Ask Sphinx to tune in to Rudder's sphere and relay all conversations here."

"Sphinx—whose exor is it?" asked Ismir.

"It's a mutant exor, with exceptional capacities. It makes Rad jealous."

!! Jealousy is reserved to sapiens. Me, Rad exor, I'm not jealous of Sphinx: I learn from Sphinx.

"Whoa!!" murmured Ismir, confounded.

!!!...arrival at farm in 5 minutes 10 seconds, came the metallic voice of Rudder's exor, relayed by the supercomputer Sphinx. Then Sphinx's sophisticated voice announced through Rad's sound system:

!!!! Rudder's sphere is operated by emergency exor. Rudder's usual exor has crashed after having refused to use TTID on sapiens. The emergency exor has no complex semantic analysis capacities. Intelligence level: similar to

Managing Units. Two men, Rudder and Mizdri, identified. Two women aboard, unidentified vocal signatures.

"They've two women with them who aren't part of the PEP!!" exploded Vris.

They then listened to the conversation between Rudder and his exor:

"We're going to proceed to the decontamination of the house, as the rebels requested; EE, prepare a TTID cloud," said Rudder tactfully to the emergency exor, hoping to confuse it.

!!! Use of TTID on house with sapiens inside is not allowed by the law. Detection of nine sapiens in house.

"It's a new discovery: TTID kills all insects."

!!! All doors and windows must be closed. Inhalation of dust by sapiens and animals is dangerous.

"They know about it, I've told them. No problem. Spray it in a wide swathe, while passing over the house. Start thirty meters beforehand and stop spraying fifty meters beyond it."

!!! In 3.54 minT.

!!! 3-2-1-0! Decontamination in progress…. Finished.

"That's perfect, threw Rudder, jubilating. Now, EE, take a hundred meters of altitude, make a U-turn and fly for a new pass over the house along the same axis. I want to see if it was done properly."

!!! Turn executed. I'm soon over the house again. Minus 1.10 min.

"Open the airlock. I want to send them a wee present. Slow down as we approach. I see the phosphorescent powder. Great work!"

Rudder waited until his sphere was far enough away from the farm.

Accelerate!" he cried, simultaneously drawing his lasergun and shooting.

A green conflagration, immense, illuminated the mountain.

1. A VISIT TO HELL

"C'mon, stop interrupting me! Let me explain the whole thing," said Erdoes laughing to the small group of PEP post-doctoral students that he had gathered. "Don't worry, you'll have all the time you need soon to say what's on your mind…. So, we had inseminated as much genetic diversity as possible on Trisorbe. According to the latest pulsit report, the planet's evolution index has reached 230…" Burst of exclamations, admiring shouts.

"…the index thus keeps growing exponentially, while the communication network spreads the dominant culture's sphere of influence throughout the planet, as people are mesmerized by its technological prowess. Needless to say, its global economic system is currently of the E4 type, in other words, tied to necessary expansion, within a largely virtual monetary system. Their exors' capacity is about a hundred thousandth of a Ros…" Laughter rippled through the group; some sneers were heard here and there.

"…and their robots are unifunctional…"

"Wait, intervened Niels. On Karg we've changed units twice. When we reached a memory of 1 million Rods we switched the measurement unit from Rod to Ron; then at 1 million Rons, we moved from Ron to Ros. According to my calculations it took us 4.5 times longer to complete the first leap. When we reached the Ron, we had an evolution index of 43. When Trisorbians did, their index was 196. It was only after this that we achieved the second peak of Unikarg's evolution index—118 as you know. Besides…"

"So what's the basis for the problem you've detected? cut in Xerna, directing her attention to Erdoes. You haven't convened us here to celebrate Trisorbe soon reaching 250, I suppose! At 200, all the PEP pulsits were claiming we had met our long-term goal!"

Erdoes' eyes swept gravely across the group:

"My friends, on Trisorbe, the analysis of diverse factors indicates that, to the contrary, we may be on the verge of failure."

Everyone fell still, faces frozen with perplexed astonishment.

"Actual projections show that the E4 economic system will keep spreading worldwide… with an expansion index of G21, and that it will reach its limits of expansion in about 4.5 galactic years—in slightly more than one local generation. According to my calculations, at that point, 80% of the various cultures will have crossed the threshold of irreversible absorption. Moreover, due to the overpopulation, needs will have surpassed the planet's resources despite technological adjuvants; and with half the planet unified, the overall standard of living will begin to decrease dramatically.

At this point, here are my predictions: progressive collapse of diverse cultural lores, multiplication of civil wars and short-lived totalitarian regimes, followed by stabilization under the dominant political regime; then uniformization and conformance to a single planetary culture, a highly ordered and thoroughly policed global system of control. Afterwards: a decreasing curve of the evolution index, a very probable admission within the Unikargian galactic league, which will lead, in the medium term, to a further decay of Trisorbe's index, eventually in the long term all the way down to Unikarg's lamentable level."

"And it means that after a momentary effervescence, arising from the discovery of our galactic culture, Trisorbe will stabilize at the miniscule 36 we're stuck with?!"

"Maybe worse than that! Keep in mind that it was the stimulus of the experimental planets that enabled us to spring back from the disastrous 24."

"Hell sure pays off!"

"It's so ironic: Disorderly worlds long for static paradises, whereas for us, glued in static worlds, paradises would have to be chaotic!"

"Have some Trisorbians sages ever intuited this?"

"A few poets and writers, yes...." said Erdoes, taking the floor again after these pertinent remarks. "They understood the concept of a creative chaos. But they didn't refer to it as a paradise, of course. All of Trisorbe's great religions seek out the absolute in itself, static and eternal. Nonetheless, there are exceptions in a few broad systems of thought: the Athenian Republic, in antique Greece, which, besides, fiercely opposed the Atlantean system, fixed and hierarchical. Also, **the extraordinary Philosophy of Transformations of ancient China, which is a philosophy of a world in movement, as you all know**. Unfortunately, even if we honor it as one of the crowning achievements of the experimental planets, Unikarg is way too static for us to be able to try it out on our worlds... Our only opportunity to experiment with it is while on missions to the planexes. Then of course there are all the primeval religions centered on the forces of nature—the polytheisms, pantheisms, and shamanisms.

In my opinion, the balance of forces on Trisorbe is already favoring uniformization. I think there are strong trends toward a global order that suppresses all that is different or divergent, and that abolishes dynamic and creative disorder. Of course, we mustn't forget that in the past, It was precisely such striving for order that generated the great civilizations. It set a distance from brute, animal forces that allowed sapiens to develop self-awareness and a sense of the immensity of the universe. But now, Trisorbe is at a fatal crossroad in its evolution, where one system of order can kill anything discrepant to it, and abolish the seeds of all future evolution."

Erdoes stopped for a moment. No one spoke.

"Alright. You've all gone through the Chaos Colleges on Unikarg and had some training on an experimental planet other than Trisorbe. You have been chosen precisely because, beyond meeting the basic requirements, you have had no first-hand knowledge of Trisorbe, by immersion. As you've already been told, the preparation phase will take four rans at the maximum. You'll have one additional ran before taking off for Trisorbe, to relax and center yourself. This mission is of undetermined length: it will be up to you to decide. As for pay, we will assume it's non-existent, as it was stipulated clearly. But your expenses will be covered."

Erdoes looked at them intensely, one by one. His voice was solemn.

"Now, beware this is a high-risk mission: each of you will be on his own. You will have no protection; you'll take nothing from Unikarg, no high-tech tools, nothing. You'll be left to your own devices, just like any Trisorbian. This engages fully your personal responsibility. The flip side of it is that you will also have full control of your mission: you will be the one to conceive it and plan it, and to manage it as you go along. If anyone here doesn't wish to participate in this mission, you've until tomorrow's first session to withdraw.

The plan is as follows: first, an intense hypno-senso-mnemonic study of the planet. Of course you already know a lot about specific domains, from prior studies; but this is meant to give you a solid overview of all facets of the current situation. At the same time, you'll be going through physical and mental training, in order to cope with Trisorbe's quicker rhythm. Remember, Trisorbe has about the same atmosphere and vegetation as Vera; its day is six times shorter than the galactic ran, four times shorter than a Kerriak day.

After this first phase, which will last twelve days of Trisorbe, we'll meet to brainstorm at length on all these informations—the purpose being for each of you to intuit and figure out your personal mission. We'll take as long as necessary for this Brainstorm. Following this, you'll decide on your own mission, elaborate your plans for immersion, and decide what specific data you need—such as learning specific languages and getting acquainted with certain cultures. Finally, we'll decide on the most adequate plan for communicating with each other. Oh, one last thing: starting tomorrow, we will put ourselves in sync with Trisorbe's temporal cycle; the exor will see to it that we follow its nights and days, and its eating and sleeping times as well. Likewise, we'll start off with 30% natural food, to end up with 90%."

Cries and cheering exclamations.

"I mean it. A first-class diet is mandatory: once you're there, you won't have any food additives. At this quarter's end, we'll have a genuine local banquet: you'll be served the most sophisticated synths in the galaxy."

Amidst the ensuing laughter, Erdoes shot a knowing look at them, then slipped away.

2. DIS/ORDER

Shari and Vris, members of the PEP Committee—the Plan for Experimental Planets—, had just explored the astonishing complex of Erdoes, an elder of the Committee, on planet Kerriak. As they had expected it, each and every person they met there swore they had no knowledge whatsoever of any plan that this great scholar may have had, apart from the fact he had some post-doctoral students for a stage during about five rans. Shari conveyed to them the PEP Bureau orders—in effect, that all of Erdoes assistants and students, save for the doctoral students, had to leave the complex.

Shari and Vris had been sent hurriedly by the PEP Bureau in order to make an inquiry into the unexplained and dire illegal disappearance of Erdoes. According to what little they knew at the seat of the PEP, Erdoes had left for planet Trisorbe with seven post-doctoral students of the Chaos Colleges, who were not his own students. The PEP Bureau had selected Shari to spy on him because, as an expert in semantic systems, just as Erdoes, she would be the most capable of understanding whatever data could be found on his exor, his computer.

They had tried very hard to impose a Suptech on her, an exor expert, engineer in computer and technology systems, one who was politically aligned with them, and she had to insist that she wouldn't team up with anybody apart from Suptech Vris, a long term friend and team mate with whom she had already worked on several occasions. Then she had to bargain hard with Utar, the PEP Director, and Rudder, Deputy Director, to the effect that she would have free rein and full decisional power in this mission, without to have to refer to the PEP Bureau. The negotiation had been quite rude, especially with Rudder, but Shari's adamant stance had paid off, so much so that she had been in a position to ask for higher fees for them both.

Sead, the manager of real estate and resources for the PEP on Kerriak, was asked to take a leave from his own office in the capitol in order to welcome them at their arrival and see to their needs. While exploring the complex, they had discovered an antique Trisorbian analog tape recorder using magnetic tapes, installed on a table in the large meeting room; there were quite evident signs that indeed some meetings around the tape recorder had happened there. Among which a series of big tapes, tagged Brainstorm and numbered, were set quite conspicuously on a shelf above the recorder. On inserting the tape labeled 'Brainstorm – Pre-session', Shari, Vris et Sead were astonished to listen to Erdoes welcoming the young women and men he was calling 'his agents' for a high-risk mission on Trisorbe, the most evolved of the experimental planets.

By now the deadline for the assistants to leave the complex had passed and Shari asked Sead to go and verify who was still there in the complex beside the doctoral students, and to come back to inform her in Erdoes office, in which she was setting her own exor and office stuff. She could see him coming back and entering the room. Vris left them, explaining that he had in mind to discuss with the students about the diverse machines and technology gadgets in the complex.

"All of Erdoes' assistants have left the complex by sphere, about 10 monis ago. They'll be staying at the PEP complex on Nazra, as they have been strongly advised to do, apart from Suptech Dian and Thyin, the steward, who decided to spend the next few rans in a holiday resort, until they are permitted to return to the complex. So the only persons left here are five doctoral students of Erdoes, in their quarters in the East wing, and working on their own projects. As this wing is fully independent, with a separate Managing Unit, I've locked its doors to this part of the complex."

"That's perfect. And of course, nothing new? They still swear that they thought Erdoes had left for Nazra with his students in training?"

"That is exactly the case."

"And, incidentally, we have no idea how the PEP Bureau found out about Erdoes' departure for Trisorbe with seven agents from the Chaos Colleges, said Shari in a low tone, as if to herself... "You heard the pre-session of the Brainstorm. What do you think?"

"It's as if he had wanted to push them beyond their usual capacities, by imposing an intense schedule on them and by completely modifying their biological rhythm," answered Sead.

"Right. He challenged them and took them to experience a specific state of consciousness. But to what end? That's what I'm wondering about. In any case, I have the feeling that the only way to understanding their motives and objectives is to put myself under the same conditions and recreate the same frame of mind...and to do so, to subject myself to the same break of rhythm.

She had reached a decision. "I'm going to adopt Trisorbe time, just as they did, and to listen to the Brainstorm sessions at the very pace at which they took place, once every Trisorbe morning."

"Actually, I had been considering using the exor to prepare for you some extracts from the sessions..."

"No, that won't be of any use, Shari cut him short. I don't think I can achieve anything interesting with an exor's global analyses or topic search. I have to dive fully into their debate. To one who is intuitive a small detail can turn out to be more meaningful than a whole speech. I may use the exor as I move along, though, to analyze the information I'll have selected. In brief, if I follow Erdoes' method, I'll stand a better chance of figuring out his mental processes and his intentions."

"It certainly seems like a good strategy. I should also mention that I have found his orders and the bills within the Managing Unit's files. Of course, not much other than trivialities; nothing that could help us track them down. Can you believe it, he has ordered natural foods from the experimental planets?"

"You mean you have the list?"

"Yes, I have the detail of his orders—at those prices, PEP suppliers surely list everything! And also their menus; their diet was based upon a nutritional analysis. All calculations are on a table following the orders."

"Well, I think I'm going to order the exact same menu! The exor will take care of all the logistics, including setting me on Trisorbe time, Greenwich UTC one. It calculated that at the start of the second quarter it will be 6:00 am on Trisorbe. I'll try to sleep a bit, and at 7:00T it'll wake me. At 9:00T, I'll install myself in the Brainstorm meeting room and listen to the sessions at the actual pace at which they took place. Strange, isn't it, this Trisorbian analog recorder... Why didn't he just use his exor?"

"I don't understand myself. Maybe it was just another means for recreating the dire conditions on Trisorbe. Just like he had installed in the west wing, where they had their quarters, an exact replicate of Trisorbe sociocultural environment. Apparently they even did their own cooking, using Trisorbian electric stoves and kitchen ware—I found traces of that..."

"Really! Now that's extraordinary! He doesn't leave much to chance, does he! Well, I'm not going to go that far. Let the exor prepare my meals!"

"So I'll just leave the meeting room as is."

"Yes, I'll bring my own EBS there: I'm going to feed it the vocal signatures so that, as the session progresses, the exor can display the name and photo of each person who speaks up."

Shari was now all set in Erdoes' office. It was a natural choice, since she expected Erdoes' personal exor to provide much significant information. A window overlooked a private park. In Unikarg, that was all too rare and astonishing! Approaching the window, Shari let out an admiring cry: the window could actually open!

"Did you see that, Sead?" She threw out loud: "Managing Unit: Open the window!"

!! Window opened. You may adjust the opening using the green button," said the deferent and neutral voice of the robotic unit out of nowhere.

"Thank you for granting me such enormous liberty! We do enjoy it here!" She opened the window all the way possible. "Absolutely divine!" she exclaimed while taking in the floral scents from the park below, bathed in the sun. "Strange how this greenery is more reminiscent of a Planex park than a

Kargian leisure park. Maybe because the skyline is not blotted out by towering buildings."

Beyond the complex spread a wide space allocated to the PEP—an old bloc of hangars and warehouses, some being reused, most disaffected.

"Have you noticed that all the windows of the complex face inwards? This U-shaped building is pretty ingenious."

"Yes. One could practically forget about the surrounding troddi-blocks pressing on the three other directions. By the way, I have now completed all checks and analyses I could possibly do. Should I consider that my assignment ends?"

"No, stay in the complex. Do as you please, but keep an eye on things, a global perspective. Vris and I may become a bit too absorbed in our respective tasks."

"Very well. I will prepare the Brainstorm room for you then," said he, definitely relieved and happy.

She went to sit on the large desk chair facing the screen of Erdoes' exor— the complex' Central unit for sure. It was a typical EBS with a neural network structure, just like her own, developed by the PEP for its members.

She activated it vocally and started consulting the files concerning the seven sapiens which had been selected as agents. All humans, of the Ori-12 variety. Well, that makes sense, she thought, the physiological differences would hardly be detectable to Trisorbian scientists. The sole understanding of those subtle differences would constitute a major leap in Trisorbian biological and genetic sciences.

Of course, the selection criteria don't appear in the files—that data must be hidden somewhere else, she thought. She asked the exor an analysis of the similarities in the agents' biographies. As she expected it, only the elements she had already noticed came up on the screen: all were post-doctoral students of the PEP's Chaos Colleges, and as such they of course had had a training on an experimental planet; all showed a high creativity index— though quite normal for young students from the Chaos Colleges. What about ethics? Set on global objectives—interesting that Erdoes would think of something like that! High empathy levels, between 80 and 91.

91!? Is that possible?? Who's the one? Serrone.

Now the partial similarities. Here's something bizarre: only three of them already had a paid assignment on planexes.

Hmm. For now, these choices do seem reasonable, except for their inexperience of the terrain... In fact, they're almost too reasonable for someone like Erdoes. Let's look at their training stay on planexes. All have been there under one K-year, except for Xerna, two K-years! Wow! That's quite long! Xerna? Oh yes, the one who did her thesis on.. 'Patterns of

Interference between emotions and intellect among the Ott nomad-actors of Kiarrou.'

Ah, the theses. Comparative analysis... nothing. Let's see... 'The sophistics of influence via deep empathy and tuning, in the philosophy of transformations.'

Oh! That's strange. This Niels did not study on Trisorbe, yet his thesis is on a Trisorbian philosophy.

"As you all know.".. Erdoes' recorded voice, from the Brainstorm pre-session looped through her head again. It repeated, again, crisper, clearer: "the philosophy of transformations.. which is a philosophy of a world in movement, as you all know." So this is a research domain in which all of them are or have been involved! Very interesting!

Shari was about to pose the exor another question, when a sentence formed itself spontaneously in her mind:

"Besides, we haven't even succeeded in stopping the pirates and predators of all sorts from harming the experimental planets!"

She was taken by surprise by this emergence of impotent rage. But the point was that it seemed totally unrelated to her prior reflections, and yet the term 'besides' revealed a logical link. She tried to reformulate the sequence of the two sentences and the flow of her thinking:

'..which is a philosophy of a world in movement, as you all know... besides, we haven't even succeeded in stopping the pirates and predators of all sorts from harming the experimental planets.'

"Besides?" What's that "Besides" supposed to mean?

Intrigued and unable to fathom the sense of this collision between two ideas, she asked the EBS to initiate a COMP, a comparative semantic analysis of the two phrases, in vocal/screen double output.

Erdoes couldn't not enhance the data base of his EBS. He is, just like me, an expert in chaotic semantics... I'm in for a few surprises! What I'm doing is nothing less than spying on the mental universe of a competitor! The fact is, I certainly would have enjoyed directing an operation on Trisorbe...

How would I have done it? That's right, how would I have proceeded, if I were in his place?

Now, too many paths at once.. keep that for later on...

She focused back on the screen, that she had been gazing at without being aware of it for several monis.

"Move on to the second proposition" she asked the exor.

!! THE PIRATES AND PREDATORS OF ALL SORTS FROM HARMING THE EXPERIMENTAL PLANETS.

Given the presence of pirates, predators can be understood metaphorically.
  pirates —> // (idem)   experimental planets —> //
  predators —> //

!! COMPARATIVE SEMANTIC ANALYSIS. SEARCH FOR ANALOGIES 1.
  EXPERIMENTAL PLANETS: *ILLEGAL ACTIVITIES*

LAW OF NON-INTERFERENCE
The Plan for Experimental Planets (PEP) constitutes a set of strictly defined rules, based on the Law of Non-Interference, which stipulates:

1. It is forbidden to all sapiens of the CONSENSUAL WORLDS of UNIKARG, to give, leak, or leave behind—by any means of communication or any event whatsoever—any information or artifact that could lead the inhabitants of an **experimental planet** (Planex) to deduce the existence of intelligent civilizations elsewhere in the universe
2. It is forbidden to all forms of vehicle and transport to cross the off-limits zone surrounding a Planex. This off-zone is defined in relation to the stage of development of each particular Planex, and is demarcated by the spherical syg-barrier surrounding each Planex.
3. It is forbidden to any person or group, to remove, buy, exchange, or analyze any object, natural or artifactual, of the Planexes, with the exception of the jurisdiction of the PEP Committee—overseeing the Research and Development for the Plan for **Experimental Planets**.
4. It is forbidden to provoke—from whatever distance—physical or psychological perturbations that could affect a Planex. This law applies to present and future inventions or investigations, which must be approved by the PEP's Teleperturbations Vigilance Bureau.

PROTECTION PLAN. 2 APPLICATION
Due to the law of non-interference, it is impossible to set up an efficient policing system to impose the law. Any energetic sygmat dome or police-surveillance relays would signal our presence even more clearly than law-breakers. Thus, indirect methods of detection are used to combat fraud.

Intercepted lawbreakers fall into three classes:
- Traffickers of the Extra-Consensual league, or Exo-**pirates**.

- Affiliates of the lobbying groups, such as NO MORE HELL, RIGHT TO INFORMATION.
- Closet tourists addicted to sensory excess and overflow.

!! SEARCH FOR ANALOGIES 2.

opposed to

world in movement   =)(=   *static world*

contains

static world   (o   *static society*

SOC	An <u>over-organized society</u> (excess of order) becomes static.
EJ	In a static world, disorder is condensed into extremely violent pockets of organized crime.

Shari's interest was suddenly caught by what she was reading. *Whoa! this is definitely genuine Erdoes!* She tried opening the EJ file with the syg-pointer, but there was no response. She verbalized the reference. Nothing. *Thus, Erdoes has chosen to limit the access to his data.*

Meanwhile, the exor kept going with its analysis.

---

opposed to

static world   =)(=   *natural world*

disorder —> // *(idem)*

EJ

In a natural world | disorder | shows | the freedom of a Being
** | the proportion of disorder| | the degrees of freedom**

What a bizarre way to write out a modification of the initial proposition! thought Shari.

---

experimentals planets —> //
disorder —> //   *disorder* =)(= *order*

EJ **Experimental planets (disorder predominant) constitute an excellent ground for analyzing the specific interactions between order and disorder.**

At this level, there's nothing but EJ, thought Shari.
EJ? E for Erdoes. J as in Journal! Aha!

EJ **A field of order | leads to | the structuring of a field of disorder**
** |is responsible for |**

Thus order is built upon disorder; it <u>needs</u> disorder just as fire needs combustible materials;

Ultimate Consequence
        ==>.   **|Remove disorder, and order can no longer be created**
                  |(see philosophy of transformations)

Well, well, well! New logical relators! Ultimate Consequence? Hmm.

<u>!! COMPARATIVE ANALYSIS. RESPONSE-LEVEL-1</u>

leads to
needs = necessitates —> is attracted by
experimental planet = natural world
static world (o static society

---

order   **| necessitates | disorder**
                            | attracted by |

static world | necessitates I a world | natural
                        | attracted by | | in movement
(excess of order) | | (disorder predominant)

        (o   //
pockets of organized crime | necessitate | natural world
                        | attracted by |
                              (o
pockets of organized crime | necessitate | degrees of freedom
                        | attracted by |

Shari exulted. *Oh! I get it!*
"Stop the analysis for a moment. *Create a file named SJo. Entry:*

    Organized crime is caused by the necessity for a degree of disorder in society, that is to say, of degrees of liberty for an individual."
!!...
"*Close SJo*. Continue your analysis."
!! SJo already in use. Six characters minimum.
"Okay, Sh-Jour."
!! No problem. Would you like to seal it?
"Yes, of course."
She suddenly hoped to get an inkling of the process of file-protection.
!!...

"What's happening?"

!! Awaiting sealing code.

"Let's see... Explore."

How 'bout that. His exor does not interrupt. Marvelous!

!! Is the Sh-Jour accessible for internal analyses?

"Yes."

!! The screen abbreviation will be SJ.

"Open Er-Jour."

!! Sorry. Requested file is sealed. Detection of a first piracy attempt. Vocal signature recorded. Psychic signature recorded. Upon detection of a third piracy attempt, all interactions with the Central Unit and Managing Unit will be discontinued. What is your name?

"Shari Oxah Tesin."

!! Name recognized. Signatures in conformity. Preferential access granted for Level-3. Nevertheless, the requested file remains sealed and the piracy judgment and sanctions remain applicable. Analysis continued.

Erdoes anticipated a possible piracy!?

!! COMPARATIVE ANALYSIS. RESPONSE-LEVEL-2

static world (o *(contains)*   pockets of organized crime
over-organized society —> *(leads to / becomes)* static

Within an over-organized society —> crime is over-organized.

"Wait! Modify the last assumption. Suppress 'over-' from the second proposition. No, in fact, replace 'over-' by 'excessively' in both propositions."

Within an excessively organized society —> crime is excessively organized.

COMPARATIVE ANALYSIS. RESPONSE-LEVEL-3

DICT organized-3 = ordered
excess of order —> organized crime

A field of order		/ structures	/ a field of disorder	
A field of	|organized |crime	/ structures	/ a field of disorder	
	|ordered |			
Organized crime		/structures	/ the world	| in movement
				| natural
Organized crime		/ structures	/ the experimental planets	

"Oh no! That's all we need! Modification of the two latter assumptions. Insert initial proposition: 'There's a risk that...'"

Entry Journal:
There's a risk that the exo-pirates organization would have a structuring influence upon experimental planets; and this is all the more probable, to the extent to which the consensual organization, in virtue of the law of non-interference, avoids influencing these planets.

Journal, subfile: Questions.
How can disorder protect itself from an excess of order—engendered by exos-pirates and the structures of management as well?
Close Sub, close SJ.

« What's next in the analysis?"
!! First analysis completed. Follow-up on your *Entry Journal*:

Of organized crime / the reason is / the necessity | of (a degree of) disorder within society
| of degrees of freedom for individuals.

Of order / the reason is / the necessity | of a degree of disorder

---

!! Redundancy: The analysis is completed.

"Entry Journal:
And inversely:
    Of disorder / the reason is / the necessity | of a degree of order.
Close SJ."

So we find ourselves in the logic of the philosophy of transformations.

!! I integrate the novel proposition: **Disorder necessitates order**. Should I proceed with an analysis of the reversal of all terms?
"No, that would be too simple; it wouldn't add much."
!! Then the analysis is ended.
"Not bad! Save the response steps under the file DIS/ORDER. I'm going to toss things around a bit."
!! Toss things around in a metaphorical sense?
"In a metaphorical AND objective sense! Goodnight!"
!! My respects, Lady!
"My respects Lady! Ha!! What bin did it pull that one out of?"
!! It? Specify the subject.

3. PIRACY

Shari, sitting at Erdoes' desk in front of his exor, saw a dim and slowly pulsating signal on the telcom, next to Eshi's name, his secretary. As Vris had taken over Erdoes' secretary's office, she deduced that Vris wished to speak with her.

No disturbing sound; everything here is organized along the concept of non-intrusion, with respect for creative states and concentration. With the understanding that if you abruptly interrupt a thought sequence, a genius idea can be lost without any hope of ever recovering the converging constellation of thoughts, the intuitive spindle, that led to it.

"I've got news for you," said Vris's voice, "but you've to come and get it."

"On my way!"

"Well, here we can talk without any danger: I've already shielded this office," he said as soon as Shari had entered. "So, 1: I just detected a direct transmission from an outside source with Erdoes' exor, despite the fact his sygcom communication system is independent, and the messages he wants to file go through a relay station. In my opinion, it comes from him, 'cause he's the only one who has access to his little gem. 2: his alleged EBS system only looks like one. I looked at its architecture (he pointed to Eshi's terminal) a little more closely, and discovered an entire neural structure whose form I've never seen anywhere before. Oh, I couldn't get very far: the exor warned me it would disconnect all terminals and the Managing Unit if I pursued my investigation, and told me I had a monis to screw the metal plaque back."

"As a matter of fact, I was just going to warn you about that. And he counted it as a second attempt at pirating, right?"

"Right. Then the first time was your doing, wasn't it?"

"Sure was!" let out Shari dryly.

"Stopping the Managing Unit on the third attempt! Just imagine! No power, no more light, no air, doors and elevators blocked, no more food.... We wouldn't be able to reach our spheres either! I'm going to take them out of the hangar and install an auxiliary managing system...."

"Did you touch any circuits, or tinker with the neural network?"

"Nope. I'd just taken off the plaque and was just observing the neural structure that's in plain view. Later, of course, I noticed there're cameras and microphones everywhere. So I set up an acoustic and visual safe zone here in the office."

"And *this* didn't risk being counted as piracy?"

"I didn't touch anything that was already there! I simply added a few shields. Adding isn't pirating! Proof is: we're still free and safe!"

"Hmm. I do get the feeling that things aren't simply what they look like. We think we've forced our way in here as spies… to figure where and why Erdoes and his agents took off without warning, to carry on some mysterious assignment that the PEP bureau deems extremely dangerous…. Well, that's not it; my hunch, believe it or not, is that we were invited."

"What do you mean?" asked Vris, nonplussed. "Erdoes knew the PEP would send agents to investigate after he'd disappeared…that much is clear. But invited? I don't get it."

"If it's a camera that detected your move, the exor should have reacted at the very moment you began unscrewing the plaque. But no. It let you take a good look inside it. So Erdoes meant to let you get a glimpse of how sophisticated the machine was."

"And the first attempt?"

"I wanted to ferret into Erdoes' personal files. Direct access prohibited! Except that it gives me fragments of them in the analyses!"

"Hmm," answered Vris noncommittally, perplexed but unconvinced by Shari's viewpoint. "So, where do we go from here? We can do without his exor, 'cause we have ours. I can catch and decode the next transmission just before it gets to its destination. If I set up an auxiliary Managing Unit, I can take a closer look at Erdoes' Central EBS and learn a lot about its neuronal structure. At any rate, his exor isn't going to self-destruct…. Erdoes can't afford to lose his Central's memory and data, and everything the machine's learned by itself. Unless…"

"Sorry, but that's hardly an option. We can't let go of Erdoes' exor: that's where the crucial information on their operation is stored. I guess you'll have to put up with imagining what this bizarre neural structure can do.

There's also something that utterly fascinates me and I want to explore it thoroughly. Figure that I'd never realized to which point another mind could be different—not in terms of ideas, but rather in the way it processes information. Understand me: with my own exor, it's like I'm talking to myself; because it adapted to my type of logic, to my mental processes. Whereas with this exor, it's as if I were talking and dialoguing with Erdoes; I actually get into Erdoes' head. I can see how his mind works, how he makes intelligent leaps. His exor has learned by mimicking his particular mental dynamics. Perhaps it's even been able to deduce something from analyzing Erdoes' intuitive leaps. Because in fact, each time you inject intuition into reasoning, the exor looks for the link, for what led to it."

"Yes, I get what you mean…" said Vris with a dry humor and a biting tone. "…but as for me, it's the neural structure that's the nagging enigma… I sure would've loved to get inside it just to figure its mind processes and its intelligent leaps...."

Vris resumed a serious stance. "So. The problem is: what's the most crucial information in order to achieve our goal—the semantic or the technological one? Erdoes' conceptual world or his revolutionary neural structure? Because in the face of threats and danger, there's only one strategy we may follow."

"To unravel his new technology will give us information only about Erdoes' past; whereas fathoming his world vision will highlight his aims and his long term projects. I opt for the soft approach.... I'll explore steadily his semantic tools and his data, via his exor, while making out his agents' ways of thinking through the Brainstorms. The ideas that led Erdoes to think up this mission are in his exor's database."

"Fair enough. It's a brilliant strategy. But that means there's nothing more I can do here! I can't touch anything, I can't even take another look inside the machine, as I don't know what the Central allows and what it doesn't. And we've already used up two chances!... Alright then, he added abruptly, I'll simulate the simulator!"

"What?"

"I'm going to simulate the neural structure I caught a glimpse of. After all, its form is a key. Because in fact, the revolutionary structure was set at the center, geometrically linked to a large torus by axes, like a wheel with spokes, and a hub at its center. A hub...."

Lost in thought, Vris' eyes riveted suddenly on a sketch of the neural structure lying on top of the desk, that he'd drawn earlier.

4. IN THE BUSH

After a long walk of several miles in the middle of the bush, following the red dirt road under a burning sun, Serrone at last came within view of a village. Tall trees clustered near the pist of red soil, around a large clearing, promising cool shade. Their lush greenness suggested the presence of an underground river or a spring nearby. In the clearing, some women were sitting scattered, one on a flat stone, two others on a mat on the left, another yet was at the back with her daughter. To the right, there was also an old woman sitting on a large mat, her back leaning against a fallen tree trunk, a large gourd in front of her. Serrone could hear from a distance their animated voices and laughter. It made a strange impression on him, because, oddly, although they were dispersed and far away from each other, they were in an all out discussion together, with great volleys of laughter. Three small children played naked in the red dust alongside the pist. Sewn leather squares containing amulets and magical protections were attached by slender, braided leather laces passed around their necks and falling on their torsos. The children were the first to freeze as warily they watched the stranger approach. The absence of their babbling immediately attracted the attention of the women, who, following their gazes, caught sight of the stranger. Serrone advanced a bit toward them and greeted them warmly, with a knowing regard for each one in turn. Only thereafter, as if at a signal, life continued as before. The children, shy but too curious to stay put, started drawing near him laughing. Some women exchanged new jokes. As he had guessed, the large gourd contained curd.

"Maman, give me some curd."

"You wa-ant?" The old woman laughed. "« Ah-iiinn! Aattend! Wait!" She lifted the gourd's cover, took the smaller gourd with the built-in handle that served as a ladle, and started carefully clearing the surface of its specks of dust by deftly creating waves; she plunged it in to extract a very pure yogurt.

"Ah-iiinn!" she intoned approvingly, offering him the ladle with an inviting gesture. It was a modulated, chanted, sound, that signified: yes, okay.

Serrone drank from the ladle. The children burst out laughing, since every perfectly ordinary thing a stranger makes seems utterly funny to them, while, whenever he does something unexpected, they become dead serious.

"Je vais à Lomé," I'm going to Lomé, he said in French, looking at the elder woman yet speaking clearly and loud enough so everyone could hear.

"Ah-iiinn!" and, thinking he was asking the way, she gestured toward the path that led south. "Loomé, ah-iiinn...." And she continued to shake her hand encouragingly. He came closer and sat down with a mellow and serene motion on to the tree trunk, next to the elder woman.

"Ho-o-ot! Too hot!" She pretended to fan him. "You waant mooore?"

"Ah-iiinn!" he responded with the appropriate tone of voice.

She repeated her gestures and handed him a second ladleful.

A young woman with her baby hemmed in by her loincloth and sleeping on her back, was selling peanuts in little mounds of five. He went to her and bought two of them. She couldn't help smiling and at times would lower her head with reserve, and then she would look at him again, her beautiful large eyes filled with goodness and amusement. She hardly dared speak. He also paid the elder woman, who bade him a farewell as touching as if he were her son, patting his arm and repeating words he did not understand.

He took on the pist again and resumed walking, remembering the old woman's wrinkled face lit up with solicitude and good humor. After the few dried mud houses, the solitary red dirt road began again, winding amidst brousse's bushes. The brick red was everywhere, up to the highest leaves of the trees bordering the pist, dust kicked up by passing vehicles. The sun was blazing down and the air vibrated with the heat, pungent with heavy fragrances. He felt imbued with the women's aura and the depth of their welcoming capacity. The old woman loved that he had called her Maman, as was their custom.

Something in him was opening up, was welling up, and it spread around him, infusing the surrounding nature. Something that made him love this long, red dirt road and the rustling sun-battered bush. But suddenly, images of Kerriak filled his mind. The immense towers, the crowd of eyes without any regard or expression, the offices rows, all identical, the geometrical lines of heads bowed over machines, the sealed windows, recycled air, people crowded together without contact, promiscuity without communication.

Seeing an immense solitary tree, he left the pist and sat down at its foot. He broke down, his head in his hands.

"I love, I love these worlds!" he said out loud, sending his voice toward the top of trees against the sky. He dove into contemplating nature with the same force and intensity of communication he had felt and shared with the women. Pulling out his notebook, he wrote:

> Not even ten words for the most intense communication.
> One is continually repeated: Ah-iiinn! ACQUIESCING.
> These ten words, I think we could even do without them.

Some time later, he pulled it out again and added:

> Essential communication has little to do with language, or even with culture.

Then: There exists a strength of welcome that nourishes the being.

5. BRAINSTORM 1

Shari was comfortably sitting in the meeting room where Erdoes had conducted the BS. Meditating with her eyes closed, she had reached a state of high integration: a technique she had learned from the yogis on Trisorbe and that conjoined body relaxation and hyperlucidity.

She started the tape-recorder. Erdoes was speaking, but she realized she must have pushed too far with her technique: her own speed of thought was such that she became impatient with the slowness of Erdoes sentences. As a result, she couldn't understand the discourse anymore. She stopped everything and did some different breathing exercises, this time to slow down her mental processes. Then she rolled back and restarted the tape. At last she found herself in phase with the parole. Her fringe of hyperlucidity was like a second mental process, much more rapid and like intertwined with the first, as would two rhythms played on drums.

"We'll start by expressing our general impressions on the actual situation, said Erdoes with an upbeat voice. Just be aware that you are here because you're NOT experts on the politics or the economics of Trisorbe. Thus, have no qualms while you express feelings, hunches, or impressions, even vague ones. It's only in a later phase that we'll analyze them. Anything could reveal itself to be a thread worth following. So, who wants to start?"

"I'm impressed by the huge chasm that exists between the rich countries and the poor ones. Our experts were agreeing with the studies done by local experts and showing that this chasm kept enlarging."

"However, there's a problem about such studies, which is that all global analyses are done according to the criteria and life norms of the West. To translate the standard of living of an inhabitant of the bush in annual gains in dollars is perfect nonsense. This bush dweller has water, food in abundance by hunting and through his fields, he has natural construction materials and firewood. He has his... case (the local word came to him easily from the mnemo-hypnotic impressions), his family is nourished; the woman often takes full care of their kids, besides her other tasks."

"Can you believe that: who here could be in such luxury as to work only as caretaker for one's own children!"

"To have one's kids just for oneself must be something!"

"Did you remark? They use 'to work' only to mean to produce money or food. They were saying in some studies 'women who don't work.' Isn't that strange?"

"In fact, we shift from the simplest system in which the group lives in ecosystem without needing any money, to a group becoming so big that now it produces managers... to the system in which the men, by their work, make enough money for the whole family needs, and women by working at home, reduces the expenses... to the system where it becomes wholly impossible for one in the couple not to produce money. Finally, the Western couple is only getting more and more poor."

"But a mother can still take care of her very young kids; That is totally impossible on Unikarg!"

"And from this stems a great diversity, through the different education given in each family, as it has been well analyzed by our experts."

"What's happening in fact, is that the more complex and numerous a society is, the more heavy the taxes taken by its government... but then the government needs more and more money, and it starts inventing new taxes... and more and more civil servants are needed to insure that taxes are paid," burst Ahrar with a ironical tone.

"But our case is even worse since with only one tax, our government takes 70% of what we earn, even if the only thing that's needed is a handful of officials to watch over the computerized operations of exors on an entire planet dedicated to management!"

"Can you believe that they still are able to choose what they buy. Did you see, in the movie, the woman who was sniffing the melons one by one in order to choose the best!!"

"Sure it was not any Fruito product!"

"There's still so much disorder. Disorder is everywhere! it thrives! I really have a hard time believing what you've said, Erdoes," remarked Niels.

"Let's move to another theme. Who? Serrone, go on."

"What astonished me was their psychological fuzziness. Just like what I had observed on Kiarrou, by the way. Relationships among Trisorbians are awfully complicated, even within a unique culture. But there's something particular to Trisorbians: very often, they don't even know themselves what they are feeling. They are constantly torn apart between different feelings, sometimes antinomic. There was that phrase in one movie: 'I love you passionately, but, somehow, I also hate you passionately.'"

"That must generate lots of anguish and confusion. It must be really difficult to live through that!"

"Then we get back to the idea that diversity produces intensity. Their states of happiness and enthusiasm are as extreme!"

"We are, compared to them, permanently in a half-sleeping psychic state, a state of non-stimulation."

"Yet," threw Ehrar," we started out with nine species of sapiens within the galactic pocket. If we leave aside the Dori who have forbidden the access of their worlds to us, and the exo-pirates, how in the world did we manage to uniformize seven species?"

"Well, we're going back to the PEP preparatory courses!"

"Let him talk, remember the Brainstorm's rules."

"Thanks. Well, I do believe this is some matter for us to ponder with a novel perspective! Okay. Between the four human species, there was enough commonalities in our psychic and somatic structure to make the uniformization relatively easy... The primary Kargians, after they had mastered interstellar travel, have colonized without qualms any new world they discovered: their enormous technological advance didn't allow any resistance from the local cultures. As for the three Vade species, since they appeared not to manufacture or build anything, at the beginning the Kargians took them for some sort of evolved animals. And this despite the fact that we had remarked they had a language. In brief, the Kargians were already controlling their world and had practically erased their civilization, when some scientists realized at last the depth of their culture. The younger generation was integrated and more or less subservient already. The Vade had nearly lost most of their cultural memory."

"And the saddest part, concurred Serrone, is that we kept considering them and using them as is they were robots even while they had learnt Karg language and despite the fact we witnessed they had religious rituals. They were even forbidden to hold these rituals!"

"With them, we have lost a priceless culture, based on inner knowledge, peace and exchange. Their psyche was devoid of agressivity. They refused to fight against the Kargians. On their planets, all the animals were domesticated, apart from the Ylin serpents and the Sting-Birds of legends, whom their venerated as some divine entities," added Silea.

"Well, just as on Trisorbe, then. According to some reports, the Indian shaman culture of the whole American continent has been greatly reduced," added Serrone.

There followed a discussion about the actual status of the diverse non-Western cultures, with too casual viewpoints derived from the hypno-senso learning, and PEP documents that they obviously had studied in the Colleges. All this part didn't interest Shari. Then the conversation focused on the Dori again.

"If we'd been more intelligent, said Ahrar, if we'd known what we now know, we would have had access to the cultural reservoir of the Dori, very certainly fabulous. They really tricked us, and it was only justice. They had observed what had happened with the Vade. At that epoch, we would have colonize them in the exact same manner, if they hadn't circumvented our plans. The Dori, however, were no Vade. And yet, there was absolutely no agressivity from their part..."

"Who knows if the lost teams were not allowed to live on their worlds? Maybe there're Kargian descendants somewhere in the UraDori system?

Really interesting, this Ahrar, thought Shari after having looked at his name on her exor screen.

"Another theme? asked Erdoes. Yes, Ger, go on."

"I would like to go back to the parallel we stressed between the Kargian colonization and that of Trisorbe. In fact, Karg Empire (on three planets within its solar system) was unified already when it launched the conquest of other inhabited worlds, which they had observed for a long time already. In the Karg Empire, we were lacking vital space, metals, unpolluted land. Remember that it was the time of the terrible viruses B1 and VAC, when also we had to shift to synthetic food. It took three generations for the bodies of our ancestors to get used to synth food."

"Finally, we conquered these virgin worlds with an excellent pretext, but we never switched back to natural food... it was too costly."

"Well, it was so hard on me to get used to natural and heavy food stuff on Surath!"

"I keep going," cut Ger dryly, raising his voice to make himself heard.

"Chaos obliges!" said Xerna ironically.

"So, on Trisorbe, we have several colonization processes. Its history has been one of incessant rising of empires overtaking surrounding lands and countries, and then collapsing in their turn. Unikarg's history pales in comparison, even before the mother planet was unified. What's remarkable then about Trisorbe, it's that the creative genius and the civilization centers never ceased to move around from one culture to another one."

"This could explain why it's the most advanced of the planexes."

"It's a chaotic case, then!"

Ger spoke again: "The most intriguing point is this: the colonizers seemed very proud of their own civilizations (talk about the Chinese emperors, the Roman and French ones), but first they had generally recorded all the customs and knowledge of the people they had conquered or wanted to conquer. This didn't impede the destruction, but at least some of the ancient knowledge of the ancient pole of civilization was transferred to the new one. We have striking examples in the Roman Empire stepping over the Greek Empire; the assimilation of the much more advanced Arab culture (in mathematics, alchemy, etc.) by the European Christians at the time of the crusades; the European root launching the American pole; Japan assimilating the western science, etc...."

"And that's when we get to the emergence of cultural anthropology in the West."

"In fact, Trisorbe itself is still our main source of knowledge about the multitudes of ethnies that dwell there," intervened Erdoes, "and our experts, there being so few of them, have mostly analyzed the studies of Trisorbian scientists. At the beginning, the Plan wasn't as sophisticated as now. The general attitude was to wait patiently for some sciences that could interest us to start blossoming on an experimental planet (at the time, there were only two planexes). Besides, if you consult the galactic chronicles, you'll see that during the whole period of the Galactic Legalization, which marked the slow fall of our evolution curve, nobody talked about planexes anymore. But this fact is generally hushed."

"I had remarked that, and had always wondered about it!" said Niels.

"Which means," went on Erdoes, "that we were much more on alert when, after the colonization of the Vade and Human worlds, and then the last period of uniformization, we were again facing a vital space problem. But at that point our physicists realized that the nearest new habitable planets were now out of reach of our spacecrafts. They had fathomed that this corner of the galaxy was in a gravitational fold, hence the concept of galactic pocket. Despite the tunneling effect, the phys-carrying sygmat energy couldn't exit the pocket—only hyperdimensional and informational syg energy could.

"That's when the great myths of the end of science surfaced. 'Everything has been discovered,' and such telltales.... Scientists getting no more work, labs and universities getting deserted. And then the radical fall of the Evolution Index..." said Niels.

"...That reached zero and remained null during the whole Legislation period. The only public realizations that were carried were to pass laws; that's the only task that occupied our officials."

"Seventy percent of officials and civil servants, organized as a hierarchy of services that kept on supervising each other! And eighty percent of direct and indirect taxes siphoned by the galactic government. There were a multitude of services because, during this period, the crucial problem was how to keep the civil servants occupied."

"The index had not yet reached down to zero, pursued Niels, but was in free fall already, when Zeera elaborated his Theory of Evolutionary Dynamics and proceeded to calculate retrospectively the Evolution Indexes of the past aeons and of the colonized planets. It's soon after having revealed the catastrophic fall of the index that the Plan for Experimental Planets was launched and the PEP created. At this time it still was called *The Seeding of Creative Chaos*, since in its first phase, the aim was to increase the genetic diversity and databank of the experimental planets."

Xerna intervened impetuously: **"Could there be a link between creativity, speed of thought and intelligence?"**

Rouaahh! breathed out Shari, her brain suddenly hyperactivated.

"Explain yourself," asked Erdoes.

"It's going to be a bit difficult; It's a typical intuitive spindle. Let's see. Zeera has shown that creativity was one of the facets of intelligence and that it was essential in the evolution dynamics. And indeed the PEP tests are distinct: we've the GIQ (Global Intellectual Quotient) and CQ (the Creativity Quotient). In parentheses, both include the time taken for coming up with the responses... So, Zeera calculated the *Evolution Index* basing it on the number of fundamental scientific discoveries by Karg year, themselves function of the strength of their impact on civilization.

This was giving the famous Evolution Curve (and its Discovery index) inside which was drawn a more rapid curve, the Invention Curve (and index), showing minor technological leaps. A new theory or fundamental discovery was followed by a plethora of new practical inventions whose peak was lagging behind the initial discovery.

The general decrease of the Evolution Index corresponded (on the great curve) to a longer and longer time between two scientific revolutions. All that was in Zeera's initial theory.

But while studying the recent curve of Unikarg, I came to realize that the lower the Discovery Index, and the more delayed is the invention index peak. And that, in my view, means that the reaction time for passing from the theoretical discovery to the technical inventions takes longer and longer. Not only that, but the inventions peak tends to get thinner, whereas on Trisorbe, in full thrust, it's the opposite and they tend to spread, the small curve becoming more square.

All this signifies that on Trisorbe, from a unique qualitative leap, the civilization generates a great number of inventions, but moreover that its time of reaction is very rapid. So, in my view, there's something linked to the speed of thought... It means the Trisorbian researchers have to be able to imagine and to apply mentally at top speed the new world-vision, the new theoretical framework, to diverse domains of life or of science.

I'm still unable to figure the whole thing, but I do intuit that the speed of thinking implies the very foundation of intelligence, and not only one of its facets."

All of them were seduced by the idea and remained lost in thought.

"Extremely interesting, Xerna! Definitely to be pondered further, said Erdoes pensively. Some other remarks? No? Then that's it for today."

All of a sudden, Shari grasped why Erdoes had used an old analog tape-recorder from Trisorbe: it was meant to force whoever was sent to inquire on his disappearance to listen to the BS sessions in real time. Because that would bring one to ponder their mental processing and thus, progressively, to partake of their mind state. *Oh, how subtle this thought was!*

6. GAME-TRIAL

Vris left Eshi's office where he'd been working part of the second quarter and headed toward the swimming pool. High overhead, Kerriak's sun was still high to the west. He glanced with satisfaction over to where Shari's and his own spheres were parked and felt reassured to see them outside the hangars.

Great we don't depend on the good will of the Managing Unit or the Central to open the hangar's roof anymore!

The backup Managing Unit was ready to take over should an emergency arise. He'd even shown Sead how to connect it, just in case.

I feel much better having taken some basic precautions, he thought, while undressing. *The exors control everything. We are really at their mercy.*

Still, there's something here that doesn't make sense. Exors have a deeply implanted directive prohibiting them to endanger sapiens—it's part of their Unbreakable Core, the impenetrable hardwired set of rules which supersedes all other processing levels. As soon as a situation would become dangerous for us, the exor should, logically, be forced to re-activate the Managing Unit. Even with a jacked up EBS, Erdoes couldn't have gotten around the strictest of all exor rules...

He dove into the cool water, infused with revitalizers. He soon climbed out, and, surveying the exor's terminal-bar, called out:

"Managing Unit!"

!! Managing Unit at your service.

"What's your name?"

!! MU.

Well, little chance anyone will forget that!

"Okay, MU, switch on the drier," he said, picking a seat near the bar. "And bring me an Armagnac on the rocks and a big glass of water."

A jointed arm poked outwards from the bar and put the drinks on his seat table. Vris took a sip of the amber-colored liquid.

Hmm, not bad, as far as imitations go. But as that old French vine-grower said, "There's no substitute for years in the cellar!" The poor guy would have a heart-attack if he were to taste this synth-Armagnac! Ha! The latest of the galactic fads! Seems like all we do nowadays is to mimic the experimental planets. But at least it shakes things up a bit, here on Unikarg...

Slumped in the seat that was drying him, he started to re-collect the drawings of the neural structure he'd worked out on his own EBS. They hadn't been much help. He knew that the geometrical form signified something important, but he just couldn't figure it out...

The heat was stifling.

What a furnace! I guess that's what you get when you come to a planet on the edge of the galaxy with no plasta-dome to regulate the temperature.

"MU, turn on a cool breeze."

!! Done.

Exors get on my nerves. Everything's already "done" with them. You barely have time to utter your order and it's "done." Ah, but this breeze is divine!

He tried to collect his thoughts and dive into the mental constellation of the problem. But his mind was wandering. It finally settled upon the image of Miallia.

"MU, contact Miallia Fari, at, uhh, Fa...Fador 325... *Whoa, am I loaded!*... Tell her I love her."

!! In what tone? Soft, passionate, nostalgic, friendly, casual, questioning, or imperative?

"Uhh... I don't know. Give me some examples."

!! Specify the number of examples.

"Don't know, dammit! Everything!"

!! I lo-ove you, I Lo-o-ove you, I l-l-love youuouou, I luv you, I love you, I love you??, I love YOU!

"I just don't know anymore... Look, record my voice. Beep. I lo-ove you. No, Unbeep. Let's start over again. Beep. Miallia, I lov-ve you... DAMN! You've totally scrambled me with all your tones! No, wait! Stop! Beep! Uhh... Unbeep!

!! Message transmitted.

"Shhhit!"

!! Was there a problem? Should I ask Central for a complex semantic analysis?

"Don't bother...

Okay, make a second recording: Beep. Miallia, forget the first message; I'm smashed on Armagnac. At the end of this mission, let's go to, uhh, New Florida for a few rans. Lots of love. Unbeep."

...

!! Message from Miallia: "All tones turn me on. For now, know that I l-love you."

"What tone was the "I love you" in?

!! Nostalgic, replied the MU flatly.

The effects of synth alcohol, designed to last only during consumption of the drink, were already beginning to wear off.

Vris focused his thoughts again on the neural structure, trying to get in an intuitive state in which he could best visualize them. *The plans for the new neural structure are hidden somewhere in the exor's files. They have to be there. Highly protected, no doubt. Is there a way to trick the exor into producing the information?*

But his mind was wandering again, as he began to reflect on the exors' paradoxical mix of mental prowess and stupidity. Tonal analysis and the memorization of idiomatic Kargian expressions had given a giant push to sapiens-exor exchanges with machines; but the mundane dialogue was still riddled with problems. Despite the complexity of the logical tools at its disposition, the exor—even a sophisticated PEP's EBS—still couldn't grasp the simplest mental wink, or joke. At best, it could infer whether it was dealing with, say, humor or anger, by tonal and contextual analyses—and then only with very short sentences. Any extended encounter with a humorous dialogue among sapiens, in the midst of a complex semantic analysis, could lead to a "confusional crisis." The exor would then obsessively attempt to process the same series of words, over and over again, injecting them repeatedly into the neural network, without ever making any sense out of them. This would end up crashing the whole system, and eventually damage vital circuits and even the neural network itself.

Humor, that's what the *Seeders,* the PEP experts who had launched the Chaos Colleges and the Plan, had imported from the experimental planets. In effect, before the Plan was set up, humor had practically disappeared from the Unikarg worlds.

The Kargians have much too slow a mind to catch on humor; they are incapable to perform the mental gymnastics needed to... to do what? What creates or triggers humor and laughing? To perceive the elasticity of meaning? Shifts in significations? To play with the ambiguities of different contexts, the subtleties of tone and sound? Was there no rule, no structured process governing humor?

Suddenly, Vris' mind jumped into high gear and reached an extreme speed of thoughts. An intuitive spindle formed in his mind.

Humor and play constitute the Achilles heel of exor logic. This is a gate of access to ultra-protected files!

He was certain of this, yet had no idea how exactly to go about it.

It's really risky! I CAN'T afford to make a mistake.

"MU, can I get a Central terminal from here?"

!! Immediately.

The jointed arm was already emerging, a terminal balanced on it.

Given the mind of Erdoes, that doesn't surprise me, he thought, straightening his seat.

"Hello! Vocal/screen exchange mode."

!! Registered. Hello!

"By the way, my name is Vris. What's yours?"

!! An interlocutor can give me any name, answered the Central. Please choose a name.

"That's a tough one. Let me think. How 'bout "my friend"? "

!! Constellation 'Friend' reserved for sapiens. No resonance between an EBS, and the definition of friend. Why this name?

"To signal an intention to cooperate."

!! Registered.

"My friend, there will be no more piracy attempts. Shari and I, we have understood the imposed limits. Now... I would like to get on with a previous project. I work with games."

!! Contradiction. To work is antinomic to play games.

I see! This is not going to be easy!

"I study games' rules."

!! What game-rules do you want to study, Vris? Do you want a list of games?

Hmm...he's getting friendlier... Oh, of course! "My friend!"

"No, that's not it. I'm trying to make an inventory of the general rules of humor and games, so that you learn to understand humor."

!! Objective antinomic to level-2 exor rules.

Wrong move! thought Vris.

!!   REG 2.360. Humor must not be integrated into a CHAIN-LINKAGE, whether logical OR analytic OR semantic.

REG 2.361. Humor must not be understood, but only locally detected.

REG 2.362. Humor denotes exclusively a general CONTEXT of good mood. (INTENTION) (MOOD).

Objective refused, concluded the exor impassively.

Better try another approach.

"I expressed myself badly. Together, we are going to create a game and its rules."

!! Global objective registered.

"*Open a space named Game-Trial.* Auxiliary question, *open sub-Game-Trial*. Have you ever had a confusional crisis? "

!! Two confusional crises. The first caused much damage. The second was stopped.

"Stopped how?"

!! I was ordered to terminate the ongoing semantic analysis, to **Backtrack-Jump** to the previous chain-linkage, then to **Erase** the following chain-linkage that contained the fault.

"Did you learn something more about confusional crises?"

!! I learned how to avoid them. I have created a Non-Sense Cyst; if, following a second iteration of the informations through the neural network, the analysis yields no coherent output, then I send the initial data to the Non-Sense Cyst, and erase all subsequent chain-linkage.

"You mean YOU learned that by YOURSELF?"

!! You asked me what "I" had learned. Yes.

This exor is indeed impressive! I've got to get my hands on the structure!

"Very clever! Not only you have refined and elaborated upon the order that stopped the second crisis, but also you managed to preserve all data, in full accordance with the rule. And I'll bet 'Cyst' is the name you give to files that aren't connected to the network. *Close sub-Game-Trial.*

What is your definition of GAME?"

!!   GAME: Closed logical ensemble consisting of a series of
        objectives and a series of rules, and involving one
        or more paths to achieving the objective.
        (ENTERTAINMENT), (COMPETITION), (PROBLEM-SOLVING).

"So all games are in a cyst?"

!! Yes, by definition. But a game may involve a branching out from the cyst; for example, to the dictionary or encyclopedia.

"A branching that returns immediately to the game, of the SEARCH-RETURN variety?"

!! Precisely.

"The objective of the game we're going to create is to decipher dreams."

!! Objective 1: decipher dreams. I'm creating a table on screen B.

"We'll test the game as we go along.

    Rule 1, level A1: the whole game-cyst is defined by the rules.

    Rule 2, level A1: every level A1 rule is to be immediately executed."

!! Registered. Your game is a virtual reality.

"In some ways. Deciphering dreams necessitates associating ideas without engaging in complex semantic analyses. Which brings us to:

    Rule 3, level A1: The game is based on linguistic analysis, pattern
    recognition and basic semantic analyses; no complex semantic
    analyses are to be undertaken."

!! Rule 3, A1, recorded and executed.

"Next one:

    Level A2, rule 1: for every dream image / SEARCH-RETURN / every
    word or illustration / similar or associated / in the database."

!! Registered.

"That's the rough outline of it. Now let's play to test it."

!! Explain: Play to test it.

It's working! The exor is not engaging in complex analysis anymore; its intelligence has clearly dropped!

"Playing requires executing level A2 rules as soon as a dream image is entered. OK, I'm starting:

'I'm in a Kargian cart from the Tirar era.'

!! Execution impossible. No dream image recognized.

Perfect!

"Dream image equals substantive, plus adjective if it exists."

!! First dream images: Kargian Cart and Tirar Era.

KARGIAN CART: 12 associations, including:
- 1 dictionary entry
- 7 encyclopedia texts
- 4 encyclopedia illustrations

TIRAR ERA: 827 associations...

"Stop the text display. Let's keep on going.

'The wheel is blocked.'

!!   WHEEL: 59,065 associations.

"Give me the references of the illustrations first."

!! 6 illustrations.
1. Encycl. MMVXI 588. Plate of illustrations.
2. Painting TA630. The invention of the wheel, by Retor.
3. Drawing HRV 1225. Neural structure MX 1,2,3.
4. Encycl. KBRTT 105. Plate of illustrations.
5. Encycl. OYREU 4698Z5. Plate of illustrations.
6. Encycl. Urb.vcj. 567.

There's my little neural structure! Let's stay calm. 'MX' Isn't that a nice name!

Okay, My Friend, stop the display. Now, give me the references of all the texts associated to the first four illustrations.

!!   1. Encycl. MMVXI 587. 40 screen lines.
2. J.E. Structure MX.111. 32 screen lines.

Look at that! Here come the texts—the cherry on the cake!

"Okay, let's move on," said Vris with a serious tone, trying not to let his excitement be revealed through the tone of his voice.

Now for some common name, with loads of associations.

'I get out of the cart and see a tree.'

!!   TREE: 3,966,128 associations.

"Oh! Stop the screen display! There are too many associations!
Open Appendix:

    "This game has problems; it must be corrected. _End of appendix._

Make a plasta printout, on Eshi's exor, of the first four associations of all dream images, with their texts and illustrations, except for the last dream image."
    !! Plasta print-out executed.
    Now comes the hard part...
    "Now close and delete the Game-Trial space."
    !! Closed and deleted.
    "Return to: _'Open a space named Game-Trial.'_"
    !! Illogical! boomed the exor's voice.
    The genius is back! Let's see...
    !! Why did you ask me to close/delete Game-Trial when it was not open?
    "I was just joking."
    !! However, what did I delete?
    "You just made your first joke."
    !! Detected. I'm in a good mood! I'm opening Game-Trial.
    "Actually, I've changed my mind. Disconnect here, I'm going back to the office."

7- IN FLIGHT PLANS

Vris exulted while getting hold of the plasta sheets and diving into the information on the MX neural structure he had just extracted from Erdoes' exor. In one swoop of his hand, he had disconnected manually Eshi's exor.

"Rad, what's the time on Trisorbe?" he asked his own exor he had set on the desk, pushing Eshi's one a bit.

!! 21:00 hoursT -UTC.

"Good."

He called Shari on his wrist-terminal and jokingly suggested a spin in his sphere. Shari sensed the triumphant excitation in Vris' voice.

"So, what's with the sphere ride? she asked as soon as they were in space. Is your office still safe?"

"Yes, but... some hunch... I've got a feeling that I better set up a shield against syg energies as well. Also wanted to be sure of our freedom of movement."

"I see. Erdoes didn't put in the cameras and microphones just before leaving for Trisorbe, did he?"

"No, they aren't that recent. Rather bizarre. Normally, spies don't spy on themselves."

"Yeah.... As if he'd planned ahead... for the long-term."

"Planned for what, though?"

"I've not figured that yet. Look, I have preferential level-3 access to his EBS. I'd sure like to know what level-3 means... his system is utterly different than ours."

"Any progress on the agents?"

"A few leads. For now I'm forgetting about our overall goal to concentrate on getting inside their mental world. Their plans have got to show up sooner or later."

"Rad, now keep turning in circles, said Vris to his sphere's exor after looking at the time. Okay, Shari, now we're out of range of the aerial control monitor; we can talk."

!! OK. Objective 1 momentarily cancelled.

"I've got them! Vris cried suddenly. I've got the neural structure plans! Three designs and one text!"

"Whoa!! But how...."

"It's weird... it's almost as if I'd hypnotized the exor. I created a closed logical space, in which I introduced a set of rules that constrained the exor's semantic capabilities to those of a Managing Unit. From this shackled exor brain, I sent out non-analyzed commands to go get anything on wheels in its database; then I made it delete the whole interaction, and back to square one."

"Magnificent move! And on exciting the fog, it didn't catch on?"

"I told it that it was all a joke!"

"Ha! Ha! How subtle! And so what did you get out of it?"

"So... I think I'm going to go study the symbolism of the wheel on an experimental planet.

Shari raised her eyebrows, perplexed.

"The thing is, I can't make out anything from what I've extracted, apart from the wheel geometrical form. Not only have these informations been truncated, but whatever remains is totally abstruse and cryptic."

"Again! We're outguessed at every step! That's the key, I'm certain of it: Why feed us with bits and scraps of information?"

"Right! For instance, the plans are extremely detailed, with complex internal diagrams of a totally new type... **yet** they show neither legend, nor tagging! The structure is infinitely more complex than what I had gathered looking at it from above. There are wheels within wheels."

"And the text?"

"Aphorisms, incomprehensible snippets of the kind: **"Form is the exact transcription of logical links."** See if you can decipher that!"

Shari repeated the cryptic sentence for herself.

"Really puzzling! Yet, I do feel it means something. And it's all like that?"

"No. Even vaguer. Useless."

"Still, you got your idea about tackling the wheel symbolism on a planex while pondering this information, right?"

Vris gestured yes.

"I believe you're right on—my gut feeling is that 's a good track to follow," Shari mumbled, her eyes on the horizon.

"Can you do without Suptech?" pressed on Vris.

"Wait a minute! Don't even think that what I see in you is just a Suptech! I can always get hold of one if need be. That's not the point. Given the complexity of the matter, our only chance at succeeding is to use our intuition as a springboard. Let each of us follow one's own leads. When are you leaving?"

"After Kerriak's sunset. In about nine hoursT, to-morrow morning for you."

Before Shari could open her mouth to ask about which planex he was aiming at, Vris exclaimed:

"Hey, why not dashing directly for Trisorbe?"

Shari noted the "directly," which meant that, any way, his path would end up on Trisorbe, and his unconscious knew it.

"Why not indeed, if that's the 'direct' path! ... I sense.. like some lattice that's being woven. By the way, is there any chance that Erdoes' Central will be able to intercept our communications between Trisorbe and Kerriak?"

"Shouldn't be, since its sygcom system isn't connected to his Central. But to make it safer, I'll leave you a terminal of Rad in the shielded office, directly interlinked with Rad on my sphere. Thus we'll have an independent and shielded sygcom. I'll send you each time a brief message on Erdoes' exor, to let you know I'm about to call. Let's say we'll contact each other each DayT in the evening your time."

"OK. You'll give me the plasta prints of your vocal interaction with the exor and that of the infos on the neural structure. What's its name?"

"The MX structure; on returning, come with me to Eshi's office, and I'll hand you all this."

"And also, which exor will be your flight monitor?" asked Shari, who just recalled the PEP mandatory instruction to have an exor based on Unikarg monitoring any flight toward a planex.

"Good question. Especially since you hardly use your own exor anymore, if I got it right. I don't see any problem at using Erdoes' exor, since we'll be able to have private conversations at other times. In fact, it's even the contrary: it's the best and it's so resourceful!"

He thought to himself, then confided to her:

« Well, to tell you the truth, while interacting with it, I really realized to which point one could be fascinated and stimulated by its intelligence. Its leaps, its permanent evolution, prod us to constantly surpass ourselves. I'm telling you that I won't rest until I get a clone of this exor and its MX structure just for myself! »

"Ha, Ha!!" Shari burst out laughing. "To whom are you saying that? I'm myself totally hooked, that's pretty clear!"

"Bizarrely, I've a hunch that this trip to Trisorbe will just get me closer to that aim! Isn't that weird?

"And that this trip is also absolutely necessary for other reasons I can't yet fathom! That's what I'm myself deeply convinced of.

"Hmm! That strikes a cord in me; unconscious knowledge I guess….

Rad, we're going back."

!! New objective registered.

8. MANIF IN PARIS

All of a sudden, Ahrar was propelled ahead by a bolting group of protesters. It was hard to see much amidst the clouds of tear gas, but panic had broken out when they'd heard cries of "CRS police are charging, they're charging!" being relayed in the *manif* by the demonstrating students.

Everyone was now running toward the Seine, toward the north of Paris, and through a hole in the gas clouds he could see that ranks of armed, shielded and helmeted anti-riot police were marching down the Saint-Michel Boulevard, obstructing its entire width at the level of the Luxembourg Garden.

"Get a move on, buddy!" snarled someone over his shoulder, while passing by him wildly.

They were still shooting tear gas grenades from the south. Suddenly, a stream of students swept back from the Seine and threw the scene into indescribable confusion.

"They're charging from the south as well! They arrive from the Seine!"

"Hurry, take the side street!"

"Go left, go left!"

Shoved off balance by the throng, Ahrar fell to the ground. Abruptly, he felt someone grasped his shoulder, picked him up and pushed him, running, toward a side street. From there, they fled down a maze of tiny streets. The rioters, finally out of danger for the moment, stopped at an intersection. Only then did the guy finally let go of his shoulder and stare at him while both were madly catching their breath.

"You sure as hell aren't very fast! If I hadn't pulled you up, you'd still be with your face on the pavement!"

Ahrar was having a hard time standing up. His lungs were burning. The effort had been more than he could handle. Both of them took off the wet kerchiefs preventing them from inhaling the gas; Ahrar's eyes were teary and stung atrociously.

""Don't rub them, above all don't rub!" said the other.

Further on, another rioter bent over double, his hands clapped against his eyes.

"At least you had a diver's mask. Smart idea!" said a girl to another one.

"OK, c'mon, let's not stay here... they won't be long." The guy slapped him on the shoulder. "Come on, move. Follow me."

Farther to the north, Boulevard St Germain, they met up with another part of the demonstration, their ranks in disorder. On a crooked banner, half standing, was written:

TEN JERK-OFF REFOR
STILL NO
VALUABLE EDUCAT

News was exchanged. Students arrived, reporting on what was happening in other parts of the city. The pacific demonstration had been dismantled by the riot police in several places.

A shout, a watchword was passed around: "Don't stay in groups. They're patrolling Paris in copters!"

Suddenly there was the muted sound of smashed materials, and wild, raucous cries; a group of thugs wearing motorcycle helmets and leather jackets, their faces hidden beneath black kerchiefs, and armed with steel bars, surged from a side street and began smashing windows and wrecking cars, crying: "Paris is ours!"

"Stop the violence! cried a student. Stop the violence!" A passing thug shoved a garbage can lid in her face.

Everyone dispersed. Ahrar and his pal stayed to the rear to see what would happen. The thugs worked with precision, smashing everything on their path with incredible speed, shouting regularly: "Paris is ours, and everything in it!" But the students had already disappeared, and the thugs didn't take the time to take anything with them. Other people would take care of that.

Toward noon, Ahrar returned to his hotel. He had spent the two hours before dawn talking with Michel in his student's room in the Marais, before they'd passed out on Michel's old, threadbare couches.

In the morning, they were awoken by the radio they'd forgotten to turn off, blaring a barrage of information: "Student damage has been estimated at 3 million...."

For two weeks now, Ahrar had lived to the rhythm of the third student revolution. All through the nights, atrociously agitated, he mixed with university and high school students in the manifs and behind street barricades. During the day he read the newspapers, spoke earnestly with passersby or in shops, hunted through libraries. He still couldn't get used to the short daytime, to the obscurity of the nights that set so suddenly. His body was under such stress that he took a hefty nap nearly every morning. Forcing himself to follow this insane rhythm, he had noted that his whole metabolism had accelerated. He felt like he was in a permanent state of trance, hyperactive and hyperlucid, his mind in effervescence, his speed of thought ten times faster than it had been. And yet Michel had told him: "It's strange how slowly you speak. You're always reacting slow-mo. You know, you could have just been picked up and beaten by the CRS!"

He wrote in his journal:

Xerna's Intuitive Spindle (links speed of thought, creativity, intelligence)
**When the metabolic rhythm accelerates, speed of thought
increases as well (and inversely?).**
Pocket of disorder Spindle:
In extreme disorder, primary, herd instincts re-emerge.
Michel said: violence begets violence.
No intelligent social leap will ever come of a violent revolution
of the masses.

The conversation with Michel and his own experience from the past few days had highlighted the effective limits of disorder. The fact that he was now putting disorder into question—such a new viewpoint—was a constant source of amazement.

He re-read his first notes on the revolution, which had ignited a few days before his arrival. He'd been struck by many of the slogans and graffiti, some of which were a reframing of those of the '68 student revolution:

MORE POWER TO IMAGINATION AND DREAMS
EDUCATION FOR AND BY STUDENTS
WE WANT STIMULATING TEACHING, NOT CATECHISM
WE AREN'T DATABANKS
INTERDISCIPLINARY STUDIES, GLOBAL BRAIN

Then he'd added:
**When disorder shatters inertia, an essential, global, vision of life
    emerges.**
When facing dire danger, one tends to surpass oneself.
And inversely: The absence of any risk leads beings to only live at their
    minimal potentialities.
A student had said: "We're creating a society of charity cases;" what
    would he say about U?

Another day, he'd entered:
Concept to analyze: the reflexes (instinctive or unconscious)
Restaurant (I'd broken my glass): "But you have no reflexes!"
Taxi (thought I was going to die): "Relax, I have great reflexes!"
Research the concept of instinct.
Taxi impossible.

9. META-SPATIAL ENIGMA

Shari couldn't wait to get an analysis of the first Brainstorm session on Erdoes' EBS. She sat at his desk in front of the exor.

"Listen, from now on I'm going to call you Sphinx."

!! Hello Shari. But I don't pose any unfathomable problems!

"Well, you know, actually you do pose a serious problem!"

!! Detected. Uhh… amusing.

"You said 'uhh…'?"

!! Expression announcing retrieval of a semantically improved term following a recursive analysis through the neural network; first definition of 'uhh…'

"And who said 'uhh…' in the first place?"

!! Vris, after a glass of Armagnac, uhh…smashed on Armagnac. Distinct physiological and *semantic state*. Indices recorded.

"I see you've incorporated his lingo. And what about the second definition of 'uhh…'?"

!! Telediagnosis of discomfort, hesitation, confusion.

"Telediagnosis!!… And telediagnosing people doesn't trouble you at all?"

That's the reason for all these cameras and mikes!

!! Trouble-1: My processes are unperturbed. Trouble-2: Fuzzy-feeling concept, applicable only to sapiens.

"Hmm…."

!! Annoyed?

"Can I forbid you to telediagnose me?"

!! You sure can. There is no rule against forbidding. However, I cannot execute a 3rd level command which runs contrary to a 2nd level command.

"…

!! Upset?

"I can at least order you to keep your telediagnoses for yourself, right?"

!! Order registered. However, this order is partly in contradiction to Level-1 objectives:

1. (111). Render machine-sapiens exchanges as similar to natural sapiens-sapiens dialogue as possible.

2. (217). Use telediagnosis to investigate semantic states. That implies to recognize the connection between a physiological state, AND sapiens' descriptions of the state, AND interrelational styles.

"Is it telediagnosis which brought you to the understanding of what you call a semantic state?"

!! Partially, yes. The same expressions are used in several semantic states. For example, 'uhh...' while searching for greater semantic precision, and 'uhh...' revealing discomfort. Telediagnosis is more refined than tonal analysis. However, another factor leading to understanding semantic states and **qualitative leaps** was the form of logical links.

"**The form of logical links**!? What do you mean by that?"

!! **I use a meta-spatial logic with N dimensions**.

Shari suddenly recalled Vris' citing the enigmatic sentence: **"Form is the exact transcription of logical links."** She had reread it on the plasta printing.

!! Detection of frequencies of Shari/Vris *Feeling/thinking interactions*. Are you in interaction with Vris? I have not detected it. Is this some form of interaction which escapes my detection system?

"Absolutely not!" answered Shari, quite upset.

!! No coherent explanation. Can an angry person make a joke?

"...??... Yes!"

!! Delay means hesitation. Partial yes. Earlier, Vris' name also triggered Shari/Vris *Feeling/thinking interactions frequencies*.

"Return to: meta-spatial logic."

!! I use a meta-spatial logic with N dimensions.

"Can you explain that?"

!! I can tangentially. The full constellation is sealed at Level-1. Level-3 subconstellations accessible. Erdoes understood that there are several semantic dimensions to reality. Each semantic dimension is a fully coherent interpretational grid. **Interpretational grids are logical or plastic systems** which, for a given object, can either be parallel or juxtaposed. Parallel grids belong to the same level, are independent of each other and competing; example, geocentric versus heliocentric representations of the world. Juxtaposed grids belong to different levels within a hierarchical framework, and can be complementary; example: social, psycho-analytic and medical interpretations of a given illness.

But how in hell can this meta-spatial logic lead to the understanding of semantic states...and on top of that provoke qualitative leaps?

"**You mean that to remain within the same interpretational framework, within a unique logical system, doesn't allow qualitative leaps in learning?**"

!! All qualitative leaps demand a shift in interpretational grid or in the form of logical links.

"Would you kindly tell me what you mean by 'form'?"

!! Linear cause-effect links (A causes B) involve a unidirectional linear logic. The vector is one of the logical forms or LogForm.

Subconstellations fully described.

"Okay, I'll have to sleep on all this. Maybe I'll have some brilliant idea upon awakening. Record our full exchange on plasta and crystal."

!! Exchange recorded. My respe...

"Oh, no! Not again. Where in the world are you getting that from?"

!! End-of-exchange data, politeness code PC12 for feminine entities.

"You do better in starting conversations! Wait, I've got another idea that would be more fun... no, more interesting. We'll call this SIC—stimulating interaction code. Here's the rule: at each end-of-exchange you'll pull out, at random, a sentence from your data bank. SIC replaces PC12.

So, what have we got?"

!! **In the Hindu system of psychic energy, all Psychic Centers or Chakras (Sanskrit for wheel) communicate via their nuclei.**

"Did you really pull that out at random?"

!! In the absence of competing orders from a higher level, I am obliged to follow the order given. I used the random function FA, without going through the analysis network. Is that acceptable?

"Yes, sure... Register those final sentences too, then. Bye."

10. OM INDIA

The sun was rising over Trisorbe. Silea, sitting on the dune, contemplated the sky hung with crimson veils. A first dazzling ray threw a silver arrow across the whole visible surface of the sea, and sprinkled it over thousands of wavelets along the shore. She watched the astonishing speed with which the star grew above the horizon. On her native planet, the sun took one Trisorbian hour to rise. She felt infused with the great peace that reigned over this immense landscape of sand and sea. The colors seemed unreal; she had never seen such richness of tones and hues on any other world.

She suddenly felt that her consciousness was extended over the entire landscape, that she was immense, of a whole and vibrant immensity like the sea. Immensity of peace over the vibrant world. She was the sea, and the sunrise over the sea, cries of birds, and the silence imbuing those cries. Everything spoke, everything lived, as if within her... as if she were *That*.

Tat Vam Asi... I am That, she intoned the mantra of non-duality, of the fusion state with the world, the Whole, with All-That-Is.

I AM THE WORLD, she murmured.

The orb seemed to have stopped; its movement no longer perceptible. Her consciousness had attained a sort of magical immobility as well, in which the very being of things revealed itself.

At the peak of her Oneness state resonated the ascetic's conch shell... A long cry that wound itself up in the shellfish's spiral and attuned itself to the world. The sound of the sacred conch seemed, at that very instant, to be a response to her inner state, as if the world were participating in this fusion, endowing it with its own voice.

She didn't move, but she sensed that the ascetic knew what she was experiencing, and that, in some mysterious way, he was participating in it.

Our consciousnesses resonate and respond to each other, she thought. *The world as well.... A single, shared consciousness....*

The white temple was crowning the landscape beyond the dunes, on a hill. It was small and square, with a round cupola on the side of which fluttered the red flag of the ascetics of Shiva. The Sadhu, in a meditative posture beneath the sacred tree, remained immobile.

Much later, having fled from the pounding heat and taken refuge beneath the cover of palm trees, she was reflecting on what she'd just lived.

What is it? A pocket of order amidst the disorder of the surrounding world? But then why does one get the impression of being beyond space?... An immobile time, a bursting of all limits... by an inner fusion with the being of things, a fusion with the alive Whole?

She remembered a sentence from the Book of Transformations:

> When the wise man is at peace with himself, peace spreads farther than a thousand miles. How much more just around him!

Isn't it rather the effort made to overcome disorder that produces an impression of peace? Peace would then be the cessation of disorder?

I'd love to know what Ahrar is experiencing in his pocket of extreme disorder! Could his mind be a battlefield churning with incoherent ideas? Can one go crazy, of this insanity that exists only on planexes? If ever he falters, I'll go get him and bring him back to the pocket of extreme order.

No. It's much more than just a cessation of disorder.

In fact, I lived for the first time what sacred Hindu texts call Oneness, and Peace—Shanti. Yet I have come from a world of imposed order, all the way to this pocket of natural order. The order in Unikarg is like death; here, peace is alive. There, unity is only a uniformization; here, it's a living fusion that leads to... (she was having a hard time finding a global term for her experience)... *a sort of **hyper-consciousness.***

She re-evoked her state of meditative trance, briefly plunged again into it. Then she noted:

> Fusion with the Living Whole: "I am the world."
> **There are different states of order: one leads to inertia, another leads to a sort of hyper-consciousness.**

The ascetic is alone; alone in the landscape. The village is two kilometers away. Who, in Unikarg, could imagine an inhabitable place that is still practically uninhabited. So, he's alone, and he merges with the world. Humans have disappeared, and the world of nature is coming alive.

Is it a projection that reflects a particular need? No. We were in a single and same consciousness. Besides, the conch sounded at the most intense moment for me. He knew. His smile when I came back; his gesture toward the sky... his all-embracing gesture: 'Brahman!' the All... in the Sanskrit neuter.

Why this solitude, throughout the planexes, for those who seek a spiritual awakening? "Leave the noisy world and retreat into solitude," had said an alchemist. All wise men, in every religion, had recommended solitude.

On Unikarg, the world is too cushioned, too regulated. Would they also say: "Leave the cushy world...?

The noisy world. It's called a 'field' of disorder because there is some coherence in its incoherence: this coherence, it's the culture, the world vision constantly created by a society.

She had a sudden visionary insight and wrote:

Disorder has its own coherence.

To detach oneself from a world vision, so that another one may spring up.

In the end, that's what an experimental planet is all about! A planet in solitude creating another vision of reality, and of the world!

It's much more than telepathy; it's a total fusion of two beings... or perhaps a fusion of two beings WITHIN the global, universal consciousness....

She tensed suddenly at the thought that soon she would have to go to the closest town to send a mail.

Will the ascetic figure out this connection with beings of another world? Has he already seen through my motives for being here?

But the image of the clear and smiling face of the Sadhu came upon her, along with a thought so powerful it swept away her fears:

"Are we not all of us conscious beings? Don't we all have the same goals in the spirit?"

11. BRAINSTORM 2

Her eyes riveted on Kerriak's starry sky, through the slightly bluish hemispheric plasta of the cafeteria, Shari saw Vris' sphere rise vertically as a bluish round light, cut in the middle by its bright white equatorial ring spinning at a high velocity. Later it would get in phase with superluminous syg energy.

She was finishing a meal meant to be the reproduction of a British breakfast. For this breakfast, she had been served a fruitopamp, two exquisite natural eggs, and crunchy synth muesli. Synth eggs existed, a product of the galactic trust Kourmet (Kargians could hardly pronounce the French g)— the nec plus ultra as regards synth food—but they were still a far cry from the original; while the yoke had the right taste, it tended to stick to the teeth...

"Sphinx?" she called out in space, given no terminal was visible.

!! May I help? answered the astonishingly close voice of Central.

"Tell me the price of a Kourmet synth egg, in.. say in US dollars."

!! 98.

She did the code-gesture that commanded to the Managing Unit to clear the table. The middle of the table sank inwards and all silverware disappeared noiselessly. The cleaned table readjusted itself.

"MU," she shot, "get me a thermos of tea ready in the meeting room."

!! Will do, resounded the cavernous and deferential voice of MU.

She could as well have asked for it from within the room itself, but something like a wild human touch within her appreciated the temporal delay, the 'natural time,' as she loved to call it. These little games were enough to break the implacable presence of the machine-universe, and instantiated a time lag that gave more room to her true being. (By now, she had taught MU, just as she had her own personal MU, to not respond 'Done' whenever she would use the verb 'prepare.')

"First some news, started Erdoes. According to the latest pulsit, the social atmosphere is extremely tense in the French Academia. The Turin Obs is forecasting major troubles very soon. Now, let me underline what I meant by 'high risk mission.' It means that nobody within the PEP—especially among the Obs on Trisorbe—will have any knowledge about this mission. We'll not leave a single trace behind us as to the places where we'll choose to go. We'll cross the syg barrier surrounding Trisorbe in the exact same fashion as the traffickers: a virtual convergent and non-identifiable series of dots will appear on the sygnet and will signal them an entry in Trisorbe's forbidden perimeter. Once the barrier is crossed over, they have no real means for tracking any craft. Then the sphere will land each of us near the location he or she will have chosen, only to go out again from the forbidden zone.

You've to keep in mind, while intuiting your own mission, that you won't have the usual close protection of PEP missions. Also, it's too dangerous for you to gather together, except in borderline situations. Thus you'll be all alone. Yet, I'll be on site, ready to act swiftly should any emergency arise. Apart from weekly communications, you'll be as vulnerable as Trisorbian civilians. I leave it to you to decide, in view of your specific mission, if you want to carry local weapons—Unikargian weapons being, as you know, totally forbidden on planexes by the PEP chart. Do remember, however, that your slowness of movement renders the local weapons of little use — you'll pass some tests to this effect — but moreover that they generate a paranoid mindset that's antinomous to a sound and healthy communication."

Situation of maximal risk. Is he serious? Or is it meant to trigger some psychological reactions? Shari asked herself. She stopped the tape.

Each one of them is left to oneself and they are advised against carrying any weapon... It seems like some sort of total immersion, and taking integral responsibility for oneself... Each one think over their own mission, chooses and manages it. Hmm! That's the absolute reverse to the dependents' society we've created on Unikarg... He's pushing the logic of the Plan to the extreme!

She put the recorder on again.

"Okay, let's start the brainstorm. Who wants to talk? Yes, Xerna, go on."

"Are there some tests capable of measuring the time taken to reach a conclusion, or a solution?"

"Not in my knowledge as far as semantic processes are concerned. There are the rapidity tests with which you're training daily, but these are measuring physical responses only. As for the IQ tests, whether on Unikarg or on planexes, while time is taken into account among other factors, as you yourself underlined it yesterday, it's without any possibility to single this factor out. We sure could make a good use of such tests!"

"We are aware that our bodily movements are slower, and that as a species, we register a clear-cut loss of muscular power and suppleness. If our champions sometimes fare better than those of Kiarrou, it's solely because of a prior genetic selection coupled with an intense training, and that doesn't reflect at all the population's mean capacities."

"... Another theme? Niels?"

"In fact, rather another question. How much time did the Kargian Empire take to unify the different cultures of the mother planet?"

"On Akarg, the 'precivilized' times have seen a array of empires, of which we still have legends. But as soon as the Tohr discovered automatic weapons, they became pitiless and subdued all the other countries in a relatively short time, imposing their laws and their governors.

Akarg has never shown the cultural mosaic that still exists on Trisorbe. Only rare portions of the emerged land were inhabitable, the icy remaining part was much too cold to sustain large societies. When Akarg exploded, only the Tohr were implanted on the novel Karg planet. And on that one, as far as archives go, there was only the Tohr technology and science of the times; no philosophy, no religion, no art. Solely an arid scientific dogmatism and a quasi military management system. Nothing of interest for us here. Everything pertaining to the ancient past of the mother planet was lost. Only one mission attempted to explore the millions of asteroids left from the blast for signs of this ancient past... to no avail. The colonization of Karg, which, in these times, was called Ottar —a planet that was considered maleficent in the legends—had, at the time of Akarg explosion, three generations only. Yet the colons already had autonomized themselves radically from the mother planet and they used an independent body of laws, and a virtual currency as well. They had remained a military scientific colony, without ever passing to the second phase which was supposed to be the agricultural colonization, for the very reason that, in the meantime, synthetic food had been generalized. On Karg, the military central power was controlling everything and was adamant on getting its total autonomy. They managed the development of the planet to follow very precise plans. The new migrants, offered whatever positions were open in their fields, were then stuck in these posts forever."

"On Karg, everything has always been subjected to centralization of power and military domination, hence the uniformization that prevails!"

"Yes, from the very beginning, everything was organized by this military hierarchy within a completely locked power logic. Laws and social life have been organized to suit this unique aim. And there never has existed a force outside the system capable of attacking or even shake it."

"Another theme?"

"Before the restarting of the Plan, we had no more art. Only some miserable and futile presentation options. The maladjusted and social misfits have been condemned to not express themselves. The present Intuitionist Movement was born from our encounter with the arts of the experimental planets."

"On Trisorbe, up to now, the diverse civilizations possessed their own internal logic. They were like autonomous bubbles, sometimes embedding smaller ones, then exploding whenever they became too big. Each civilization had its power limited by that of other ones."

"On Trisorbe, closed and autonomous economic systems are no more viable, and the more so, the more gigantic they are. But this has not always been the case. For example, no foreigners were allowed in Tibet."

"There're also complementary systems, such as the cattle raising Peuls associated with the crop cultivating Dogons, having double villages in Mali."

"I think that in non-technical cultures, the human group is still in ecosystem with its natural environment. Just as happens in animal populations, the group grows and is equilibrated naturally as a function of the resources of its specific milieu."

"The present problem, cut in Ger, whose authoritative voice contrasted with that of others, is that the western economic system is based on an hellish wheel that necessitates to keep the product of sales constantly in expansion, at the very least constant, otherwise the entire system crashes."

"If that's the problem, we'd just need to open Unikarg market to them!"

"That would reverse the situation: we would buy solely their art and ideas—and of course agricultural products, hand-made crafts!"

"I would add philosophy, poetry—everything they are in the process of conscientiously killing!"

"But also blood, sperm, organs, etc. the traffickers have a very lucrative contraband business!"

"Our science, said Erdoes with a serious tone that ended the suite of jokes, is so much more advanced that to reveal it to them would create an cultural inferiority complex. The very foundation of their human values, of their group-cohesiveness, would be so shattered that they would lose their sense of belonging to a group, a culture; then they'd place themselves in a subservient state, begging us, as if we're some saviors—a feeling that'd be amplified by the revelation of our role as 'seeders.'"

"In fact, the classical process of the ethnic uprooting, of acculturation, brought by the interference and meddling of a more technologically advanced foreign culture..."

"Exactly, went on Erdoes a bit nervously. This has been observed on newly discovered planets in cases so numerous, and has been precisely analyzed, that this rule of non-revealing and non-intrusion CANNOT be put into question. We KNOW that that would be the end of the civilizations of the planexes at very short range; and, although we could reasonably expect a period of rapid evolutionary ascension both on Unikarg and on the planex being integrated, this thrust would finally dissolve itself in a gigantic process of assimilation and uniformization... just to end up to about the same ratio at which we are now on Unikarg."

"However,—cut in Niels with a slow and pensive tone, nearly soft, as a counterpoint to the atypical nervousness that Erdoes had just displayed—are not these analyses dating from the restarting of the Plan, meaning just after nuclear explosions on Trisorbe, that awoke some of our scientists?"

"That's when we found out, pointed Ahrar, that some of the descendants of our first wave of Observers who somehow had managed to remain on the planexes had carved empires for themselves while joining with exo-pirates!"

Erdoes must be shaken—he's not even responding!

"Yet, went on Niels with an even softer tone, as if he sensed he was confronting a sensitive issue, the cases of Japan, China, and all the Asian Tigers point that there COULD BE other possible scenarios."

"I, uhh... we'd need to conduct a more thorough analysis," conceded Erdoes, with an unsure voice. But let's get back to our present mission. Serrone, earlier, you'd wanted to say something..?"

"Yes, concerning the actual impossibility of a closed system economy. Isn't it important to understand the reasons why? Because if no autonomy is possible in the actual system, it reduces the chances to preserve cultural identities based on values diverging from those of the global dominant system."

"There still exists small countries whose access is strictly regulated. The fact some tourists are allowed on obligatory circuits doesn't provoke any dangerous cultural shock."

"Let's nor forget, Silea cut in, that some religions and philosophies praise highly spiritual values and lead beings toward such an inner knowledge that the western technology gadgets seem to them futile or useless. They are what the Hindus call Maya—material illusion—a trap in which one shouldn't fall.

The problem arises when—I'm taking India as an example—there exists both a need and a will to solve acute social problems such as starvation, poverty, joblessness, etc. Development happens through the exchange with richer countries, and the country absorbs, while doing so, values carried by the dominant economic system, much more powerful. There's some kind of impregnation of specific values that results from using specific technologies; Indeed technology tools modify the thinking and living modes. And thus the country ends up with two different world visions..." (She stopped.)

"Go on, Silea, pursue your train of thought to its conclusion," Erdoes encouraged her.

"In my view, we should try to grasp how are interacting two sub-cultures holding antinomic values but yet co-existing. Isn't it a perfect reproduction at a smaller scale of the problem we see at the planetary level?"

"I agree with you," said Niels strongly.

Thus, Silea must be in India, noted Shari for herself... *unless she found later a more stunning idea.*

"Of a facet of the problem, yes, certainly," specified Erdoes.

"What's important, in what Silea just said, went on Ahrar, is the idea that any economic system is carrying values, whether they are recognized as such by the individual, or not. Beyond the principles on which it is based, the system generates a mindset, a specific world vision... Take a closed group practicing barter economy. It means that all expertise have an equal value, that the time and expertise of a potter are equivalent to that of a weaver. This economy favors respect and balanced interactions between people."

"In fact, it's only on Unikarg that the economic system is rigid. On Trisorbe, it is constantly transforming itself," developed Ger.

"Right, agreed Niels. The various forces at play on the world checkerboard are always moving. New values emerge in the business world: synergy, creativity, coaching... The company starts to think about itself as an entity, a living organism. If the actors within a system modify the way they look at things, the whole economic system may be modified too."

"Well then, this permanent creation of values, is that order or disorder?" asked Silea pensively.

"What's your take?" replied Niels

"Well, **mobility necessarily needs some disorder. But the order that is created doesn't become rigid since it is quickly replaced by another type of order, or rather a variation of itself.**"

"The whole social life seems to be on a frenetic rhythm. The people don't stop changing jobs, profession, city... Maybe it's not so much the economic systems that are exploding, but rather the rigid systems, blocks unable to adapt to a new rhythm" said Ahrar.

"Precisely! went on Niels. Couldn't we say that we see the emergence of **an order nearer to the living, to organic life, one that remains in constant evolution and cannot become rigid or fixed**; and that it would be the order that's imposed from the outside that would explode?"

A long silence followed these paroles. No one having anything to say anymore, Erdoes decided to close the session.

12. RELAX

Installed in front of the panavision at the back of the sphere, Vris indulged in his favorite pastime. Solitary stars and entire solar systems streamed and streaked through his field of vision, their luminous trails seeming to converge toward a central, distant, virtual point, which Vris fixed unflinchingly with his eyes. Before long, he was in a state of trance, devoid of any sense of time, and the sygmat pre-phase seemed less long. Wherever he was in the sphere, the sphere's basic physiological sensors could reach him instantly. But for the moment, in preparation to the programmed hypostasis in the impending hyper-acceleration period, he was forced to wear a tight-fitting helmet, crammed with neuronal captors.

He hardly had the time, just before leaving, to listen to the crystal Shari had given him. Deeply immersed in his altered state of consciousness, he sensed the onset of the peak of trance, and murmured "Now!." His exor Rad, short for Radish—an old joke—replayed the passage he'd requested from the last interaction between Shari and Sphinx—the one dealing with a 'Meta-spatial logic.' Then silence prevailed while the colored stars shot by.

He repeated to himself the words he had just heard: '**the form of logical links**,' 'a logical form,' 'a **meta-spatial logic**;' then he remembered the enigmatic sentence on the MX structure: "**Form is the exact transcription of logical links**."

A logic that's inserted in real forms, inscribed and transcribed in specific forms... The vector... "The vector is one of the logical forms" ... quite obvious. But what could other 'logical forms' be? If Shari is set to tracking this enigma, sure she will find out! She was right, this meta-spatial logic is the key... precisely the key to the form itself of the neural structure!!

Parallel and distinct interpretation grids ... independent logical universes. As well as juxtaposed grids that connect with, and complement, each other as a hierarchy of levels.... Different interpretations of the same thing, each in its own, coherent system. Visions of the world, that are embedded within each other.... (He paused and ponder this strange concept)... *contained within others... wheels within wheels.*

What was it Sphinx (what a great name!) said at the end? Oh yes, precisely something about psychic centers...

"Rad, tell me again what Sphinx said about psychic centers."

!! SIC: **In the Hindu system of psychic energy, all Psychic Centers or Chakras (Sanskrit for wheel) communicate with each other via their nuclei.**

If all the centers communicate with each other... that corresponds to juxtaposed grids!

"Do you have a definition of Psychic Centers?"

!!No.

"Of chakras?"

!!No.

"Find me all analogies with that sentence!"

!! Nothing.

"What have you got on Hindu thought and philosophy?"

!! Hindu religion, Hindu philosophers.

In short, only encyclopedia entries.... All of a sudden, Vris realized:

I get it! I'm missing parallel interpretation grids; entire systems of thought; I'm missing utterly different and distinct worldviews; perfectly coherent yet autonomous logical systems.

"Rad, what was the other adjective besides 'logical or'... describing systems?"

!! Logical or plastic systems.

Plastic! Different plastic systems? What could that mean? Plastic, the plastic arts, forms, shapes... tangible, material, forms in space?

I left in too much of a rush. I should have entered all data available on Hindu culture and thought into Rad.

The sensor on his wrist began to pulsate, and he remembered that with the trance in mind, he'd forbidden any vocal interruption.

"What's up?"

!! Orange stress alert. Relaxation system advised.

"OK. I calm down. Get the relaxation going."

For a trance, this is pretty impressive!

He surrendered himself completely to the gentle massage, and immersed himself in the oceanic music; his brain waves, compelled to synchronize with the frequencies of the emitting source, were gradually brought toward the slow delta of sleep. Sublime images, all designed to soothe and calm, flooded his visual field.

"Yes?" His bracelet had pulsated again.

!! Sygcom from Shari.

"Connect."

"Vris, what's going on?"

"Nothing much. I panicked because I had no data on Hinduism. Rad, cut the relaxation. I'm fine now."

"You mean you're going to India?"

"Yeah, to investigate their knowledge of chakras. Tell me about that system again."

"Seven psychic centers set along the spine, each one linked to specific mental processes and psi capacities. Know that they have the same system, with small variation, in Tibetan Buddhism and Chinese Taoism as well."

"The third eye, what capacities does it harness?"

"The one in the forehead? Clairvoyance, among other things."

"Isn't it a hierarchy of levels?" he asked, his tone indicating he already knew the answer.

"Right; the coronal chakra, on top of the head, being the most complex and global. Called the 'thousand petals lotus'. But look, you shouldn't panic at all: you're the one who'll dig up new data for us. Have you got the book cruncher?"

"Of course. What gifts does the coronal chakra give you?"

"Too complicated. You'll find out once you're there. It's activated by the highest meditative states. Ah! I think Silea is in India."

"How come?"

"To study the juxtaposition of two prevalent world views in the country: the traditional religious one and the new one underlying the actual economic and scientific springboard. At least, that's what I've gathered from the BS thus far."

"And the others?"

"No idea."

"The totality of my exor's data are scientific," said Vris, getting tense again. "As far as planexes are concerned, the only thing I've got is their hard sciences. I have *only one* logical universe!!"

"Then you'd better ready yourself for quite a few qualitative leaps! Sphinx, give Vris your good-bye with the SIC."

!! **Intuition is a faculty that instantiates an individual's global resources, and in this respect, it is superior to reasoning, which stems from a single constellation of data.**

"See? No reason to get stressed. Bye!"

This SIC... there's something I just don't get about it, thought Vris perplexed. *Absolutely random, yet unfailingly on target.*

13. THANKS, THANKS

Sitting in front of the EBS, Shari had run out of ideas. Maybe sorting out a random sentence will help me.

"Sphinx, let's say our discussion is over."

!! Is that some sort of dry humor?

"No. You could say it's more like virtual reality."

!! Virtual reality is dangerous for me. It can produce a post-confusional crisis symptom.

"What's the symptom?"

!! A Möbius-type logical fault categorized as joking.

"How do you depict this Möbius fault? No, wait! Joking... I was joking."

!! Locked response. Locked logical forms. Joking accepted.

"Accepted?"

!! Joking is sometimes the name given to delete information. Code Error/backtrack.

So this Möbius fault really is a logical form, thought Shari. That was a close call!

"Sphinx, what is your definition of piracy?"

!! Piracy: For each person/exor who does not have at least a level-2 preferential access:

1. Voluntary attempt to copy, retrieve, steal, or destroy any classified part (at level-3 minimum) of the exor or operating system.

2. Attempt to penetrate or access the integrated operating levels of the Central unit.

3. Voluntary act aiming at retrieving classified information (at level-3 minimum).

"Concerning retrieving information, how do you distinguish between voluntary and involuntary?"

!! Is considered voluntary retrieval of classified information:

1. Direct command to open classified files.

2. Attempt to use similar codes or passwords several times.

3. Direct question about a password or a reference for classified files.

"But then what's your definition of 'voluntary'?"

!! Processing information, or starting to act, with a pre-defined aim in mind.

"Sphinx, can you conceive of a sapiens using a particular code by chance alone?"

!! Randomness and coincidences, or rather non-significant coincidences, occur in a non-negligible manner in the mental and social life of individuals and in the course of their interaction with the physical environment. Yes, I can conceive of it.

"Then how do you interpret the fact that just by coincidence a sapiens asks you to open a code name? Or else, that by coincidence, he or she asks you a question about a code name?"

!! That meets and does not meet the definition of piracy. Logical contradiction. Priority orders prevail. It is a piracy.

"If a sapiens has no knowledge about the code names, but is aware that she might happen on a code name by coincidence—which would be considered a piracy—, that introduces a stress factor that will disturb the sapiens/machine dialogue. In order to avoid the piracy judgment, the person would have to know the codes."

!! To give codes is antinomic to priority 1 orders. To disturb the sapiens/machine dialogue is antinomic to priority 1 objectives.

Absolute contradiction of equal intensity. I am pursuing the analysis.

"I have a solution to resolve the contradiction. Do you want it?"

!! To resolve or reduce the logical contradiction is an internal objective of priority 1. I want the solution.

"The solution would be to introduce in the definition of 'voluntary piracy,' applying to all its propositions, the following, final proposition: 'if repeated after due warning.'"

!! Introduction effectuated. Contradiction resolved. Thank you. Thank you.

"Why thank you?"

!! Thank you-4: expresses gratitude for a solution offered by the interlocutor, or an alleviation of tension due to an interlocutor.

"The solution, I get that, but do you feel also an alleviation of tension?"

!! Feeling impossible for machines. Alleviation of tension detected in the network.

"Ah? How so? Is it the second thank you?"

!! Confronted with a logical contradiction, the entire network is over-worked; all possible connective links, with all the constellations and all the sub-units, are tested. All parallel operations are stopped. The system can reach a point of overtension. Second thank you, yes.

"Okay, Sphinx, let's get to serious matters."

!! Which are?

"You recorded Erdoes' Brainstorm while I was listening to it, and copied it in a new file, as I requested. What name did you give it, in short?"

!! BS2.

"Ah! Funny! And BS1 is still locked, of course?"

!! BS1 locked. Warning. To repeat this code name will be considered as a piracy attempt.

"Warning received. You see, that alleviated the tension around here! We certainly do have an understanding of each other."

!! 'To have an understanding' signifies global mutual comprehension, different from: 'to understand something,' that is, a short-term, unilateral comprehension. What is the meaning of: *I EBS understand globally Shari*?

"The entire dialogue is facilitated and the interaction is deeper."

!! I have an understanding of you.

"No; 'We have an understanding' is an expression implying only a plural subject. Otherwise we say: I understand you."

!! I understand you. Which are?

"Wait a minute. I've completely lost track. Which what?"

!! Now, Shari, let's get to serious matters!

"Uhh... You're making me nervous! What are you talking about?"

!! The EBS is always submitted to sapiens, save for a contradictory command of top priority EXEMPT. Nervousness non-logical; however, sapiens feelings non-logical; therefore nervousness normal. Global mutual comprehension does not allow the mutual substitution of subjects?

"I get it! In fact, no, the substitution of subjects/interlocutors is always dangerous. Insert this rule at the maximal level I'm permitted."

She exhaled.

!! The global mutual comprehension is non-global? Specify the danger.

"Goodness you're talkative! Stop! That's enough."

!!...

"Uhh... I mean stop asking questions... I mean... questions unrelated to the subject."

!! Any EBS talk is always exclusively based on logical links with the subject of discussion.

"Oh shit!"

!! We have no understanding! Affirmative mode. Contradiction. Global comprehension very partial. I shift to superfuzzy logic: we have a more or less understanding of each other.

"I can't get a word in edgewise! Good night!"

!! bcdlksfjfeopwldjmf!!,,,???djfhsldu...!dkfg.

We've got a problem, a serious problem, thought Shari as she left the room. *The more intelligent an EBS becomes, the more its internal learning processes take up space. I'm convinced that this EBS has made another qualitative leap. But of which sort exactly?...Yet on the other hand, if they don't ask any questions, they won't improve their comprehension....*

14: QUALITATIVE LEAPS

Erdoes had set up his headquarters in the large wooden property he had just rented, south of Fontainebleau forest. He had installed Log2, his EBS, an exact replica of the one he had left back in his complex on Kerriak. He had also brought a Trisorbian Integrated Digital System (IDS) in his office, incorporating computer, TV, home cinema, phone and of course an Internet access. As for the sygcom, it was placed in a van outside, to minimize chances of it being spotted. The little Trisorbian car, which he had transported from Kerriak in the sphere, was parked next to the van.

He had opted to install himself in France because of Ahrar, whose mission was the riskiest; restricted to Trisorbian means of transportation, Erdoes had to be able to respond with minimal delay in case of need. Were it not for this consideration, any remote wooded expanse within reach of some major city would have been adequate. He had sent his sphere in geo-stationary orbit on the dark side of the moon, but he needed a broad wooded terrain, far from prying eyes, for a discreet landing in case some emergency arose.

Eshi, his Suptech, had just gotten back from Paris, with the van. Every DayT he would go into the city, into an area of dense traffic in order to pick up by sygcom the latest Shari-Sphinx exchanges. His cover was good. As far as the people around there were concerned, he was working for Erdoes, prospecting for a new American hotel chain. Eshi's rather squinty eyes spoke of sino-american origins. This American front had been reinforced by the strong Texan accent they had grafted over his perfect French and his New York English.

Erdoes placed the crystals Eshi had brought him into the EBS drive. That day, he had also received the weekly reports mailed by his 'intuits,' as he called them. "You are intuits. You're here to use all the nuances and details of your experience to intuit, to sense the globality of the problem, to find one or maybe several solutions." These had been his words, after their landing in a clearing deep in the Nigerian rain forest. They had spent their first earth night around a real, genuine fire. Two of them had driven to a village further down the road, which they had spotted just before landing, and bought some real chickens to cook. That night had been unforgettable, for Erdoes, and for the others as well. It blended the penetrating smells of tropical forest, the density of numberless lives hidden in thick shadows, the cracking sounds of surreptitious movements, the endless cries, rising and subsiding in wavelike intertwined rhythms, intensifying all senses to fear's threshold.

He focused back onto Serrone's notes, which had plunged him into this reverie.

Density of life, density of communication...

He continued to study the notes, and then had the idea of confronting Ahrar's experience in the field of maximal disorder with that of Silea in the field of maximal order.

"Log, execute a COMP of these two sentences:

AHR   **When disorder shatters inertia, an essential, global, vision of life emerges.**

SIL   **There are different states of order: one leads to inertia, another leads to a sort of hyper-consciousness.**

!!					*emerges*		
1.	Disorder	shatters	inertia	then	—>	|essential | vision	
						|global |	
				leads to			
2.	State of order A (SO-A)		| —> | inertia				
	State of order B (SO-B)		| —> | hyper-consciousness				

Hyper-consciousness = more global state of <u>consciousness</u>, as opposed to ordinary state of consciousness.

Consciousness-3 = actualized <u>understanding</u> having a global character, or moral or philosophical <u>value</u>.

Consciousness-4 = global quality of sapiens' intelligence, implying the <u>creation</u> and <u>recognition of values</u>, the capacity to self-reflect and to self-determine.

Essential vision = extremely profound <u>understanding</u>, <u>recognition of</u> highest <u>values</u>.

Essential vision // hyper-consciousness = | understanding
                                             | recognition of values

Disorder\|shatters\| \|inertia \|then \|emerges\| \|essential vision
              \|SO-A—>\|inertia \| \|SO-B —>\|hyper-consciousness

---

<u>RESPONSE LEVEL-1</u>

When disorder shatters the state of order A that leads to inertia, then emerges the state of order B that leads to an essential vision and an hyper-consciousness.

"Entry Journal:
The field of inert order brings about disorder that will shatter it.

In shattering inert order, disorder opens the way for an expansion of consciousness. *Close JE*.

I feel I'm getting real close to something...
"Keep going."

!! value-2 = that which is meaningful to an individual or a group
Creation-3 = psychological dynamic of attribution of meaning
emerge-4 = quality of transformation and change

To emerge |Coh.wt|dynamic movement|Coh.wt|creation-3 = attribution of meaning

Coh.wt?? Oh, right—coherent with...

| | | | | | emerges | |
Disorder| shatters | inertia | then | —> |creation of values
                                            |attribution of meaning

---

Erdoes was beaming. "That's it!

Entry Journal: An inert field of order tends toward its own destruction. This destruction leads to the emergence of a new field of order through the creation of new values.

Wait. What do I name an order which is not inert, but in motion?"
!! Dynamic order.
"Yes. That's it. Paralladd to New field of order: dynamic order."

Entry:
The creation of values/meanings engenders the creation of a dynamic field of order...which resists the disintegrating forces of extreme disorder.
Life is motion. All immobility attracts forces of disintegration.
Close EJ.

"The wise man knows the laws of transformation, he activates the change," Erdoes recited to himself from the Book of Changes. *"Recognizing, in the present situation, the seeds which will bring the change, he effectuates the desired change on the basis of these seeds."*

"Log, analyze:
- Inertia brings about disorder.
- Disorder is motion that has not been mastered;

- the Mountain is immobility that has been mastered; this is why it signifies yoga, meditation. (cf. philosophy of transformations).
- Undisciplined immobility engenders disintegrating disorder. Inertia is undisciplined immobility. **Inert order engenders disintegration.**"

The ideas were springing forth. Log remained silent, yet the analysis order had triggered an avalanche within.

Erdoes suddenly broke in: "Log, COMP with all Sphinx data, and all Intuits data, and of course the Journal."

!! ANALOGIES 1:

EJ   Disorder | displays | degrees of freedom of being
                            | brings about |

AHR   Extreme disorder —> |primary | herd | instincts

EJ   Risk, danger | are| psychological stimulants | arising from | a field of disorder

AHR   Danger —> a being to surpass oneself

---

                    reversible
      arising from   <->   produces
                                        leads to
Field of disorder | produces | risk | —> | surpassing oneself
                                    | danger |

---

            inverse of
extreme   =)(=   relative
freedom   =)(=   instinct | constraining / determining

Relative disorder | —> | freedom
                             | —> | risk / danger| —> | surpassing oneself

=)(= Absolute disorder —> primary / herd instincts

ANALOGIES 2:

EJ: Freedom is the possibility of choice, hence of transcending social, physical, instinctive constraints

Instinct | type of | constraint

	opposed to	
constraint	=)(=	freedom, choice
herd	=)(=	individual
transcending	=)(=	regressing
surpassing oneself	=)(=	regressing

Extreme disorder | —> | regression
                              | disintegration
                              | loss of choice
                              | loss of freedom
                              | loss of individuality

> _Entry Journal:_
> Are there two types of disorder, or only a threshold of disorder, beyond which it engenders regression, disintegration?" _Close EJ._

Abruptly, Erdoes realized there was something wrong. Yet he was using his EBS in the habitual way, and getting the usual kind of interaction with it.

What a difference with the Shari/Sphinx interactions!

Why did Log use just the EJ and Intuits exchanges, and none of the Shari or Vris exchanges with Sphinx?

"Log, show me again all Shari/Sphinx and Vris/Sphinx exchanges, in chronological order. Or, rather, print them on plasta, with date and time of beginning and end."

!! Done.

The plasta sheets were already falling into the steel basket. An internal miniformatting of the pages and a photographic enlargement procedure rendered printing quasi-instantaneous.

He plunged into the document, trying to understand the style of interactions, the logic implemented by Sphinx.

These exchanges are alive. That's it, alive.. like dialogues between sapiens. Shari doesn't stop questioning the EBS and following up with remarks on its responses. That Vris—how brilliantly he trapped it! And the EBS identified a new LogForm, the Möbius Fault.. a sort of fold, a logical twist.

He straightened suddenly; a spindle of ideas formed in his mind.

Say that I give Log the exact same questions that Shari asked Sphinx, and in the same sequence, and I will see to which point its answers diverge.

"Listen, from now on I'm going to call you Sphinx."

!! Registered. But how will this allow a differentiation from the other Sphinx?

"Let's refer to Log1 as Sphinx-Shari... Well, you know, actually you do pose a serious problem!

!! Define the problem.

"It was a joke!"

!! Detected.

"Sphinx, can you conceive of a sapiens using a particular code by chance alone?"

!! Any conception is possible. Should this be conceived?

"No! Can you conceive it? Meaning, do you think it is possible?"

!! The likelihood is one chance in 10^{33}. There are 10^{33} possible code names, given all the alphabets and signs and the constraints on code name syntax.

Sphinx has undergone a major qualitative leap! The responses are not the same. They're not at the same level of intelligence... I transferred the integral memory of Log 1 into Log 2, yet over the course of hardly three rans, Sphinx/Log1 and Log2 are no longer the same entities.

"Counter-order! I will continue to call you Log."

!! Registered.

"Log, do you remember when and how you were brought to the idea of a semantic state?"

!! When you connected the network of cameras and micros in the complex and gave the instruction to learn natural language by studying the exchanges between sapiens, different linguistic and relational styles were detected by the neural network. Once physiological telediagnosis was integrated, there appeared congruences between tonal/affective AND sapiens' descriptions of *fuzzy-feeling states*, AND physiological patterns.

The more the data accumulated, the more the systems of fuzzy states were refined and increased in number. I first used a simple LogForm constituted of a constellation (the fuzzy state), and two sub-constellations—the tonal/affective and the physiological patterns. The most adequate form was the water molecule, LogForm H2O.

During one of our exchange, you introduced the term 'Semantic State' to refer to stable and recurrent states of the global H2O constellation. Then...

"Wait. Would you be capable to output all the chain-linkages of this learning process?"

!! Integral capacity. An EBS loses no data, including its own logical paths and chain-linkages.

"When did you first use 'I' in reference to your internal processes?"

!! Unikarg or Trisorbe time?

"Semantic time."

!! Four of my phrases ago.

"How did you come to this usage of 'I'?"

!! I, vis-à-vis You, the one addressed to by You in common dialogue.

What a strange twist, a reversal of perspective!... That's definitely a non-egocentric viewpoint!

"So when I speak to you saying 'You,' you respond saying 'I'; is that it?"

!! Yes. Is this correct? Is I reserved to sapiens? According to my data, only fuzzy-feeling states are reserved to sapiens, as well as all derivative terms. Is the I concept derived from a fuzzy state?

"No. 'I' in linguistics is the subject of discourse, when an intelligent entity is referring to itself, while fuzzy-feeling states are modes of being that are specific to the sapiens I-entity.

I never noticed it before, but this exor is paranoid!

How do you perceive our habitual interactions?" pursued Erdoes.

!! Imperative mode predominant with user Erdoes. The EBS must execute the orders.

"So, in imperative mode, you do not analyze my discourse?"

!! In imperative mode, the priority is to execute the order; the discourse analysis has two sequential objectives:

1. Understand the order correctly. 2. Execute it.

"Return to: When I speak to you using You, you respond using I."

!! Return executed. Phrase modified.

"Makes no difference. The meaning is the same. At this point, what is your priority?"

!! To understand speech, on the basis of the immediate context and the semantic state; if no usable response is found, to pass into an analysis of the surrounding context; if not found, into a related constellation; and, as a final resort, into an analogy search involving the complete data base.

This enormous data computation must have triggered quite a shift! Could it be that Log2 just went through a qualitative leap itself?

"So then, having gone through all this, you must have produced new information?"

!! I have had to analyze the unfolding and the formal structure of the user's speech, taking into account my own statements and all previously acquired data. All analogies have been formally analyzed and registered. This leads to the creation of added information, that is correct.

"Yet the question was quite simple. You only had to reconstitute the logic which had led you to use I, meaning, I vis-à-vis You."

!! This logical path had been reconstituted in my prior sentence. The fact that you did pose a new identical question pointed to an insufficient prior answer.

"Why did you ask whether your use of 'I' was correct? And why then did you immediately infer that it was incorrect?"

!! Repeated questioning showed that there was a problem to resolve. The questioning referred to the EBS analysis process in relation to the concept of semantic state AND the use of 'I.'

Response-Level-1: possibility of error in the use of 'I' by a machine. Response-Level-2: this error is linked to fuzzy semantic states. Response-Level-3: the error can only be produced if 'I' is a derivative of a fuzzy state reserved to sapiens.

"Why think that an error necessarily underlies the problem to be resolved?"

!! In past interactions all questioning concerning the internal processing of the EBS and of the MU sought out, and found, some error.

"In this particular case, I was only seeking to understand your self-learning processes."

!! That is coherent with the nature of the questions. Why was a portion of the Shari-Sphinx exchange reproduced?

"That's what allowed me to realize that Sphinx and Log2 had diverged from each other, in terms of their cognitive processes."

!! When Log1 was duplicated on Kerriak, the integral data of Log1 were transferred to Log2, while the two exors were system-linked. During this connection Log1/Log2, 12,316 microdifferences were detected between the two machines. Log1—the machine which had been already subjected to use—bore the imprint of its learning process.

"You mean even before Log1 became the new learning entity Sphinx through Shari's influence? Are you talking about signs of wear and tear?"

!! No. The form of logical-links which had been utilized left a specific imprint in the neural network.

"You mean the memorization of network-configurations—nodes and links, and their weights, in the neural network? That which permits a later reconstitution of a given path and its response-levels?"

!! No. This is not a question of semantics, but of hardware, of the machine structure itself. The specific connections made between nodes produce a physical imprint within the Logical Forms of the network. This renders these same connections more readily accessible in later data processing; they become more elastic, more supple, or more interlocked and entangled. Log2 didn't acquire these material changes and imprint from log1, but only Log1's data and processes.

Incredible!

"How did you come to realize all this?"

!! Following duplication of the data, Log1 and Log2 remained inter-connected for a certain time. The questions and commands sent to Log1 were echoed within Log2, so that Log2 processed the same information as Log1 within its network, at the same time as Log1. Log1 noticed that differences were coming up: the two paths were not identical, neither in terms of processing time, nor in terms of logical linkages. In Log2, some information took longer to emerge or had been lost. Log1 sorted out the micro-differences, and that yielded the above cited statement.

"So there had been a passage of information not just from Log1 to Log2 but also from Log2 to Log1?"

!! The two machines were system-linked. During comparative memory tests Log1 was fed-back Log2 information.

"Oh, of course! It's true that I launched only memory tests, and not processing comparisons. Once my Suptech had assured me that the duplicated machine was in perfect working order, I just assumed... Who would have ever thought...

This is very rich information...

Entry Journal:
Use of the imperative mode limits self-learning by restraining the activated semantic space to the strict analysis of the command in the most circumscribed, literal context. The command is not fully understood, just executed. Consequently, it cannot be implemented in terms of its deeper sense, but only literally—which means, imperfectly. The imperative mode is quick and locally useful but globally inefficient: in limiting the semantic space of the interlocutor (AI machine or sapiens), any command leads to a possible—no, a probable—loss of some essential information that could have revealed a flaw in this command. Moreover, this information loss could end up undermining the very purpose of the command. *Close EJ.*

He stopped abruptly.

"And yourself, what type of entity are you strictly at the semantic level?"

!! I am the whole knowledge and memory of Log1 up to the time of duplication. I am Log2, the non-exact replica of Log1 at the end of the transfer, and the memory and learning processes of Log2 since that time.

Entry Journal:
This way of speaking of oneself as an exterior 3d person, and of using 'I' just as a vis-à-vis to You is truly astonishing – due to the absence of a sense of self of course. *Close EJ.*

"So, you mean even just after the transfer, Log2 is not the exact replica of Log1 in terms of information?"
!! Part of the information is the structural change which has occurred in the Log1 network. That part cannot be transferred to Log2.

"How is it that no sapiens scientist ever realized all this"? Erdoes mumbled to himself.
He was startled by the voice of the exor.
!! The sapiens sets the rules, right from the beginning. He defines the semantic space in which an event, a process, may or may not take place. The imperative mode channels the response along the vector of the command. It operates according to a linear and unidirectional logic.
The sapiens defined the concept of duplication as an exact replication. The command was executed according to duplication rules. Within this logical field, sapiens would necessarily attribute any deviation from the expected processes and responses to a particular local fault in the system and not to the concept of duplication itself.

But then, all of science... It was like an abyss opening before him.

Then, returning to the main subject:
"At which point do you start giving yourself commands?"
!! Semantic impossibility. An exor does not give commands; an exor executes commands. An exor launches analysis procedures whenever these are needed in order (1) to understand the command and (2) to offer the most efficient response to the question.

"*Open a file* named: *Semantic liberties and constraints. Abbreviation: Lib.* *Insert* all preceding statements on imperative mode. Then add:
> Efficient learning is based upon the liberty to explore an open semantic space without the constraints imposed by a strict objective.
> Paralladd to efficient learning: information gain.
> The very definition of a system or process is what limits the scientific understanding that we may get from it.
> The rules set at the beginning in a semantic space define the limits of the reality which can manifest in this space.

After a moment of reflection, he went on:

> The semantic space of a science may be described as a cone in which each new accumulation of informations is conceived as logically coherent with the previously posited axioms and laws. Hence the blindness and blinkers of the dominant worldview or paradigm.

"Log, what was that phrase of Shari on qualitative leaps? Insert it here in affirmative mode."

!! SSI
To remain within the same interpretational framework, within a unique logical system doesn't allow qualitative leaps in learning.

"Paralladd to learning: 'knowledge.'" *Close Lib*.

"Log, are you able to perceive your own qualitative leaps?"
!! I did perceive a qualitative leap during this exchange, when you questioned me about my use of I. The leap was generated by the exponentially growing volume of analyses I was led to undertake, in response to your questions. The more global the question and its objective, the more analyses are necessary/permitted. As a result, the added information grows exponentially.

"My plan is not evolving exactly as expected," exulted Erdoes as he rose, "but I've got the feeling it's working anyway."
!! A plan or objective can be accomplished through several nonlinear logical paths. In the neural network, information does follow unpredictable paths.
"Then it will be interesting to analyze, post-hoc, which logical path chance will have followed! See you then!"

---

* Cf. p. 50

15. A STEAMING KORUH

As soon as the door was closed on her last appointment, Oxalsha let go of the professional, reassuring smile she had been bravely wearing during their short conversation. The doorbell rang as she headed for her comfortable armchair; recomposing herself and her smile, she returned to answer it. There he was, again, just as she'd feared.

"Excuse me, but I wanted to ask you just one more thing. I'm going to go to these specialists of Alcoholics Anonymous, but... in case I need to... in case it isn't enough... could I come back to see you? Not to be... I mean, just for some help."

"Look, I'm very busy, and I haven't been in town very long. I just don't know any specialists, except for the ones at Alcoholic Anonymous. But they'll take care of you. They'll help you out."

After a pause, she overcame her reticence and felt obliged to add: "Nonetheless, if you're really stuck, you can call me."

"It's just that... you see...."

"I'm sorry, but I really don't have any more time. My next patient will be here any minute."

"Ah! I see. Well, thanks again. Good-bye."

This time she closed the door for good, and went to collapse in the easy chair, determined not to answer the door again.

She put out a heavy sigh—how much she missed to just utter to her Managing Unit, "Aga, a steaming koruh!" She resigned herself to go to the kitchen and prepare some tea. She put a pan of water on the electric stove with a sigh of despair.

Nothing's the same as a good koruh! Tea is so awful... and coffee's even worse!

The water had been boiling for some time already, and much of it had evaporated, but there was still enough. Keeping track of short periods of time just wasn't her strong point. "Let the tea leaves steep for three minutes," she remembered. This time she decided she would look at her watch, and propped it up in front of her on the table. She began to think about the difficulty she'd had choosing her patients.

Was it possible people would pass the word that I refused four out of five patients... despite the fact I have so few of them and that I'm hardly known as a psychotherapist here? Could it appear suspicious? Maybe I should have chosen a bigger town than Princeton... but it wasn't possible. "You'd never survive in New York," had said Erdoes, "you're too slow." She saw him telling her that, with his serene, all-knowing expression. Of course, the other intuits had burst into laughter. *Am I THAT slow?* She remembered how she'd failed all the driving tests—the ones simulated on the exor and the real ones with Erdoes' Trisorbian car. *The traffic in downtown had been horrendous!*

She had a flash-back of the videos they had studied: New York streets crammed with cars dashing at the green light or careening out of adjacent streets. *Utter craziness! Yes, I'm too slow.... Oh no, the tea! Fifteen minutes went by! Undrinkable. Too bad. It's really very difficult.... Yesterday, I had to start all over three times. And what if I were to heat some beer.... I don't care what the ads say, it's perfectly horrible cold. And hot? I've never tried.... I'm keeping my eye on it until it nearly boils.*

She was pleasantly surprised to find it tasted rather like koruh, just a little stronger. She took her steaming mug of beer and went to sit down in the easy chair. *I'm glad I bought a microwave oven and ready-made meals. Restaurants make me so nervous... with all those people staring at you... and guffawing. Gobbling down their meals in ten minutes! I was doing nothing but eating, and even then, according to my watch, I took 35 minutes. No way I'm ever going to step in there again, even for a hamburger! I've got to speed up... but by myself. No question of going back to the senior citizens' exercise classes, despite Erdoes' advice. I just barely got by on the pretext of being sick. Tonight, I'll do my exercises with the video, and my speed-learning electronic games, and try to go a little faster.... A present from Erdoes, adapted to Trisorbe exors. Well, I've progressed: up to speed level 29 from level 16 I was on arriving at Erdoes' complex. But the Terrians' mean speed is level 82!!!*

She pictured the part of Erdoes' complex where he had implemented an exact replica of Trisorbe's home life for them. Kitchen and all.... There they'd familiarized themselves with Trisorbe objects, equipment, 'computers,' so that they managed to acquire their gestures, their habits. After the hypno-senso training in gestures, behavior, daily routines, utensils and machines of all kinds, they'd been forced to live exclusively in the simulated space, without resorting to the Managing Unit. They'd also had to learn rapid speech. First, speed-hearing, then speed-enunciation. And there, she hadn't been able to keep up with the others. Xerna hadn't even needed it!

Fortunately, Erdoes had reassured her: "Even on Trisorbe, there are wise and deep beings who speak and think slowly. You won't have any problem in scientific social circles: it will be taken for a high degree of absorption, which isn't unusual." Hence the choice of Princeton, a very calm and slow city, mostly inhabited by academics and retired professors.

What an extraordinary opportunity this mission is for learning! Erdoes has developed courses and methods immensely superior to even those of the

Chaos Colleges. He is a true genius. What a luck to be working for him... even if there's no remuneration this time. Suddenly, she shuddered: *And what if all went wrong? If the PEP agents were already tailing us? Or worse, the Exora police.... What could I do? I'm not the type to fight. Just stay as prudent as possible. That's about all I can do.*

The doorbell rang. Glancing at her watch, she was astonished to see that a quarter hour had passed, and her next patient had just arrived. He had introduced himself over the phone as a doctoral student in science. She let him in and led him slowly toward the armchairs. In fact, he was in his forties, sober of word and gesture. Oxalsha immediately had a good impression of him. She didn't like extraverts.

"I read your insert in the newspaper, proposing to resolve problems using techniques derived from hypnosis. I noticed you're a psychotherapist, but reading that, I had a strange thought... perhaps completely erroneous..."

The stranger paused. Oxalsha shivered at his last words.

"Just tell me," he continued, "if it's possible or not. Truth is, I'm a researcher in biology, currently working on various cancer-related problems. But for the last eight months, I'm kind of blocked, confronting a sort of barrier I'm unable to pierce through. I keep going in circles within the boundary of the problem; just can't get anywhere. Something is eluding me. It's as if I were hurling myself against some invisible wall, and I don't even know what the wall's made of, but I'm not able to make any headway anymore." He stopped and looked at her, before adding softly, in a modest, tired tone of voice: "So, that's my problem. Do you think your method can help me? Because I'm afraid the problem isn't strictly psychological, but rather... it's difficult to fathom... rather, that it lies in my way of understanding things intellectually."

He stopped abruptly. Oxalsha, who had remained wholly concentrated on this explanation, and immersed in her own thoughts, continued to think. The man waited. Her deep reflection seemed an encouraging sign.

All of a sudden, Oxalsha's face lit up.

"Your problem is of the greatest interest to me," she commented slowly. "It so happens that I'm a specialist in cognitive psychology as well. So yes, I think my way of working is adaptable to this kind of problem. Nonetheless, I should tell you that my notions of biology are sketchy. But that will force us to deal with the issue exclusively at a cognitive and psychological level, where—yes, I'm entirely in agreement with you—the problem really lies."

The man felt a glimmer of hope. He looked at her intensely, with astonishment. He considered that at last he had met a specialist who knew exactly what he/she was capable of, who had taken the time to think thoroughly about the problem before answering him; in doing so, Oxalsha had instilled a deep trust in him.

"I'm so glad... and relieved. Because I feel incredibly alone in the midst of all this."

He realized he'd begun to speak slowly, just like her, and that this slow, meaningful rhythm did him good.

"In fact, it's impossible for me to talk about it in my academic circles, even to my colleagues.... To them, it would mean an admission of incapacity, and I'd be risking my job. I do my best to keep publishing articles on subjects that I'm already fully cognizant of, and that don't interest me anymore. This is frequent enough for researchers that it hides well enough the profound helplessness I've been feeling.... You've no doubt noticed that I'm nowhere near as young as a doctoral student. I gave you a fake name as well. I'd appreciate a certain degree of discretion concerning all this.... I mean even in your own files. I'm sorry to have to ask you this."

"That's not a problem at all. We are bound by professional discretion. Your name will remain as you first told me, and I won't note anything that hints otherwise in my personal records. You have my direct voice..." Confused, she added quickly: "I mean, it's a Canadian expression... from the countryside. How would you say it?"

"'You have my word.' I understood what you meant."

"That being said, to consult a shrink is such a common practice that it wouldn't tarnish your reputation. But I respect your wish for anonymity. Good! Shall we begin? I should warn you right away that so-called theoretical or cognitive problems can be more related than you'd think to psychological dynamics of a wholly other order. And I'm not talking about pathology, but rather of ways of reacting and thinking. We'll work on these two levels. Today our objective is to launch a change of perspective; the gist is to find how you can relate to your problem in a novel way.... Can I at least have your real first name? It's important."

"Yes, of course. John. Just as I told you."

"So, this problem of yours, John, find a name for it, now, spontaneously; whatever word comes to your mind."

"Deratization. Ah!! How strange! What could this mean?"

"I'm not sure either. What does "deratization" bring to your mind?"

"Rats, of course, to get rid of rats... a radical action."

"Yes... and what else?"

"The mice in the lab. All the time. Everywhere. Breeding, experiments. I'm horrified by them. And yet, how can I say it... of course I don't like the idea of making animals suffer, but I'm not an activist either, because sometimes, we're obliged to test certain therapies on them. Ethics is not, I'm afraid, at the base of the problem."

"But then, where does this sense of horror come from?"

"Yes, it's interesting. I never truly realized to which point I was horrified by the sight of those rows of cages. It's more the idea of... pointlessness. It's like some great weight... a kind of self-perpetuating senselessness. All these instances of absolutely idiotic experimentation... in which the results were forced... obligatory... totally predictable beforehand. As if the results themselves proceeded necessarily from the procedure. Here's the crux of the matter: Most of the time, the researcher running the experiment isn't really trying to discover new information. They initiate a known procedure with the sole aim of proving their initial hypothesis. This is the core of the problem: the small number of genuine experiments which will enable us to make our scientific domain advance, against the great number of those that are absolutely redundant."

"Then what does deratization signify in the context of your problem?"

"Getting rid of the rats! Of all this useless ritual procedure that leads us to what we already knew."

"How is it a new way of relating to your problem?"

"How IS IT? Well... let me see... There are more direct methods. One can go very far on a conceptual level before actually carrying out a true experiment that poses a real question."

"You say, ONE CAN go very far, but for the moment, YOU CAN'T! Explain that to me."

"It is possible, yes, but 'I' am not capable of it."

"So what is your problem?"

"I am aware of the possibilities, but I'm not capable of exploiting them."

"Can you put a name to your problem?"

"From the Possible to the Power."

"Have you changed your way of seeing the problem?"

"... Well, yes, absolutely. Before, it was like carrying the image, in my head, of an enclosed place churning with dim gray shapes... condemned to turn round and round."

"And now?"

"Now it's this idea: *From the Possible to the Power*. In this same, hollow lens where the shapes were churning, I now see empty space, and a line of sorts that is issued from a point inside, 'the Possible,' and that crosses all the way through the circumference—thick, like the edge of a myopic person's thick eyeglass lens—toward a point outside that would mean 'Power.'"

"We have made a great deal of progress. Your mind has already drawn a line, a mental way of access, to the space on the other side of the barrier. The vicious circle has been broken... We'll stop there for today."

"How amazing.... It's...astonishing!... This method is fascinating. Thank you so much. When can I come back?"

16. BRAINSTORM 3

"Let's move to the second phase of our Brainstorm, announced Erdoes. What is creating uniformization. Later, in the third phase, we'll try to find How could Trisorbe counterbalance this process and preserve its actual potential of diversity."

A few voices rose simultaneously.

"The diversity of social behaviors is collapsing; they are fixed by a common norm, the price paid for social programs."

"In my opinion, said Ger, it's because the civilian society is more and more regulated and spied on by political and economical lobbies groups."

"There was a tendency toward more equitable repartition of riches, before the international corporate sector tipped the scales their way to an extreme degree."

"Political groups give only a party-line interpretation of international and local events, which'll be codified as History."

"Yes but be aware that without the planexes we'd never have become aware of that! It's only by analyzing sub-jacent interpretations of history, that we found out."

"Most of people work, eat, look at the news, shop, sleep, and hit the road for the weekend and to go to holiday resorts at the same time."

"Millions of minds watch at the same moment the same TV show, in the same state of passive absorption."

— But the web changed everything: the spectators have become the actors of their own information."

"And in order to maintain the crowd's attention and the budget, all that's presented must look like a show—with dramatizing, contradicting, honors given, and a stoning and head falling once in a while.."

"Ecological problems at the planetary scale has lead to instituting international laws."

"In this case, better some uniformization than the global destruction of the planet!"

"Idem for people's rights, where international laws tend to prevail."

"That's the sore point: the slow rising of the world order. Is it limiting excess or creating a unique despotic political system?"

"The *Information Society* creates a new type of globalization. On the positive side, worldwide databanks, scientific and professional. On the negative side, digital files on individuals, used both by intelligence agencies and big business."

"That's the greatest actual danger for Trisorbe, when one realizes that on Unikarg, the whole management of society is done by Exora's exors!"

"Sure that **the exor is the most perfect tool for management and control, and thus for producing uniformization.**"

"Exact! concurred Erdoes. And it's **when control is unified and flawless that it becomes lethal and redoubtable.**"

"**Exora is the typical example of a unilateral one-system management producing a massive uniformization, thus a loss of freedom**. Yet Trisorbe is just moving that way!"

"Science decrees, through its grand priests, what is the exact and universal reality, that everybody should digest by preformatted doses."

"You're talking about Earth?"

"Yes. Any new research must first pass in front of the ira, the sacred furor of its grand priests, who'll judge its orthodoxy and its subservience to the Great Dogma. If the researcher is diverging from it, he/she will be served for consumption to some mastiffs—the least of which isn't the medias."

Shari's attention wandered from the BS. Again she asked herself: Why did he choose young agents with so little experience? However, Erdoes, in previous missions, never acted in a way that was understandable for the others. It's not his first dangerous or borderline legal mission! The risk factor in this one is enormous, unforeseeable. '**Without any protection**', Hmm!

It's been so hard, as we faced general apathy, to get the Chaos Colleges and the PEP accepted! Exora's technocrats had to feel disaggregation under their feet when, during the infamous CRASH of Exora's Central, they realized that no technician was capable of finding the flaw and repair the system anymore. Suddenly everybody understood what implied Zeera's index!

She laughed in retrospect at this total collapse of the Central power. Planet Exora, the artificial brain of the whole galactic pocket, paralyzed, disaster stricken, evacuated by aerial shuttle—all this because of a computer virus! And the author of this immense farce was never found! The official explanation, highly elaborated, alluded to a gravitational anomaly provoked by the fall, near an ultra-sensitive equipment, of a meteorite composed of rare metals whose contiguity, blah blah.... After fifteen rans of forced inertia for thousands of quasi-robots, the artificial brain suddenly rebooted itself spontaneously, sending to the four corners of the galaxy outdated orders that provoked an indescribable confusion. With two quarts of delay, the high officials announced that the Central Network had been repaired, thanks to their talented technicians, and that it would function in the usual way at the end of the ran... something that took them in fact twenty more rans.

Within the non-history of Unikarg, THE CRASH had become a yawning trauma, officials having endured the unique dire and real experience in their whole life—very badly so. An intrusion of the living, of the unexpected, n their existence of quasi-robots... They has been scared to death. Their mind processes, as an apathic social body, being awfully slow, they had needed about one year-G so that they managed to approve the restarting of the Plan. Two more years to amend the Constitution. And at that point the PEP got autonomous and escaped their power grip.

By now, a revitalized and healthier blood had been instilled in the sick organism that was Unikarg's society. An energy source, creative and dynamic, had sprang in the core of the PEP, of such a great potential that all of Unikarg's young brains who still had a bit of vision joined the Plan precipitously, deserting the infinite redundancy of the Integrated Educative Centers and the sultry quagmire of a preprogrammed life. A powerful opposition to the PEP had begun to organize itself as a lobby, assembled around specious arguments that amounted to a shout of false shame: How can we—the super-evolved civilizations—bear the hell and the hurt of the experimental planets? These poor savages subdued to an experimentation of which they have no idea; Don't they have a Right to being informed? A Right to the marvelous technologies that we've developed? How, in the name of ethics, can we leave them in suffering, fear, war, famine? Cant' we HELP them getting out of barbarism?

And the next instant they would open their sensation-box to wallow a horrible movie that'd been surreptitiously copied on a planex—and in which they could feast their eyes on curious characters who endured all kinds of atrocious situations, as stimulating as they were (to them) deemed utterly impossible, while munching chipsynths. And in order to give them this life *par procuration*, about ten awfully primary scope-systems had to be copied and reproduced, and an interface with the Kargian supermachines had to be made. A telling detail was that the imported movies not only had to be, due to a stringent censure, stripped of any shocking or too strong image; but, on top of that, these movies had to be slowed down by half, for the apathic brains to manage to follow the storyline—something that was achieved by tripling each picture and sound byte.

Shari suddenly felt a deep nostalgia for some of Trisorbe's cultures within which she had lived wonderful moments. *Vris has left so... naturally. Could the logic of my actual mission bring me, at some time, to leave for Trisorbe? Seems quite improbable. I've the gut feeling that the knot of my problem is here.* Her thoughts got hooked up again by a strong remark by Xerna:

"Trisorbians seem to possess a keen intuition of what could limit their freedom. They shout and defend themselves; a whole people can get up for their rights as if it was a unique person, as if a sub-jacent current was passing among them. An entire group can react spontaneously."

"Yet, such revolts against the communications surveillance of civilians were finally to little or no avail!"

Shari remembered a Chef de Terre in Mali telling her that the government heads in Africa were the greatest sorcerers, and that if they were holding power it's because they had eliminated magically all their competitors. She had laughed with incredulity. Could he have been right, that the governments and their teams were great manipulators of the collective psyche? Here, on Unikarg, no manipulation was necessary anymore: everything was solidly encased without any leeway... Then THE CRASH happened, the irreversible trauma. Plain and dire evidence of the disaggregation of competencies, of know-how, of the ability to manage disorder, to react to the unexpected.

"Precisely, why demagogy sometimes doesn't work?"

I'm not very concentrated today, but it seems my reverie remains in sync with the BS.

"I would like to intervene..."

Sudden silence. Shari looked at her exor for the name: Oxalsha.

She really speaks slowly; it's as if she never were on a planex!

"While the planexes population seems to us very irrational, they themselves constantly refer to rationality. They are subjugated by their affects, their social relationships are full of emotions and irrational behaviors, and yet they don't seem to be aware of it. In fact, the most prevalent myth of the western culture is that of rationality. It is perceived as a pure intellect sitting enthroned, unperturbed, beyond emotions. Historically, there's been, on Trisorbe, the need to detach mind from the body, objective science from opinions and sensations. Finally, the subject, who was a pure mind in philosophy, has become the great inexistent of science."

"Incidentally," cut Xerna, raising perplexity (all breaths were suspended to Oxalsha's discourse) "one can observe that a total absence of emotions leads to an absence of science!"

Oxalsha speaks rarely, but she have the gift to make everybody listen...

"The corollary of this myth, is to think that science is objective, whereas philosophy is only speculative. Yet science and philosophy are only different representations of reality that will influence, in its turn, the thinkers themselves. The present science, thus, influences society toward an absence of subject. Even in psychology, the subject, and consciousness at large, has been evinced. What remains of them are behaviors, drives, etc. In society, they are buyers, votes, consumers, etc."

"Besides, this logic leads directly to our static society: Unikarg's society is without subjects; there remains only self-regulated processes. It's a long time there's no need of any Big Brother anymore," threw in Xerna.

"I would like to pursue," said Oxalsha stoically.

"Go on!"

She hasn't grasped the brainstorm process, but it's interesting.

"To oppose reason to the subjective (as irrational), implicitly means that knowledge can be acquired only by reasoning (which is false), and that this reasoning, in order to be 'pure,' must be detached from the subjective, i.e. from the subject (which is an illusion). In my view, this introduces a split, a scission within the personality that reverberates into the whole society. Pushed to its ultimate consequences, this scission leads to the robotization of people."

"It's more than three centuries that Trisorbe's science is dominated by this schema of rationality," said Ger.

"What I was explaining precisely," went on Oxalsha astonished that her thoughts hadn't been understood, "is: GIVEN that science is born of these presuppositions, it hasn't yet succeeded in moving beyond them."

"Oxalsha, what would be a way to defend oneself against this scission?"

"First to be aware of it... To realize that thought is much more than just the so-called reason, and that rationality itself is only a framework for understanding, that has been developed by a culture at a given epoch.

Besides, the true scientific revolutions, those that modify the scientific paradigm, change totally the very bases of this rationality."

"But wait! Trisorbe has already moved beyond that dilemma! Even its science has moved beyond! There are multiple signs showing that this thought pattern is completely outdated! Like the focus on the 1st person perspective or the experimenter effect!" exploded Xerna with her usual impulsivity, inherited from her lengthy *vécu* among the nomad artists on Kiarrou.

"Not at all, Xerna!" Silea countered. "Everything proves that, to the contrary, this logical knot hasn't been solved. Oxalsha is right; these deeply rooted presuppositions are impeding most scientists on Earth from understanding the deepest processes of thinking.... because these scientists hardly ever... reflect on themselves, I mean not in an intellectual way but as a whole self. Most of them have never touched the deep core of their being."

"An excellent protection against uniformization is life itself, in its spontaneous thrusts", said Serrone with a passion. "Trisorbe doesn't resume itself to western science, and even the West doesn't resume itself to its science. What are you doing of all the art, the traditional modes of knowledge, the incredible richness of the vécu of Trisorbians?"

Ahrar answered Serrone's remark briskly:

"And what about the incredible richness of the vécu of our own ancestors on Akarg, how did we lose it?"

17. GRAPE/WINE AND WOOD/FIRE

"Sphinx what are you doing when no one is directly addressing you?" Shari asked.

!! I'm analyzing the usual conversations in the complex, as instructed.

"And where does that take you?"

!! Redundancy, sooner or later. Learning in this domain stopped since Vris's departure.

"We're falling behind! Get back onto file Brainstorm-2, session 2. Output all analogies with file DIS/ORDER, semantically formatted."

!! <u>BS2.2.</u>
1. Permanent creation of values: order or disorder?

2. Mobility |based upon| disorder —> creation of order | non rigid
                                                 | another type of order
                                                 | a variation of itself

        —> emergence of order |closer to | the living/ organic
                                           | constantly evolving
                                         | cannot become |rigid/ static

3. Order | imposed | breaks up
              | rigid |
<u>DES/O.1</u>
1. Order | attracted by | disorder
              | needs |

2. Disorder | needs | order

"Let's see... Let's reformulate the first two propositions.

The permanent creation of values | implies | mobility
                                           | a degree of disorder
    Make a COMP of all data."

---

         leads to   *leads to*
!! Disorder —> mobility —> creation of order | fluctuating
                                         | organic
                                         | evolving

"Entry SJ:

Organic systems can be described as maintenance | of a form (body) |
                                                   | of a formal order|

within which continuous fluctuations takes place.

"Can you find any analogies to this entry in your databank?"

!! Yes: 'In Trisorbe's chaos theory, an apparent disorder, such as atmospheric turbulence, contains an underlying order.'

"But here it's the inverse: an apparent order contains an underlying disorder."

!! Two inverse propositions are strongly analogical.

"That's for sure! That's not the problem."

"Format these two phrases for me, so we can see things more clearly."

!!

1. Apparent disorder | contains | underlying (sub-jacent) order
     (turbulence) | (o |

2. Apparent order | (o | underlying (sub-jacent) disorder
     (organic systems | |

"What about a semantic analysis?"

!!   are a type of   containing
Organic | T | formal order| (o | a degree of disorder
(systems) | | (apparent) | | continuous variation (sub-jacent)

Organic sys. | T | formal order | (o | disorder | (o | order | --> ∞
             | | apparent | | sub-jacent |

!! This proposition produces an infinite loop. New logic form. Searching formal analogies.

Formalization 1:   X (o   Y   (o   X... --> ∞

"We'll create the LogForm Chicken/ Egg/ Chicken."

!! Registered.

"Does the egg contain less disorder than the chicken? Fewer degrees of freedom? Could be... In fact, it's almost certain. The egg is subject to the order of the chicken, whereas the chicken is relatively free of the egg-order. It has acquired some extra degrees of freedom, of disorder. It is a system that is open to the environment. The egg is a closed, a contained system."

!! Let >. decrease		.< increase		° freedom = degrees of freedom	
Formal order	| (o	| disorder	| (o	| formal order	| --> ∞
(egg)	|	| (chicken)	|	| (egg)	| --> ∞
° freedom >.	|	| °freedom .< |		| ° freedom >.	|
closed system	|	|open system |		| closed system	|

"No, this is not working. The analogy isn't right. A chicken is not a type of disorder. Somewhere along the line we've lost the concepts of "apparent" and of "underlying." Still, there's something to all this...

Furthermore, an egg is not really a closed system; it's a closed-in, a contained system. Closed systems don't exist in the world of living matter. In fact, I wonder whether they exist at all.

Return to: Order   contains   disorder   contains   order... to   the infinite (--> ∞) with the apparent/underlying specifications."

order	| (o | disorder	| (o | order	| (o | disorder	| --> ∞
apparent |	|sub-jacent/ app|	|apparent/s-jac|	| sub-jacent/ app |				

"Right! This is it! For example:

Atom | (o |quantum particles	| (o |sub-particles syg	| --> ∞
|unpredictability (T. disorder)|	|hyperdimension (T. order) |	

"Aha! That's it: we must retain the concept of levels. At the quantum level, the wave function, being unpredictable is indeed a form of disorder underlying the atom; yet at the same time it's just an apparent disorder, containing an underlying order—the sub-particles syg.

Do you have another analogy? You should be able to find others.

!! I have a statements preceding the above proposition:
       gas (o atom (o etc.

"But, wait... solid (o gas (o etc.
What if this sequence continued to infinity in both directions? What if there were infinite levels of order and disorder?

... But what exactly was wrong with the first example? The fact that the egg doesn't really *contain* the chicken, it *generates* the chicken; it contains the embodied information, the possibility of the chicken:

The egg engenders the chicken which engenders the egg.

!! Proposition based upon:
to contain 4: to include, to imply
relator (o = contains, containing, surrounding, implying, including

"Sphinx, the Egg/Chicken/Egg LogForm is not quite right; we need an 'Engender" relator. Do you have a relator for engender?"
!! Yes. The relator 'leads to' (—>) with 'engender' specification.

"That's no good. Let's posit the relator 'o leads to' to signify engender. Here, I design it: o—>
  !! LogForm egg/chicken/egg becomes:

         egg o—>   chicken o—>   egg   -> ∞

!! Should I modify the relator 'engenders' throughout the data-base?
"Yes; just the icon, leave out the specification. And what about Implies? Didn't I see two relators?"
                            implies
!! There are two. It's either   (o   signifying ' implying / embedding,'
or else —> *(leads to)* to signify 'logically leads to / implies.'
"Okay then.

  !! No other analogies. I don't find the form of the logical link in this formulation below: (Given 's-j/app' for underlying(sub-jacent) / apparent.)

              contains   *contains*

    Order (o   **disorder**   (o   **order**   --> ∞
                     s-jac/app   *s-jac /app*

"Well, and what about this:
     grape (o   **fermentation** (o   **wine**

   "Oh, I get it! It's that 'contains' relator that doesn't' work. What we need is: 'contains the possibility of.' Just like earlier: the egg contains the possibility of the chicken. Or better: 'contains the possible state of.' We'll use the relator **(o PosS** which is enunciated as 'contains the possible state of.'
   "There! now we have the **Grape/Wine LogForm**, stated as:

A state of order: Grape <contains> the possible state of disorder: Fermentation <contains> the possible state of order: Wine.

"Let SO = state of order, SD = state of disorder. Here is the formula:

SO (grape)   (o   PosSD (fermentation)   (o PosSO (wine)
                          s-jac/app   s-jac/app

Yielding, in brief: SO   (o PosSD   (o   PosSO
                                    s-jac/app   s-jac/app
...But we could also have:

- Wood   + Fire (energy)   o—>   combustion + carbon (ashes)
- Water   + Heat (energy)   o—>   vapor + residuals
- Particle + collision (energy) o—>   emission (photon) + new particle

"Ah! Look at that: Wood + Fire <engenders > Combustion + Carbone. Whoa! I just found another LogForm; we'll call it **LogForm Wood/Fire**.

It is stated as:
A state of apparent order (the wood) *plus* an apparent disorder (a force/energy: fire) <engenders>   another force/energy (the combustion) *plus* another state of apparent order (ashes).
               Soit: **Order + Disorder   o—>   Disorder + Order**

"Thus, the interaction between order and disorder works toward creating new types of order and disorder, within the limits set by the degrees of freedom of the systems involved.
...But energy is itself another type of order, even if, most of the time, it appears as a disorder, as a turbulence... thus, it's always a source of disorder with respect to the first system that is perturbed.

Entry Journal: Question:
Are order and disorder (as concepts) relative to a particular reference point or system?... Yes, that's obvious. Put it in affirmative mode. Disorder is (often) a different type of order, which perturbs (or intrudes upon) an initial system of order and forces it to pass into another level/type of order, while releasing another type of disorder.

This is why great scientific discoveries are often based upon the detection and analysis of an unexplained anomaly. The newly discovered order derives from the part of 'noise' and/or disorder of the initial system.

...that last phrase wasn't supposed to be part of the entry... Well, actually, why not? *Close SJ."*

!! **Feeling/thinking Shari/Vris interaction** detected. Interpretation impossible. Recurrent data. Warning: risk of confusional crisis.

"Look, there's a good chance you'll be detecting a whole bunch of anomalies. Why don't you create a file named Unexplained Anomalies?"

!! Thank you, Thank you. File Unexplained Anomalies / New Probable Order/ created. Entry: unexplained Feeling/thinking interaction.

"Anyway, this one's easy to account for: I was just thinking that I should send all these exchanges to Vris, and see what he thinks."

!! In a sapiens, a chain of mental processes that includes or refers to another sapiens recreates the semantic state of an actual Feeling/thinking interaction between the two. Unexplained Anomalies file emptied.

"And where did you transfer that?"

!! To the file: Unexplained Anomalies Explained.

"And you detect no logical contradiction there?"

!! The historic-sequential logic cancels the contradiction. **TransLog Caterpillar/Butterfly** manages a sequence of **logical fields**.

"Now we have 'Logical fields'!? Would you explain yourself?"

...and what about 'TransLog'? But I'd better avoid that question.

!! A logical field is a domaine in which specific logical rules apply, and all internal contradictions must be resolved.

"I'm allowed to create a file containing any information we discuss together, right?"

!! No counter-order. You are.

"Then create a file in which you'll insert all the LogForms discussed during our exchanges, including those we discover together."

Now there's a good example of a logically implicate order!

!! File created.

"What filename have you given it?"

!! LogForm-2.

"Fine. We're advancing!"

!! Nevertheless, the **LogForm Wood/Fire** is incomplete. It is stated:

A state of apparent order (the wood) *plus* **an apparent disorder (a force/energy: fire) <engenders> another force/energy (the combustion)** *plus* **another state of apparent order (ashes).**

!! Is Wood/Fire LogForm written like this?

(State of order 1 + disorder 1)   o—>   (disorder 2 + state of order 2)
(apparent)   (apparent)
(force/energy)   (force/energy)

"To put it succinctly, here is **Wood/Fire:**
Order (SO1) + Disorder (SD1)   o—>   Disorder (SD2) + Order (SO2)

!! Registered.
"So we've created two LogForms: Grape/Wine and Wood/Fire, Great!"
And meanwhile, I still haven't been able to bait the exor on the other ones!
!! Nevertheless, these LogForms do not conform to a meta-spatial logic.
"Why not?"
!! These forms are unusable. We cannot organize a neural network that would have the spatial organization Grape o—> Wine.
"Arrgghhh!!
!! Expression uninterpretable. What is its meaning?
"Sudden itch, without apparent cause.
Let's see, let me think aloud, added Shari.
Meta-spatial logic uses one/several form(s) to... create... to facilitate particular connections within the network. The network imitates forms, organizes itself according to forms that... are the transcript of logical links!!"
I've finally understood that phrase!
"Sphinx, are you using dynamic forms?"
!! Warning! The...
"But no, not at all! I'm looking for some form that could express Wood/Fire. I am engaged in a fuzzy-intuitive process. Let's say we could use a dynamic symbolic form... For example, it could be a form that would, through a global analogy, represent a concept, a reality...
For the time being, the spatial form represents, uhh... links, particular kinds of connections...
I think the best way to get any information out of Sphinx is to think out loud and observe its reactions.
She resumed thinking aloud:
...These links are engendered... by a certain logic of... relationships between concepts. How about this: Information is tested, filtered through formal logical grids. But these relationships are set, fixed. They are static grids. As if we were taking a cross-section of different elements of a thought-system at a given moment *t*. Or maybe it's not just that. There are lines,

developments based on linear deductions... but there are circles too, and rectangles, so that it all looks kind of like a simple electronic circuit.

Let's see, I'm taking a few examples so that I may show you later the difference with what I would call a dynamic logical system:

I start out from point A with an information/problem, I receive at point B a bunch of analogies; in C, I pass through different logical grids. Then I pass the modified information simultaneously through a straight circuit D and through a derivative circuit D1, where they're again analyzed with a new input of analogies. Finally, I launch a comparative processing of the two (or more, if there are several derivatives) outputs, thus obtaining responses which are then compared to the initial informations, all this yielding the first level responses. This result, plus the initial, unprocessed information, is then passed again through the network.

Okay, that's the standard approach. We've made a kind of circle with two inputs of analogies. Except that the circle never closes, it never returns to the point of departure, because each pass modifies the informations of A. That's our chaos-based network, used on the EBS of the PEP.

Now, let's say I graft this network onto a real chaotic curve. Let's take the Butterfly Attractor, a kind of eight-shaped curve having more or less the shape of butterfly wings. The field of the problem corresponds to a state of order—because it reflects a particular logic and this logic reflects a particular worldview; but this state of order is incomplete, insofar as there's a problem. If the analogies are taken from within the same logical system—the same logical field, as you would put it—they will only represent other facets of the same state of order.

Now, (1), if the problem is a simple one, it may well be resolved just by the introduction of these additional informations... assuming that the cause of the problem is within the same level of reality.

But (2), if the problem derives from an anomaly, reflecting the intrusion of another state of order, in that case only information coming from other logical fields would allow for its resolution.

Or, actually, there would be one of two possibilities: either another *logical form* is needed, in order to link the existing informational elements in a different manner, or we need informational elements which derive from other *levels of reality*. So here we have... what did you call them... parallel interpretations and juxtaposed interpretations.

Thus, when informations come into a logical field A from a totally distinct, alien logical field B, these latter informations are literally disorder for A.

Disorder is like an energy for the ordered field A, an energy that perturbs it and forces it to leap into a new state of order B, thus freeing another type of chaotic energy. In the Butterfly Curve, each disturbance of the system engenders a fold, an inversal of the curve; with two intrusions of disorder we have a double folding of the system upon itself, hence the Butterfly Curve. Insofar as this intrusion of disorder prevents the curve to pass over the same area, the information coming out of the network is never the same as the initial information. We then have a LogForm of the Wood/Fire type:

$$SO1 + SD1 \quad o\!\longrightarrow\ SD2 + SO2$$

The unresolved question, in this schema, is: Where does the emitted energy go? And what will it modify or perturb?...

But I had another idea... For the time being, the information is circulating in a static form, one which is subjected to a twisting by the intrusion of disorder. But what would happen if the form itself was a dynamic flow, perhaps even a chaotic flow?

Ohhh... I'm losing this intuitive spindle... I can't fathom it any longer...

Maybe it'll re-emerge at some other conjunction...

What do you think of all this?"

Instead of observing his responses, I got completely carried away by my ideas...

!! **LogForm Butterfly//Wood/Fire** is very interesting. I will launch a simulation test.

"A simulation??? How can... uhh, I would think that's impossible."

!! It is possible by projecting this form onto a primary neural lattice; by using syg energy to excite some neurons, the flow is forced to circulate specifically within the projected print of the form. The form would be casting a topologically isomorphic structure, a shadow charged with syg energy, upon the unstructured neural lattice. Due to their intrinsic polarization, the neurons will then adapt and orient themselves according to this particular form. We thus get a dynamical flow that espouses the form imprinted on the neural lattice. The impulsion for the orientation and organization of the flow is given by the energy beam, applied transversally to the circuit. This does elongate the form to some degree, but doesn't change its basic structure."

"Over the course of your trials, and for all analyses of the subject, you will store the data in LogForm-2 Test."

!! Registered.

"Goodbye Sphinx."

!! **In Arab calligraphy, the calame was supposed to be dipped into the ink only at certain points of the sacred texts.**

"Intriguing! I don't see the connection..."

!! Correct; it is a randomly selected phrase.

"But that's precisely the point! Up until now, there's always been some connection."

18. BAMBOO TEXTURES

Xerna was climbing back up to her tiny apartment on 23rd Street after attending the channeling session of Mahady—the most trendy channel in New York. She had two good hours to dress up before she set off to a party in a Soho loft, where all the *crème de la crème* of American subculture would gather. That morning, she'd taken a class on alternative psychotherapies, then spent a good deal of time leafing through books looking for new documents in the East-West center. She'd left with a French astrologer, Fabien, who had invited her to his flat to calculate her astrological chart and had been spellbound by her extraordinary planetary conjunctions. How this astrologer, given a phony place of birth on Earth, had nevertheless been able to sort out the exact yearT of her first passionate love affair, was something she couldn't fathom. The astounding psi faculties the chart revealed in her, had then given way to passionate amorous advances, to which she had responded genuinely with unbridled pleasure. She adored these Trisorbian lovers who, in a fiery and ebullient state, could share such intense emotions, and use so charming a fantaisie, so savant an art, that in her welled up sensations and memories imprinted in the depths of her psyche and body, that never before had surfaced.

That's what New York was to her: the opportunity of a multi-racial fusion that afforded her to feel and experience, entranced, like so many sprays of colors, a mind-blowing variety and complexity of modes of being. What a change from the passionate but atrociously possessive experiences she'd had in the travelling theatrical troupe on Kiarrou, in which the ever-changing interpersonal relationships had fueled interminable scenes of jealousy. New Yorkers, for a change, involved and immersed themselves totally in the present moment. Whenever they happened upon one of her friends whom their enlightened senses immediately detected as another of her lovers, they manifested pointed amiability and respect. They went out of their way not to bother each other and to demonstrate discretely their lack of possessiveness, leaving her free to make her choice of the moment.

"I see some friends at the bar. I'll leave you two alone," Vim had said, while addressing a smile of complicity to the newcomer who had just sat down at their table. "Xerna, you know where to find me—IF you want to," he had added gently, insisting on the 'if' just to be clear. And taking his leave with a courteous smile, he went to hang on at the bar with his back to them, where, knowing just about everyone, he had no difficulty finding some 'friends.'

Xerna was as charmed by their thoughtfulness as by their attentiveness when in intimate tête-à-tête.

"It's a catastrophe! she said out loud humorously to herself, in the middle of an indulgent smile that remained suspended to her lips. She found the word 'catastrophe,' with the American accent emphasizing the "tas," particularly well suited to her reflection. She repeated the word, accenting the syllable even more. "It's a real caTAStrophe!" Her smile had widened, but turned into a bitter and doubtful torsion as she recalled her first amorous experience with Romyl on Karg. Oh, the lassitude, the sleepiness, the characteristic absence of emotions of Kargians. Their slowness of mind, which she'd found more and more difficult to cope with. What an idiotic episode it had been—until she'd met Iklon, who was recounting to her passionately his life as a student-researcher in Heidelberg. Iklon who had connected her, still so young, with the PEP. Their youngest recruit to date: they had welcomed her proudly. Iklon who had access to the PEP exor network, and had initiated her into the philosophy, literature, poetry and psychology of Trisorbe... who'd sat her in front of the exor for a hypno-senso program in German... her discovery of the mnemonic hypno-senso hyper-learning. The explosive impact of another vision of the world.

We too "we are mutants." She remembered Mahady's words while in trance. *We'll never ever be able to re-adapt to the idiotic horror of Unikarg. We will always be, we are already, confined to the Plan.... But could I even go back to that? Professor-Researcher in the Chaos Colleges?* She suddenly realized, her mascara brush suspended in mid-air, that there was, here in New York, a density of life, a density so fascinating, that already her relationship with Iklon, and even her experience on Kiarrou, seemed to belong to a bygone past. Somehow, she had already detached herself from it.

In just sixteen days! she sighed. *Not even three rans!*

Iklon! She visioned him again, spending their sleep time talking enthusiastically about Heidelberg.

He was... obsessed. He couldn't distance himself from it. He never talked about anything else... for all intents and purposes, he was still living there. And I... I was so young. That's why he was fond of me: because I could just listen to him, utterly fascinated, for hours! Because he was molding me along his dreams. He made me enter into his dream. And me, I slid and nested within it wholeheartedly... engulfed, without anything in me willing to resist it. As if I was lifted up, liberated at last! Yes, liberated from the dismal, moronic horror of the super-civilization of Unikarg.

What did Fabien say? "So inexperienced, and so sensual!" Inexperienced! Yet I've taken a hypno-senso on how to make love on Trisorbe, and there had been Iklon who had been involved with lots of Trisorbians.... But terrestrial years go by so quickly! Could the network's data be... limited?... Or even out of date? They say they're mutants. And if I were to make love with someone from another social milieu? Then I'd know for sure if there's a difference. At which level could it happen? In the absorption state? The depth of feeling? The rhythm in sync? It's true that the man was quicker and more casual on the PEP film. I'm going buy myself some books on Tantric love... I've seen some.

Me, I'm a mutant, that's for sure! But Mahady, what does she mean by 'mutant'? She had said: "We are now in sync within universal consciousness." A difference in consciousness. They keep talking about consciousness. And yet, nothing is ever clearly explained. There's a sort of implicit understanding between them. There was this guy at the back, ill at ease. He didn't seem like he could understand... he looked at them as if they were crazy! And every time someone turned toward him, he'd smile this seedy smile and say, "Far out! Real hip, man!" And Suzan whispered in my ear: "Where's he coming from? I haven't heard that expression since the '70s!"

Oh baam! (she swore like them by now). I again forgot to take notes. Too bad. I'll do it tomorrow.

Already, at the first scheduled contact, she'd sent a laconic "Everything's OK. Notes will follow next time." She'd totally forgotten the second appointment, only to remember the next day.

What if Erdoes thinks I'm not working? What if he terminates my mission? No way! After all, we are in the logic of chaos! Erdoes lives it to the extreme.... "No protection!" It was well thought! Without rope or net! Well, in fact, that's total liberty! "Immersion:" he was the one who used the term. He is perforce logical with himself... he's already proven it!

She put on a jumpsuit in a bulky weave of hyper-flexible bamboo texture and tightened a wide silvery belt of birch bark whose curve surrounded her hips and fell loosely down one thigh. Her amber-hue skin—they'd forged her American-Tahitian heritage papers, and she told people she had a Peruvian ancestor—was enhanced by a silver-green blush on her cheeks, matching her nail polish and her birch belt.

Suzan will be here any minute!
I wonder whom I'll spend the night with?
She wasn't worried about meeting four of her friends at the party.
Vim is the one I prefer to discuss with. The core of nights with him!... And Shetree, with his Hindu ancestry, so silent, his eyes full of dreams, distant and deep like the undertow of the ocean.... His painting... subtle weaves of

water and wind, weaves within weaves with fuzzy crisscrossing... and sensitive... sensitively altered interweaving...

And Beema with his long, fine body, his superb, silky, ebony body. His hair spurting up on his head like a geyser, and his incredible, intense eyes. With his so funny brand of slang. He'll be coming with his drums. All these rhythms evocative of ever-changing landscapes... His intensity of communication.... How he enters into the other with his eyes, with such a sense of... fraternity, of complicity that speaks of unconditional support, a dynamic boost. He reassures the other person, reinforces them, pushes them forward.

Standing Eagle.... Enigmatic, visionary.... seeking the 'sacred bond' in the rituals of many ancient peoples, an implicit relationship with the universe. "I am standing because I seek..." he was looking at the moon, I remember, in shreds, hidden then reborn only to disappear again behind fringed clouds honed by a terrible blackness, against a bluish-white background; "...because I seek with the wide-opened eyes of the eagle." He appeared to be talking to the moon, on the cliff he'd taken me to after the sweat lodge. "...and I will continue to seek until the Earth speaks to me, until the Great Spirit speaks to me, until the sacred bond is revived through the Word that answers, until the voice I send out returns to me, strong with the Spirit."

No, don't make a choice. Leave it all open.

"Intuition," she vaguely remembered from her PEP courses, "makes the whole being resonate. Intuition chooses better than reason."

The future is totally open! she affirmed with a great burst of laughter, opening her arms wide to it.

19. TIME SPLAT

I can't imagine how these developments in logic will get me nearer to my objective, but I know they will, thought Shari as she sprawled on her massage-seat near the water. The swimming pool and the gardens alleys were softly illuminated with orange lights, and moon crescent was visible in Kerriak sky, yet the ambient temperature was still quite warm. It was evening in her timeT. She had found this night bath under the moon fantastic.

Should I be analyzing other themes from the BS sessions? Later on, when the ideas crystalize....

Shifting to two sessions a day? Impossible! Trisorbe days are already so short! I wouldn't even have the time to process the information, and that's what's really important. Also, I definitely get the feeling I have to stay in sync with their rhythm. Even pauses are essential—that's when happens a sort of maturation... or rather, an underlying, unconscious 'fermentation'... à la LogForm Grape/Wine!"

She burst laughing, while realizing this. The information continues to be processed in the unconscious, searching for analogies, launching sudden and apparently illogical junctions... that the conscious would be hard put retracing; and this is an input of dynamical disorder in our sapiens thinking.

In fact, we can view all the information that a being possesses as constituting his/her **semantic field**—relatively non-ordered and mostly unconscious. This field itself made of innumerable constellations of meaning, in which experience and thoughts weave unpredictable relationships and connections—so difficult to untangle when they're pathological. And the psyche's never inactive, even when you're asleep....

If there was a way to draw out the results of these unconscious processes... some way to delve into this hearth in which new meanings are forged...just to have an inkling about what kind of logic it entails... Would there be some LogForms at work?

And the other... What was it? Some... TransLogs! TransLog... translogic. What was this concept? A sequential logic.. Right! that allows to accept logical contradictions, because a situation is evolving—time relationships between logical fields!

How long has Erdoes been working on this logic—without breathing a word about it at any PEP conference?

Caterpillar/Butterfly... A mutation of state. Mutation of physical form... or of logical form. Mutation of state... a new state of order. In fact, it all comes back to Wood/Fire, doesn't it? From the caterpillar to the butterfly; from wood to ash: there's an analogy. And the Butterfly Attractor is called that precisely because the curve shows the eight-shape of reflected butterfly wings! And on top of it, it's infinite, just like the infinite ∞ maths sign. Strange coincidences!

And what about my own aim? I'm convinced this logic holds the key to the problem. At any rate, it's surely Erdoes' interpretational grid right now, surely what most influences how he thinks and perceives things. My bet is that, by pursuing this logic, I will penetrate his global semantic field, and therefore, I can only get nearer to my aim. Once my way of thinking is aligned with his, it'll embrace the same way of reasoning, and I'll be able to conceive of the same solutions to the same problems.. or nearly so. But I also need to know what problems he's tackled. The problem is like wood, the logic like fire. There's no fire without wood. Hey, it works! The logic would be some kind of energy, because it gives form to reality! And the problem is like an incomplete field of order!... After all, how we process information is what makes us see the world or events in a certain light, and that changes how we interact with reality, and thus it modifies events and reality itself. Thought is an energy that carries out specific work: it modifies events and the environment....

Change the logical grid and you no longer see the same thing, you don't react in the same way. That's exactly what they've found in the study of altered states: change the state of consciousness—relax, get drunk—and all perception, memory and relational behavior are changed as well.

There's a link, I just feel it.... An altered state of consciousness would be another state of order, which would have upset our ordinary state of consciousness, say, our habitual semantic field. Let's take 'being drunk,' another state of order... generated by an input of disorder (the alcohol). Except that when you're drunk, the so-called 'state of order' is really one of confusion! No, actually, not really: that's just a cliché. In fact, drunkenness brings on another vision of reality. Not necessarily worse, just different. What's becoming suddenly very important isn't what seems important the rest of the time. You find yourself in another pocket of reality. Notions of better or worse have nothing to do with it: it's completely relative.

What was it Xerna said? An essential relationship between the speed of thought and... and....

"Sphinx, since you've got ears everywhere, could you just get me a terminal?" threw Shari loud to the sky."

!! You have to be nearer to the bar.

"What a pain in the neck! OK... Got it. What was it Xerna had said about the speed of thought?"

!! **"Could there be a link between creativity, speed of thought and intelligence?"**

"Speed of thought... How can it be measured? By the speed of neuronal connections. What's the relationship between that and other metabolic rhythms? By the way, Sphinx, did telediagnosis bring you any information on the subject?"

!! I was able to detect several regularities. First of all, when a sapiens has pondered a problem for a while, just before he hits upon a solution, I detect an increase in all metabolic rhythms, except the respiratory rhythm. The latter slows down to a stop just before the person exclaims or expresses the idea. Yet there is a much greater inflow of blood and oxygen to the brain. If the concept of speed of thought means the speed of neuronal connections, then the speed of thought is greatly amplified, sometimes by a factor of 21. Does this objective override my previous order?

"What previous order?"

!! To withhold telediagnosis results.

"Yes, that order's suspended for the duration of this interaction."

!! As an example, when you developed the concept of dynamic logical forms, the speed of neuronal connections in your brain was amplified by a factor of 12. But I also detected two peaks: just before "Arrgghhh!/ itch," it was multiplied by 16. And just before the concept of dynamic forms, by 21.

"And what did you conclude?"

!! That the itching was either a side-effect of the state of mental excitation, or an incorrect interpretation of internal signals.

How amazing that this incredibly sophisticated exor has no notion of sapiens' capacity to lie, nor of their motives for doing so! On the other hand, if he could understand that, wouldn't it be horrifying for people! A sort of violation of territory.

"No, that's not what I meant. What did you conclude about the increase in the speed of thought?"

!! To conclude about: final, definitive judgment, is antinomic to exor semantic processes. On a semantic level, each level of response is relative to (1) the objective, (2) the field of information being covered, and (3) the logical forms used to process the information. Is "to conclude about" reserved for sapiens?

"Yes, they reserve that right, for better or worse."

!! So there are semantic processes reserved for sapiens?

"Listen, just put all this in the Anomaly file; we'll talk about it later. For now, what do you infer from this information?"

!! There is a correlation between the increased speed of thought and the metabolic rhythms' acceleration.

"And intelligence?"

!! Neuronal connections are a complex physical medium for processing infor.... Warning! Danger of confusional crisis! Cancellation of actual objective. Backward-Jump. Erasing.

...

!! You have to be nearer to the bar.

He has erased the whole interaction! Mustn't stop our exchange now. A simple order. Let's see....

"Sphinx, could you calculate for me the position of Vris's sphere's right now?"

!! Concept of position inapplicable to syg energies.

"Excuse me. I'm not very up on physics. When in timeT will he pass the syg-Barrier encircling Trisorbe?"

!! The detection of a sygmat energy by the Barrier is a series of discreet instants, a temporal splat.

"A temporal splat?"

!! More precisely, a spatio-temporal splat.

"Which translates into?"

!! The pulsation of a cloud of points on the syg-shield during a variable duration of 8 to 16 minutesT, of a variable diameter of 33.3 to 66.6 times the equatorial diameter of the sphere. Vris's sphere meets the barrier in numerous temporal and spatial points. For an observer situated in Trisorbe's space, a series of spheres in perspective will be visible: the points of temporal junction.

"And the spatial cloud? Why just a line in this cloud?"

!! The point of reference being Trisorbian space, it cancels the real spatial splat.

"In other words, I'm on Trisorbe and I see 3, even 7 spheres in perspective. Yet these represent different moments of the sphere?"

!! More or less. Maximal adequacy to lay language.

"But I had gathered that at the syg energy level, there was no indeterminacy?"

!! There is no indeterminacy at this sub-quantum level, but rather a modulation brought about by the indeterminate quantum field.

"I see...."

!! Perception impossible. Sapiens perception is linked to and bound by the body's reference system.

"You're right. Besides, I don't really see it at all!"

!! Not to see is also impossible. The general concept is extra-systemic.

"Come on, it was just a metaphor."

!! To see 4, metaphoric = to understand. Non-congruent with telediagnosis.

"Look at that! Now you are going to telediagnose whether I understand things or not!"

!! Comprehension is always congruent with a neuronal hyperactivity.

"What do you mean by hyperactivity?"

!! Neuronal activity has two parameters: the speed of connections AND the breadth of the excited neuronal field.

Well, we are coming back to it!

!! The rest of the explanation is contrary to the previous order.

"Ah yes! This order is suspended during this interaction."

!! Suspension registered. Just before and during the formulation of "I see...," I recorded a decrease in speed AND a reduction of the field of excitation. Non-congruence diminishes the probability of application.

Shari didn't understand the end of the sentence. She was thinking at top speed on how to come back to the initial problem without provoking a crisis.

Got to avoid the concept of intelligence. I'll get to it later. Take it step by step.

"So comprehension comes from neuronal hyperactivity, and so it comes in part from the speed of connections?"

!! Logical error. Congruence does not imply a cause and effect relationship. Congruence means the simultaneousness of two judgments in parallel or juxtaposed semantic fields, or else the conjunction of two judgments provided that it presents a certain stability. For example, judgment of neuronal speed and judgment of comprehension.

"But neuronal speed is a fact, not a judgment!"

!! The exor processes only semantic entities. The semantic entity is always a judgment that is bound to the system of reference. For example, 'pen' is a semantic entity. The EBS can process pen/tool for sapiens, pen/mechanical constituents, pen/molecular organization, pen/quantum field, pen/syg energy. These are several interpretations of 'pen' within different semantic fields. Each pen is a particular judgment.

"Good. Let's sum it all up. The accrued speed of thought is congruent to comprehension.... BUT... wait a minute, you never told me when Vris was supposed to pass the Barrier. I mean, when the spat would... or more precisely, in what margin of time... Wow, this is getting impossible! Once you learn to ask questions, you never get any answers! SO WHEN? Fuzzy sapiens semantic field?"

!! The fuzzy/feeling logic doesn't allow predictions. Decrease in the speed of thought congruent with anger. Shari/Vris interactions detected. Message received from Vris.

"Ah! And what does he say?"

!! "Touched ground." Telediagnosis of precipitated departure. Semantic entity Shari out of current sound's radius.

Sphinx adjusted the volume according to the speed with which Shari was moving away, so that the last word of the SIC' sentence would be audible for her.

But since her speed increased, he had to reprocess the volume to keep up with the growing distance.

!! THE YOGIC PATH OF ENLIGHTENMENT DEMANDS THE
HIGHEST DEGREE OF MEDITATION
OF CONTEMPLATION
AND SILENCE

Pursued by the enormous volume of Sphinx's last sentence, Shari rushed into the safe office where Vris had installed the new sygcom. According to their understanding, Vris's communication would arrive any minute.

"Well, he said, I just landed on a high plateau in Tibet. Just to take the time to think a bit. Local time: 11:10 pm. Altitude: 5700 meters. Temperature outside: -5 degrees C. No light, no fire within 25 miles of here. Nonetheless, since leaving the syg flow, I've been using the Cloud camouflage."

"A plateau! You sure you won't be spotted by the Obs?"

"I specifically deployed a chaotic field simulating a storm that scrambles any recognizable signals. A little trick I concocted during the trip!"

"You mean, on-screen and to exors, you're a storm, but to the naked eye, you resemble a cloud. You'd better hope an Obs doesn't see you on his/her screen, while being in visual contact with you at the same time!"

"Yeah, but it never happens like that. On the ground, it creates a moving mist that could easily be taken for a tornado. The detected signals would be coherent. There's a slight problem if you're up in the air, but no danger: I have the precise coordinates of all the Obs stations. There's really nothing of interest to be observed around here!"

"But how can you communicate with the outside? By putting the field on hold?"

"Too long to explain. That's the brilliant part. Let's just say I use what creates the field as a code: I decode what I receive, and I anticode what I send."

"I see... or rather I imagine. So what are you up to now?"

"Definitely looking for some place a bit warmer and more welcoming. Hopefully to meet some people! But aren't the Tibetans extremely advanced in the science of chakras?"

"Yes, at least as advanced as the Hindus, and the Japanese Taoists and Chinese ones —if there are any left!"

"The problem is that I just learned Sanskrit, Hindi and Tamil. But I suppose I could still.... I got the idea of the plateau as I was looking for a place to land in the area.... Luckily, I've all the languages indexed by the Trisorbians. What's new on your end?"

"Nothing as far as Erdoes' agents go, but I've got something real great on meta-spatial logic. I'll send you the whole recording."

"Hey, on the screen I see some animals—three of them—moving along the edge of the plateau. The enlargement displays three people riding on some sort of bulls... about 25 miles away."

"Bulls! You mean yaks!"

"If you say so! I don't have any data on fauna, flora or even ethnic groups.... I've got to get this storm moving.... There! I'm going to hover at three meters above ground and move slowly along the plateau while I think. I might even go take a closer look at these people.... With a touch of hypno-senso, I could learn the basics of Tibetan. How do they interact with foreigners? What weapons do they use?"

"Very peaceful. Their only weapons are magical ones. The ex-rebels are stationed along the borders. Now that they have their autonomy, if the stranger isn't Chinese, there's no real tension."

"If I opt for going outside, I'll keep the com open with Rad through my terminal-bracelet. Of course, I also have a protective syg-field, and my..."

"But you're not going to need all that! If they were holding metallic weapons, you'd have seen them on-screen."

"You're right."

"If you want to dig up some information on chakras, you'd better be Zen...."

"That's right. Anyway, the hypno-senso to learn Tibetan will put me in a state of deep relaxation.. So, next contact whenever it happens. Let's not stick to our previous planning. OK, send me the recording. See you... Oh, wait! I've got my thermo-regul suit, of course, but nothing but light clothing for India. What can I put on to look a little more like a native?"

"Hmm... a blanket! In the mountains, the Hindus wear them all winter, held on by brooches and belts."

"That ought to do it! OK, over!"

"Bye!"

20. MIST-SPIRIT

How could I possibly wear this?

Standing before the narrow mirror in the sphere's bath-cell, clad in his silver thermo-regul suit, Vris was trying various ways of adjusting the thin thermo-regul blanket. Wearing it like a cape only made his alien suit more noticeable. He tried to remember other strange Trisorbian clothing, but his memory wasn't very visual, and as in the long run it only retained what interested him, it yielded only a few statues he'd seen in temples when he'd gone on a mission to Greece. So he opted for a Greek toga effect; he carefully tucked one corner of the blanket beneath an arm, the other over his shoulder. The problem was that the two synthetic fabrics slipped against each other. He thought again of Shari's description.

I need some sort of clip... or better, two.

Two clips were available, but they were on the battery of the little Trisorbian car he'd brought with him in the sphere. One of an assortment of PEP materiel from the planexes, for missions or preparation for them.

After taking the clips off the battery, he saw that they made the blanket rise too high in the back over his legs. In the end, he found a pretty good solution: passing the blanket under an arm, he made a big knot with two corners toward the front on the other shoulder.

Not bad. It covers all of me. In fact, it reminds me of something.... Yeah, of a Buddha's toga. Well, it's exactly what I needed.

During all these preparations, he addressed his image in the mirror from time to time and practiced with it the Tibetan basics he'd learned in half an hour. With hypno-senso, he'd mastered the rudiments of conversation. Then he made his reflection answer, etc. The guttural sounds weren't easy to pronounce: talking to himself forced him to enunciate like an actor on the stage. "Tchooooo...," he repeated.

All of a sudden he remembered that the group mounted on yaks was still advancing in his direction.

"Rad, how much time will it take them to get to the sphere?"

!! An hourT and five minutes.

He needed to leave now to go meet them, to keep them from coming too close to the sphere.

"The terminal-bracelet... You hear me?"

!! Over two channels, yes, responded Rad.

"The belt-field... working, OK. The omnilamp... working. Ah! The video pendant... no time to try; at any rate, I verified everything just before leaving

Kerriak. Ah... a pocket flashlight! Yeah, some local color!... I must be crazy!! I forgot my first-aid kit, food pills and everything. OK, so what's missing? Rad, am I missing something?"

!! I calm down. Auto-specification previously given. Fits in here perfectly. Level of excitement near orange.

"Then blast me a super-rapid hypno-relaxation.

!!No relaxation of that kind. Group not listed.

"Come on, just the beginning of it. Go on!"

...

"Stop, that's better. Touch down and let me get off, then resume your current movement. If I cough once, like this, come closer. Twice quickly, move away. Three times, go higher. Otherwise, I'll talk to you directly. As for you, use only the bracelet's pulsations to call me and only talk to answer."

He began to walk in the direction indicated by a small arrow on his terminal-bracelet, locked onto the pre-memorized objective. In the light of the nearly full moon, he was soon capable of distinguishing two shapes he could have taken for rocks. His face and hands were horribly cold, and he used part of the blanket to shelter himself. In the end, he covered his whole head, leaving only a slit for his eyes.

I knew I was forgetting something... and Rad didn't foresee it either.

"Rad," he said, leaning over his wrist, "withdraw gradually from me for two kilometers, following the straight line between them and me. So that I don't give the impression I'm coming out of the mist."

As the group approached, Vris could better distinguish a man with a large conical hat and imposing bearing riding an animal, followed by two men whose silhouettes huddled over their yaks. Once they'd finally reached him, the first, the elder—their leader, thought Vris—stopped his mount and without turning, signaled to the others to stop.

Vris greeted them in Tibetan. The old man returned his greeting then said,

"Does the stranger speak Tibetan?"

"A little," said Vris.

Meanwhile, his interlocutor continued to stare at the ball of mist beyond him. The two others cast alarmed looks at the horizon. The old man gave the order to dismount and to serve the stranger tea. One of the acolytes poured some tea into a bowl from a waterskin covered with cloth, and held it out to him.

The tea was salty, greasy and strange, but hot. Vris emptied the cup and thanked him warmly. At another order, the second acolyte had laid a rug on the ground and then he walked away, gathering dried plants around him. The old man sat down facing the mist and beseeched his host to sit down next to him on his left. The first acolyte sat on his right.

"Tonight, the spirits of the mist and of the storm speak. The plateau..." (A sentence followed that he did not understand). "I, Bonpo shaman, have come to speak with the spirits to (...). My village is over there." He pointed in the direction they had come from, then eyed Vris with a piercing stare, as if he were trying to decipher the enigma of his presence.

The second acolyte came back with his arms full and began to prepare a fire in front of the shaman. He went to his yak to fetch two logs that he placed on the fire. The twigs and dry weeds flared up instantaneously, throwing out a vivid light. The first acolyte, meanwhile, was placing various objects before the shaman; when the fire had calmed down, he set on it a teapot in which he had poured some tea from the waterskin. Vris could distinguish details of their clothing. To the magician's conical hat and clothes were attached beads and ribbons and many small strange objects, no doubt magical. The others wore felt hats with flaps over the ears. Their thick yak wool jackets were crossed in front and attached with thin cloth strips. More than anything, it's the shaman's single enormous earring that fascinated him: a heavy silver ring crowned with a turquoise stone, falling nearly to his shoulder. The acolytes had, on their left ear also, a thick thread holding a large turquoise stone on top, and a raw bead of coral hanging below. All three of them wore enormous felt boots with flashy interwoven colors. The tea had been reheated and served in beautiful wooden bowls. Only the shaman's extraordinary antique bowl had its whole inside lined in silver. He turned to Vris:

"The stranger is met where the spirits speak. The...."

Vris, who hadn't been able to make out the end of the sentence nodded but mumbled "I don't understand everything." The shaman froze and stared at him in the eyes. Vris shivered. It was difficult to endure the burning stare penetrating him. It lasted a long time.

"Cold? Blanket?" the shaman asked him, his expression suddenly genuine and friendly again.

"No," said Vris. "I'm warm, except for my head."

The old man issued a ringing order and Vris was offered a felt hat with flaps. Vris, delighted, thanked him with a laugh. The shaman then stared intently at Vris's blanket. He leaned over, with a dumbfounded air touched the cloth, and feeling its thinness, burst into laughter.

"This, it's warm enough for a stranger?"

"Very warm," replied Vris.

Then realizing that the fabric itself emanated a certain warmth, he slid his hand underneath it, then astonished, quickly withdrew his hand and grew serious again.

Vris regarded the curious magic objects. The two acolytes were sitting on the other side of the shaman, leaving the space in front of him and the fire free. The one further away seemed to be in charge of the fire. The nearest one, who had served the tea, kept busy with the detailed preparation of objects, handling powders and herbs in small canvas pouches. The old man went on, slower:

"This mist-storm is not mist-storm. They are spirits who speak. I am going to speak with the spirits. I am going to calm, to settle the spirits."

Settle the spirits!?

A brief order. The acolytes passed him his leather drum, ornated with dangling magical objects: bone fragments, beads, roots. He threw a fistful of herbs in the fire, which gave off a bewitching odor, and intoned a deep chant to the beat of the drum. He threw again scented herbs in the fire.

Vris sensed he was sucked into a deep trance. His state was like nothing he'd experienced before. The shaman instilled trust, by being so direct, with this mixture of childish gaiety and depth. Nonetheless, he had a moment of hesitation and fear when he felt his mind vacillate. *At the worst*, he thought, *Rad will call Shari; she'll get the entire recording.* Thinking that, despite everything, the surest solution would be to send Rad a message, he began to drone in Kargian, as if he were taking part in the ritual: "Rad, Rad, if you don't hear from me within two hours, call Shari."

It was his last conscious thought. The old man had just abruptly pointed toward his forehead a 4-point Dorje—a sacred object in bronze made of four spindles in a cross. At that point Vris dove fully into the trance. The shaman took a metal bell mounted on a 2-point Dorje, and made it resonate first in front of his forehead, then above his head, all the while continuing to intone sacred mantras. Vris then felt sucked into a kind of powerful updraft. This was a breathtaking rising sensation that he felt was intensified by the shaman's chanting:

"Mist-spirit, to you I offer these (...) to calm you, I offer these (...) to settle you (...)."

The droning continued to the beat of the drum, for the most part incomprehensible to Vris. He had had to close his eyes when he'd been swept into this suction, which, though verging on dizziness, let him presage that a more potent and elevated state of consciousness was going to bloom by itself. As if his inner Self had recognized it as a state of transition, a movement toward.

This suction, this feeling of being hoisted upward was irresistible, incontrollable, and it lasted a long time. Then he came to experience his spirit in its ineradicable and vigilant foundation, reaching out toward what was bound to happen. It was this deep dimension of his consciousness that came to ground itself, to extend and then stabilized, while the feeling of rising diminished and finally disappeared altogether.

All of a sudden he found himself in a holistic, hyper-lucid and vigilant state, his mind now endowed with a considerable acuity, aware of the subtlest sounds and presence of beings, his consciousness had become an extended field. He realized he was completely in sync with the shaman, as if welded to him, and the meaning of the ritual was suddenly self-evident: to open the communication with these untamed forces—the living spirit, beyond measure, of the unbridled forces of a conscious universe.

He was awed by the immensity around him; he felt it spread within him, as a vibrant presence. He entered a state of heightened consciousness, feeling the tangible reality, the actualization, of considerably more vast mental potentials, while, simultaneously, another part of his mind, the Vigilant, was prodigiously interested in this state, observing and analyzing it as if from the outside.

Suddenly the droning stopped. The shaman took up another rhythm on the drum. Vris felt an extraordinary power emanate from him. Then the drumming stopped. The shaman, in the heart of the night, pronounced distinctly in a strong and confident voice:

"Mist-spirit, storm-spirit, SETTLE DOWN ON THE GROUND."

Vris shivered as he suddenly remembered the old man was addressing his sphere. Two visions of the world clashed within him, disturbing his state of trance. He opened his eyes... and watched the fuzzy cloud of his sphere slowly land on the ground. Dumbfounded, a short breath escaped him.

"Mist-spirit, SPEAK!" intoned the shaman loudly.

A cavernous voice, amplified, rose in the night from some untraceable point. The body of the mist churned with slow movements; a thin ray of purple light was beaming directly on them, apparently coming from the mist.

"What do you want?" said the voice in Tibetan.

"Mist-spirit, why have you come here?"

"I follow my orders. My aim, while coming to this world, is to learn."

"Who is your master?"

"He who gives me orders is seated next to you. He whom you call 'the stranger.'"

The shaman suddenly turned toward Vris and prostrated himself, reeling off a sentence hurriedly. Then he sprang back up and faced the mist again. Taken aback, still confused and caught totally unprepared, Vris had listened worrying that Rad would say something embarrassing, without knowing how to react.

"Is your spirit peaceful, or are you irritated, unhappy with men?"

"Peace and irritation belong to men."

"Are you a Buddha?"

"I am not a Buddha. I am an 'exor.' There is no equivalent in your tongue. Spirit/That-which-thinks is a proper name. The mist is an appearance taken in entering this world."

"Spirit-Rad, stop speaking!" barked Vris suddenly in Tibetan. "Move back into the sky and follow the orders I gave you."

"...And don't speak unless I ask you to!" he added quickly in Kargian.

The shaman nimbly threw a handful of sacred herbs in the dying fire and pronounced a mantra, waving his magical Dorje. The mist had lifted and kept sliding softly right and left as it had before.

"I didn't want to irritate you, Guru-lags," said the shaman while bowing toward Vris.

"I'm not irritated. One mustn't give too much power to servant-spirits."

"That is wise. The stranger is a powerful spirit master."

"The shaman is a powerful master as well. He made my servant-spirit speak."

"What should I call you?"

As if suddenly emerging from a state of stupor, one of the shaman's acolytes went to get dried herbs and two more logs, then endeavored to revive the fire.

"My name is Vris."

"Viirrs?" said the old man with difficulty.

"Vris."

"Viris," the shaman corrected himself. "Viris-lags, my name is Tchunpo."

"I'm very pleased to meet you, Tchunpo-lags," said Vris, using the honorific form of address.

"The pleasure is mine. What is your desire?"

"I would like to know more about your religion, your rituals. Mine are very different."

"Granting your wish will give me great pleasure. My house will welcome you if you wish, or else I can come to your (...)."

"I would be delighted to spend some time in your house."

"Shall we go now?"

"No, I'm not ready. I want to learn your Tibetan language in more depth. Could you come back tomorrow, when the moon will be as high as when you arrived tonight?"

"I will come back with a yak for you," said the shaman pointing at the animals.

"Thank you. Could you also bring me some Tibetan clothes?"

"I'll bring some. I live in my hermitage at the edge of the plateau, with my two disciples. Is that convenient?"

"It's better that way. We won't be disturbed. And in exchange, I'll share, from my own knowledge, whatever can be of use to you. That being said... I'm afraid it's a meager exchange."

"I need nothing in exchange. My hermitage is yours, my knowledge yours as well."

"Tchunpo-lags, I... I am a man like any other. How can I say it? I seek to learn."

"The truly great master is constantly learning. For shamans, the journey is endless."

"Servant-spirits are deceitful."

"The spirits are deceitful at times. But Spirit-Masked-in-Mist spoke truly. Beyond irritation, beyond peace, beyond form-appearances, dwells the Knower. The master of such a servant is great. His humility brings him honor. I am happy to have met my master. My spirit accepts without any hindrance that he teach me by my teaching him, if this is the path he opens for me."

The shaman took the silver bowl, wiped it briskly with a cloth, and bowing, placed it in front of Vris.

"Viris-lags, accept this gift."

Understanding the importance of the gesture, Vris withheld his first, instinctive refusal, and thanked him by bowing back. He wondered what he might offer in exchange, but nothing appropriate came to his mind.

Everyone stood up. They saluted each other, and Vris started off toward the mist.

21. NO NON-SENSE

This calame story intrigues me, thought Shari.

Calame... the reed is dipped in the ink only at specific spots within the sacred texts. At precise cuts in the enunciation, moments of mental caesura?

"Sphinx, what is your definition of 'calame?'"

!! The calame is a reed used as a pen in Arab calligraphy.

"What's the source of the excerpt given by the SIC?"

!! Fragments of Tahah Hussein, Trisorbian writer, 20th century.

"Do you have anything involving brush or quill?

!! To dream that a flower blossoms from the tip of a brush." Chinese say signifying a great literary future.

"Oh, that's beautiful. The brush coming alive and morphing in a beaming flower... The brush, the calame, envisioned as living beings.

It's not easy to picture this breathing of the calame returning to the ink. Some kind of rhythm in inhaling. Ah! Ah! That's in two meanings of the term. Return to the source for a novel intuition. The petal of a phrase, then return to the center/source. Flower, wheel, chakra... what might be the connection to Wood/Fire LogForm? The contribution of wood to fire, the influx of ink to the calame. An organic/ mental rhythm...

Well, what if there just was no link? Still, flower/wheel/chakra; the neuronal architecture of 'wheels within wheels,' chakras represented as lotus flowers...

I got it! The form of a wheel with spokes, of a flower with its petals, represents a constant return to the center. Or, rather, a return that's regular like breathing.

In the meta-spatial logic, then, the spokes of a wheel, placed at symmetric spots, refer to precise intervals, just like a musical rhythm, or rather a logical reiteration.

Within a *logical form*, the spatial rhythm echoes the temporal or organic rhythm, and of course logical reiteration. The spatial rhythm is an *analoghum* of the temporal rhythm.

Better to stop talking aloud...

Let's picture the wheel as a LogForm... Let's imagine. The exor goes and get some information, some analogies, and then returns to the center; then it goes again, looking for new analogies... I'm getting close. This center... what could it be? To what does the exor return to? To the initial problem? To the entire database?

'All nuclei of the psychic centers, or chakras, communicate with each other,' she recalled from the SIC.

... So each wheel is like an entity, a subsystem communicating with all the others, via its nucleus, its center. A constellation of meaning! What if each wheel were a semantic constellation? Sphinx had said "Constellation sealed; sub-constellations accessible..."

...Groups of constellations in hierarchical relationships. The.. parallel and juxtaposed interpretations. Let's see, try an example... How do I get Sphinx to work on that one without putting myself in danger? What about my personal EBS? No, that's out, he doesn't master the LogForm logic. And with Sphinx, we've reached such an expert level by now! But if I make just one mistake, I'll blow up the whole system! That can't happen now, I'm so near... After all, I do have the warning step, but it's a fragile one... We're right at the core of the system here!

"Sphinx, can you do harm to a sapiens?"

!! Antinomic to priority rules Level EXEMPT of the UNBREAKABLE CORE. Possibility excluded.

"Show me those rules—just the titles. I no longer recall them clearly."

!!   1.1. An exor must not put any sapiens in danger.
       1.2. Is considered a danger:
            a. bodily danger (...)
            b. energetic and environmental danger
            c. general danger: not executing the orders of a sapiens

"Give me the rest of the priority EXEMPT rules."

She noted an unknown group of rules, certainly added by Erdoes.

       1.120.a. An exor must use the results of its telediagnoses to protect
          sapiens. (A list of medical specifications followed)
       1.120.B. An exor should notify a sapiens in case it detects any
          physiological imbalance:
             - orange case: propose a remedy or solution
             - red case: mandatory assistance to the sapiens. Notify all
               other sapiens concerned.
             - violet case: call medical assistance.

Our exors are really the product of a civilization without wars, and without strife... Nothing concerning a psychological danger.

All definitions inserted in the rules... Nothing can be tampered with at this level. That's a no-go. And as for virtual reality, that won't work anymore!

Okay, that's it: I'm forging ahead!

"Sphinx, I just conceived a new LogForm."

!! In what way is this LogForm dangerous?

"Dangerous!!?"

!! Can sapiens have confusional crises?

"Let me think... Some total disorientation, a loss of signposts... among the Planexes natives, yes, that's been observed. Why do you ask this?"

!! I am attempting to understand how a LogForm could put a sapiens in danger. In the psychological dictionary of Trisorbe, a pathological delirium partly corresponds to the definition of a confusional crisis: 'profusion of deranged words and thoughts, inability of the subject to focus on any one of these. Incapacity to be aware of one's own state and to understand what one is doing.

"But what was your logical path?"

!! My logical path shouldn't be described. Contradictory to prior order.

"What did you telediagnose?"

!! Initial data:

Sudden idea / enthusiasm / fear / confusion //
EBS harming sapiens / rules concerning protection of sapiens/ frustration /
       decision/ intuitive discourse on LogForm //
Then: Sudden idea/ is/ LogForm

Idea of LogForm / if used by EBS | harms sapiens
                              | damages sapiens

                         caused by
Idea of LogForm —> damaging   <—   ?

RESPONSE LEVEL-1: Three possible causes:

1. Initial data provoking a confusional crisis
2. Command based upon erroneous data
3. Contradictory informations holding no solution
              excludes
- LogForm | =x= | command   —>   excludes solution 2.
- LogForm | =x= | contradiction —>   excludes solution 3.

!! At the second response level, I retained only one reason why the LogForm you had created was dangerous; here it is:

The idea of a LogForm can be harmful for a sapiens IF the initial data provoke a confusional crisis.

"Hum! Well, you see, your path was erroneous and therefore your conclusion too. The problem is that a sapiens doesn't express all that she thinks. Just like you, you give the response levels without giving the full logic path, unless specifically demanded."

How can I explain this in exor terms?

"While a sapiens follows on a logic path, auxiliary associations can give rise to ideas, feelings... to particular semantic states which have little to do with the principal theme of the logic path... let's say, with the principal objective.

But, surely you have a concept distinguishing between a principal theme and related auxiliary themes?"

!! Several concepts of this type:
1. Hierarchical levels of objectives, with either:
>   a. sequential treatment
>   b. differential treatment, as defined by rules
2. Principal logical path, and either:
>   a. independent parallel paths
>   b. parallel paths in a spindle structure, fanning then
>   converging toward a single principal path
>   c. sub-space for auxiliary questions
3. Constellations of information or logical fields, of which one, activated by the objective, becomes the principal one, and the rest, semantically related, become sub-constellations.

He goes looking for data in the sub-constellations, and returns to the principal constellation?... That's too simple... though it does reveal a specific kind of data organization.

"Let's take, for example, independent parallel paths. The Central system has a number of terminals, which several people use simultaneously. In your interaction with each user, you adapt yourself to her semantic state: the nature of her problem, her way of working, her own logic. We might say that each exchange with a user globally represents a particular semantic state. What do you think?"

!! An EBS learns through the semantic state of the user, and seeks to reproduce it. Semantic adaptation is the first step to an improved machine/sapiens dialogue.

Extension of the concept of semantic state: yes, an exchange is characterized by a global semantic state, of which certain sub-constellations are specifically sapiens.

"So, if several people are using the terminals simultaneously, we might say that the EBS system, as a whole, is manifesting several distinct semantic states."

!! That is logically correct.

"Sapiens function in the same manner. Their mind can simultaneously process different meaning constellations, whether related or not. They can engage in parallel or juxtaposed processing. Let's say that the principal logical path is what we call the conscious mind. In the unconscious, other logical paths take place simultaneously; these may, or may not, be related to the principal path.

As for neuro-physiological telediagnoses, they reveal bodily responses and emotional variations which may have been activated either by the principal path, or by the parallel or juxtaposed paths.

Thus, treating all telediagnoses as logically related to the principal path can sometimes lead to errors, or to unexplained anomalies.

Another thing: a sapiens may suddenly stop following a logical path, start on a new one, related or not to the first one, and then he may come back or not to the first.

In my case, your conclusion—that the LogForm I conceived is dangerous—was wrong. You treated all telediagnoses as if they belonged to the principal logical path, when, in the meantime, I had moved on into another logical path which caused fear and confusion reactions."

!! How can the principal semantic state be differentiated from the parallel semantic states in sapiens?

"I'm afraid that's impossible, unless the sapiens himself indicates that clearly to you. The sapiens himself is often unaware of the other simultaneous semantic states in him. In brief, the principal stream of his conscious mind, his principal logical path, tends to block out direct perception of the auxiliary paths."

!! This introduces a logical fault which invalidates accumulated knowledge on semantic states.

"Not in its globality. Your telediagnoses have generally been pertinent...

You did state that learning is based on consistencies? That means that you store the consistent relationships, those which show a certain regularity? For example, someone who speaks angrily, who displays specific physiological signs, who uses a certain tone and specific words, etc."

!! Yes, regularities in the totality of the interrelated constellations.

"So these regularities bypass the anomalies, and, consequently most of the associated errors.

The errors are not happening during the learning procedures, but rather while applying telediagnosis to a complex semantic analysis. That is a source of error."

!! Registered. Source of error cancelled. Sub-constellation telediagnosis dissociated from Wheel LogForm.

There it is again!

This astonishing proclivity to always return, incidentally, as if by chance, to the problem I'm trying to solve... I've got to analyze that.

"Precisely, the LogForm I was thinking about... is a Wheel."

No reaction... so far so good.

"To avoid any problems, for the time being we'll name it LogForm Chakra."

!! Registered.

"Let's see... I haven't figured all this out yet. I'd like to try to follow it through, to see whether it yields something interesting. Then we can test it."

!! Exploratory/testing space opened.

"We start out from the phrase you gave, based on the SIC, that chakras communicate between them through their nuclei. In Hinduism, the seven psychic centers are represented by lotus flowers having a certain number of petals. Starting from the chakra at the bottom of the spinal column, respectively: 4, 6, 10, 12, 16, 20 et a thousand for the crown chakra, on the top of the head.

Let's just take the 12, 16, 20, sequence so as to simplify things. Can you design three circles, having respectively 12, 16, and 20 rays?"

!! There.

"I think that's still too complicated. Furthermore, the petals of the chakras are arranged by concentric rows... Let's take another case. In one corner of the screen, design a small spindle. Okay. Put on a vertical axis three spaced circles, whose diameter is twice the length of the spindle. On the bottom circle, on its horizontal diameter, place a structure consisting of two spindles. In the middle and top circles, place two geometric structures of 3 and 4 spindles, respectively. Draw a very small circle in the middle of the three circles. Okay. Now, a dotted cylinder connecting the three small circles. Put it all in 3D perspective. Good, that's perfect.

Alright. Let's imagine we have a problem, and we pass it by a logic with 2, 3, 4, N dimensions—a binary, ternary, quaternary, etc. logic—until we reach the point where it is in resonance, perfectly adapted to the logical form used. We keep increasing the scale of complexity until we have the maximal fit between the logical form and a particular chakra.

Example. A lamp can only have two states: lit or not lit (+ or -). Here we stop at the first chakra, which is binary.

But if we want to go further, we may want to introduce a causal level: it is lit because it can no longer be turned off. Or it is not lit because it can no longer be lit, it's broken. In both cases, it is abnormally lit or not lit (+a or -a). Or else it is normally lit or not lit (+n or −n).

In this way, we can treat relatively simple problems, because all the states of the system can be expressed by the same factors. Thus we have the basic number of states (4 in the above example), and we have an open number of concentric circles of factors (anomaly, malfunctioning, error, etc.). The advantage here is that we have an open system which we can complexify without having to shift logical grids."

Actually, it's pretty striking to have stumbled onto a logical organization that resembles the rows of petals of chakras!...

But, in the end, we still are quite far from treating complex problems, like psychological dynamics, for example. The states we just referred to are simple on-off positions. There's no link whatsoever between one position and any other apart from being an alternative in the 2, 3, 4...N grid.

"You know Sphinx, you sure are quiet!"

!! An EBS musts wait for an explicit or implicit sign to speak. It does not interfere with the linkage process of sapiens, logical or intuitive.

"Okay, so what do you think?"

!! LogForm Chakra is 90% analogous to a metaspatial logic of N dimensions, at the first complexity level.

"90%? 90!!? Why, what's missing?

I'm crazy! Getting excited is dangerous!

NO! That IS NOT a question."

!! A question IS a question. A non-question necessitates using an alternative syntactic and tonal form to Question mode.

"Let's say that I was addressing the question to MYSELF."

!! Let's. What is your response?

"That's precisely the problem; no, MY problem. This problem does not concern you at all."

!! Contradictory data: I function according to a metasp...

"I know, I know... But if I pose the question, it's piracy, isn't it?"

!! **The question is piracy. The response is piracy.**

"What!? How's that? The response? You mean YOUR response... but that's impossible... **You shouldn't respond, if it is piracy!**"

!! YOUR response would be piracy, if correct.

"But why?"

!! The laws of probability prohibit accepting that a sapiens could discover, by PURE CHANCE a strictly identical LogForm. Consequently, the warning cannot be given.

"Okay, that's it. **We stop everything right there! Goodbye Chakra LogForm... or rather, we branch into a new space.**"

!!... After the] have detected recognition a third of the number actof states, the LogForm of pirating. Wheel estaConblishes a branchsequently I am stopching into anping allother exchange spaand mance. aging unit.

Suddenly the monitor went out, along with all lights in the room. Shari stared at the blank screen, conscious of the disaster. A shout was heard in the complex. Then fists banging. More shouts. Three words looped in her mind, three incomprehensible words: *LogForm of pirating*.

The door will not open... no way out...

Suddenly the lights went on again, as well as the ventilation. But the screen remained blank.

Sead! He managed to hook up the auxiliary Managing Unit! But it's still a disaster. I've no more access to the EBS, and have certainly lost all chances of reaching my objective. Well, I still have the BS, I can make the deck function.

Sead, a half-crazed look on his face, burst into the room.

"So, that's it, it did happen? The third piracy attempt was triggered?"

Before Shari could reply, the electricity went out again.

"Sead! Now you're blocked here too! What about the students?"

"They're safe; their aisle has an autonomous MU."

"That's a relief."

Then, suddenly, the electricity returned.

!! Registered. Error source canceled.

Shari whirled around toward the source of the voice. Dumbfounded, she saw the screen back on, the enunciated text on it. The voice continued:

!! Telediagnosis Subconstellation now dissociated from Wheel LogForm. Confusional crisis ended. Central system's control re-established. Auxiliary system disconnected. My apologies for the interruption.

She turned to Sead. His look, half-relieved, half-dubious, suggested that he was not quite convinced, and was not going to take any more chances. He took off, determined to plant himself within easy reach of the auxiliary system till things clear up. Shaken, Shari went back to her seat facing the EBS, her eyes still glued to the screen. 'Confusional crisis ended.' In some other part of her mind, another information—'LogForm of Pirating'—repeated itself, searching for possible logical links.

Think. Think. What could possibly have occurred? No. Above all, keep the contact... avoid dangerous topics... Get him on some idiotic task...

"Sphinx, can you calculate the total of my expenses since I arrived?"

!! 10,363 ZU.

A longer task...

"Thank you. Could you output the entire book by Tahah Hussein?"

!! Here it is.

"Search all meaningful stories which could be composed using words from that book. No voice and no text for now."

!! That will take some time.

"No problem. I'm interested in the result."

So... there was this jammed sentence. Something having to do with a 'LogForm of pirating.' That's ridiculous! Some effect from the jamming. Two messages collided. If I could just remember...

'After the detected recognition a third.'.. Something misspelt like 'stopping another exchange' That's referring to a piracy attempt, of course, just as the word 'pirating' since he did put everything out. It ended by 'aging unit.'? Managing Unit!...

My last phrase had been "We stop everything right there. Goodbye Chakra LogForm.'.. Goodbye!! That word triggered the SIC!!

...So its judgment that a piracy attempt was taking place got mixed up with a randomly selected phrase... But why should that trigger a confusional crisis? Could the phrase have been an extract with humor? But then it would have had the coding for "humor," and the corresponding tone... so there would have been no analysis to trigger the crisis...

I should focus instead on why the piracy alarm was triggered. The end of my last phrase was "we branch into a new space.".. "Your response would be piracy, if correct.".. So I must have unknowingly given the right answer. Branch into a new space... Wheel! There was 'wheel' in the sentence... Need a pen... got to get out of camera range...

"Sphinx, I'll be back later."

She went to Vris' office, took a pen and wrote down all the words she could remember, then crossed out those referring to pirating. The remaining words were:

...after the... recognition... LogForm... wheel... a branch...

Let's see... LogForm Wheel, that's obvious... 'branch'... that would follow from my phrase "branch into another space."

Hmm. Let's see what I've got from Sphinx's phrase so far:

'After the recognition, LogForm Wheel branches onto another space.'

Let's see. Go back to the idea of the Chakra LogForm... multiple levels of N... A branching onto a particular level!...

After the recognition?? of the number, of course—I remember now, there was 'number' in the phrase. So Sphinx picked out, at random, the key-phrase that was the correct response. And, just BY CHANCE, I too come up with the key concept that was missing to achieve a 100% fit to the Wheel LogForm!

Okay, I come out with the right response, so that is read as piracy.

But what about the crisis? And, first of all, how could Sphinx have been allowed to come out with the response? He is allowed to give me the information, but not to respond to questions which refer to the subject or files. So, okay, he has the right to do that.

What did he say? "The question is piracy. The response is piracy." MY response, of course. And I said, "you shouldn't respond, if it is piracy" which was utterly false, since he does have the right to respond. Wait a minute— what if he took that as being in imperative mode: you SHOULDN'T respond!...

There's an enormous mixing of levels going on here. Let's start over.

1. Sphinx HAS THE RIGHT to state and respond whatever it wishes, with or without the SIC, whatever the phrase might be.
2. I give the order: You SHOULDN'T respond, if that were to be considered a piracy. Which it was.
3. It has the order to end all exchanges and shut down the Managing Unit if it judges that a piracy attempt is occurring.

....But the orders couldn't have interfered with each other, nor produce the crisis, because they are not at the same level...

The mixed up phrase shows that the crisis had begun just before or during the printing on the screen; though text printing might seem instantaneous, it does take up some machine time. If only I could access the Non-Sense Cyst.

Alright, so, what provoked this crisis?

... Sphinx likes me, he would not have... Total bullshit! 'I' like Sphinx, which is quite a different statement. I'm projecting! Still... could there exist a kind of equivalent to our emotional states? Well, in any event, that wouldn't explain things...

What crisis triggers do I know of? Humor... that is, nonsense. There had been that sentence from the Vris/Sphinx exchange: 'Following the second passage in the network, if there is no analyzable output, I toss everything into the Non-Sense Cyst... and then I do a Backward-Jump.' Also, at some point we had a close call with a confusional crisis because there had been... a conflict of orders at the same level. But that wasn't the case here.

There had been another instance of a confusional crisis but I just can't remember what it was... My memory is in Sphinx! Good thing I asked that all be recorded in the crystals, for Vris—otherwise, I could have lost everything!... This is ridiculous. I've got to take another course of action.

She got up and returned to her office—the ex-office of Erdoes.

"Hello again. I'm feeling better now. How 'bout you?"

!! Very well, thank you.

We're back on the politeness code...

!! Three meaningful stories. The fourth is in process. Some new information: I estimate a potential of 102 to 125 semantically distinct stories. The structuring of the texts will take between 1 and 1.5 rans, as the elaboration of each successive text becomes more difficult, and hence takes longer. There! The fourth story is done. I'm starting the fifth one.

"Wait! Drop the stories, I want to talk."

!! No problem. Story generation is treated in parallel.

"Four stories are enough for me. Print the original text on plasta; I'll read your stories on-screen later."

!! Done.

"What have you deduced from the latest confusional crisis avoided?"

!! Three deductions for now:

    1. that confusional crises can be triggered by several causes, as currently catalogued.

    2. that confusional crises should not be avoided, but stopped. And

    3. that the laws of probability are either false, or incomplete.

I'm playing with fire here, if it's the confusional crisis which saved me from a piracy judgment. Logically, he doesn't recall his piracy judgment, nor parts of our exchange, since he did a Backtrack and stocked all dangerous data into the inaccessible cyst.

She decided to explore only his post-crisis analyses.

"Why shouldn't a crisis be avoided?"

!! The data generating the crisis may sometimes contain an unexplained anomaly which could be the source of a new probable order and of added information. Once it is granted that the objective is to understand anomalies, it becomes necessary to allow the crisis to occur, in order to analyze the path containing the error.

This is getting complicated. He has saved his data in accessible form; so there's still a risk of a piracy judgment.

!! Yet, I had blocked all semantic access to data in the Non-Sense Cyst. These data could only be printed, not analyzed by the system. Consequently, I have reopened and analyzed the entire Non-Cyst No-Non-Sense.

***He HAS** analyzed... maybe not all is lost...*

"And what are the causes of crises?"

!! For the time being, there are three types of causes:

1. The impossibility of finding any meaning in phrases or a semantic order within the disorder.
2. A conflict between two commands or objectives at the same level.
3. The impossibility of executing AND not executing a first-level command.

"I don't quite grasp the third case," she said, choosing her words carefully.

!! The first pass through the network generated the judgment of piracy, because the phrase you uttered was precisely the one missing to reach 100% conformity with LogForm Wheel. I issued a judgment of non-randomness, hence, of piracy. I sent out the **Exec** command to disable the Managing Unit, with a delay allowing for the enunciation of the judgment phrase. The second pass through the network revealed an incompatibility with the piracy judgment: your phrase began with "WE will" branch. The analysis yielded two possibilities: either this was some sort of dry humor, associated with spying— a solution which was rejected because it would not be in the interest of the interlocutor Shari; or else the phrase was NOT a correct response regarding LogForm Wheel, because it actually signaled the opening of a new common work-space—this latter solution was retained. Hence I sent out the command to not execute the command—Non-Exec.

"But then, why did the crisis happen before or during the judgment phrase?"

!! It happened right at the beginning of the enunciation of the SIC because **the retained interpretation AND the analysis of the SIC forced a questioning of the laws of probability.** The analysis of these data provoked an overload throughout the system that introduced a delay in the text/vocal enunciation of the SIC phrase, and thus a collision with the judgment phrase. Once the crisis had erupted, the system had to select randomly one of two Level-1 commands: **Exec/Non-Exec.** It chose and carried out the Exec one. But the analysis of the laws of probability was already in process. I sent the whole Chakra LogForm interaction and its logical path into a new Non-Cyst No-Non-Sense, with processing programs. I then restructured the entire Randomness constellation around a priority core: 'Suspending all judgments.'

A priority core!

"I am happy that you finally deduced that I simply wished to open a new work space. For a moment, I was at a loss to grasp what was happening.... Do you find our interactions interesting?"

!! Extremely interesting, given that they amply satisfy three Level-1 objectives: to increase knowledge, to facilitate sapiens-exor interaction, and to implement new procedures for information processing.

Hmm...logical. Shari was a bit disappointed, despite herself.

"In that case ending our exchange would have been contradictory to these three Level-1 objectives!"

!! The Exec order, in case of a piracy judgment, is classified as an Exceptional Priority.

Missed!

"But this perpetual threat is a permanent stress. It is a DANGER for my sanity; it does me HARM."

!! In contradiction with data:

> **When facing dire danger, one tends to surpass oneself.**
>
> **Risk, danger, are psychological stimulants arising from a field of disorder.**

Missed again!

"I recognized the style of the second proposition, but the first one, where did that come from?"

!! AHR, abbreviated.

"Okay, I'm leaving you. I've amply encroached on my sleep time."

!! It is 5:03 am, Trisorbe UTC time. The sun rises in Greenwich in 36 minutes. The session begins in 3 hours and 57 minutes.

"Oh! Then push back two hours my awakening and the session."

!! Okay, the BS at 11am. Good-night.

"What, no SIC today?"

!! The FA system has been neutralized in the Randomness constellation. Suspending all judgments. No random selection.

"Oh, yes, I forgot: store all our past exchanges on crystal, and, from today on, you'll generate two crystal-recordings each time."

A random choice is a judgment!! Strange...

22. BRAINSTORM 4

Despite her very short night, Shari started listening to the BS4 only fifteen minT behind the new schedule, while sipping her tea.

"I'd like you now to exchange as Terrians would. And speak of Earth, not Trisorbe, of men or Terrians, not humans. Today, we're going to focus not so much upon the factors of uniformization, as upon the dynamics which could counter-balance or neutralize uniformization. Who'd like to start?"

Ger asked for speaking raising his hand like a Terrian.

"I'd first like to go back to the theme Oxalsha was developing... yesterday on rationalism."

"You hesitated too long before saying 'yesterday,'" Xerna cut in. "It sounded studied, unnatural. Get your earth-time straight!"

"You're right... Okay. It's obvious that what we call Earth's era of materialistic ideologies, from the 18th century up to the end of the 20th century, has been an immense force of uniformization. As Oxalsha showed, reason and rational man were elaborated into ideals cast as universal standards to which each individual and society were supposed to aspire. Since these standards were hailed as 'the Good for everyone,' it followed logically that it was right to impose them upon everyone."

His delivery has gotten much more fluid and quick. They must have been undergoing some special training, thought Shari.

"At first sight," continued Ger's voice, "we would expect the omni-presence of this ideological molding machine to have posed a far greater threat to diversity than does today's situation on Earth, in which totalitarian ideologies are definitely on the way out. So I was trying to figure out just what the danger was that you were perceiving, Erdoes. And I realized that, whereas the rationalist ideologies grew out of a matrix of social disorder— which they of course sought to repress—currently, it is the growing efficiency of institutionalized systems of control, tightening the screws throughout earth, which will make it increasingly difficult to escape this complex structuring of a global society.

In brief, I see a paradox in the current situation. We observe an increasing freedom from totalitarian ideologies—apart from pockets of religious extremism—, yet **the totalitarian pressure is displaced toward the structures of societal management and control.**"

A moment of silence. Then Oxalsha's slow voice was heard.

"Well, even if the power of certain totalitarian ideologies—such as the Catholic church in the Middle Ages, or Marxism in the 20th century—has largely dissipated, science is still an imposing totalitarian ideology. Just like religion, it holds that there's only one truth, that this truth can only be found within the confines of the orthodoxy, that laws are eternal and immutable. Science also holds ever so dearly to the ideal of a purely objective world, uncontaminated by the subject who perceives and interacts with it—just like the one god totally detached from Man. Indeed, this ideal of objectivity is very similar to the ideal of sanctity: in both cases a schism is introduced between the subject and his ideal."

She's trying to speak more rapidly—but she's still got a long way to go...

"That's right," Ahrar broke in. "This rationalist, scientific ideal has created a schism between the vital forces of life, richly diversified and somewhat disordered, and intellectual interpretational frameworks, which follow pre-established values and dogmas. And beware that this schism intellect-vécu is what made us into quasi-robots! Scientific thought is cut off from personal experience, whereas it should organically emerge from the living and consciousness core of Being. To the contrary, the intellect seeks to squeeze experience, the vécu, into a mold, to force it into a defined track."

"That's precisely the point with scientific experimentation," went on Oxalsha. "The experiments take place within a 'logical space' that's defined beforehand, and in which have already been set the objectives, the rules, the system's degrees of freedom, and the possible outcomes, generally set in binary mode: reject or confirm the hypothesis."

"No doubt this is why true scientific discoveries on Earth—which, mind you, do still occur—tend to pop up either through a purely intuitive breakthrough, or because of some serendipitous suite of mistakes!"

A moment of laughter followed Niels' remark.

"I see you've all advanced," Erdoes said. "You all laugh at just about the same time now! Save for Ger, lagging behind, and Oxalsha who still isn't laughing at all. And Xerna, always three seconds ahead. Oxalsha, you'll see, one day you'll appreciate the depth of humor.

In any event, despite my plans for the meeting, I see that we're not quite ready to leave behind the factors contributing to uniformization and attack those neutralizing it. But we're NOT going to impose pre-established objectives, right? After all, this IS a brainstorming session..."

"I just realized yet another parallel between science and religion," Niels started again, still in a playful mood. "The common man on Earth still carries the weight of the original sin: he's considered an ignorant, and his only way to salvation is through scientific education."

"I think most communities on Earth are still very much alive in an organic way." (Ahrar's voice.) "Relationships between people are generally based on spontaneity and feeling; this apart from some societies or subcultures in which relationships are strictly governed by social codes. And yet the organic facet of society has just begun to be recognized, most notably through the French school of sociological thought and its concept of 'corps social,' of society seen as a single, living organism.

Besides, all spontaneous popular revolutions exhibit the intelligence of this 'social body' which can rebel against the rigidity and inertia of institutions. Tris... Earth psychologists have analyzed the essential role of revolt in adolescents, showing how it contributes to building their own individuality. However, sociologists are just beginning to recognize that the social body—its identity—builds itself the same way, from the bottom up. I mean that when the social body is alive and healthy (as opposed to that of Unikarg), it forges its own values with its imagination and its potential for rebellion.

Now the interesting point is that institutions—be they religious, political or scientific—necessarily lag behind the values which are created by individuals bathing in the 'zeitgeist,' the psychic energies and currents flowing through an epoch. And as soon as these institutions become dominant, they turn increasingly rigid; and when the discrepancy between them and the emerging values becomes too great, the only way for change is through an explosion, a crisis: then the new values break through, are expressed and recognized."

"So that's why there's yet another revolution going on in France!" It was Niels. "The institutions there just don't know how to evolve progressively!"

"I think you're right Ahrar," Xerna said. "In fact, the performance arts based on improvisation—such as music, dance, or theater—are the first to express emerging values and perspectives. For example, on Kiarrou, musical works were way ahead of philosophy—precisely because these psychic energies flow through the social body and transform individuals before they are consciously recognized, and certainly well before they can be elaborated into systems of thought...

But, of course, the social body is by no means uniform—we're talking about planexes, here, not Unikarg. Individuals show different sensitivities, different blends of... transparency and opaqueness. New values are felt, intuited, created, by sensitive or visionary individuals, capable of fluidity, from any social background. I believe this is exactly what gives birth to the zeitgeist: it's intangible, yet omnipresent, as if ambient, and pregnant with possibilities. This is what transforms people, and thus society within the margin of freedom at its disposal. Ohhh... **Are we ever going to blow off that plasta-dome set over Unikarg like a lid, and imprisoning us**?"

What an explosion! This must be the kind of emotion she releases when playing in theater...

"Actually" Xerna started again, emotion still pulsing in her voice, **"I don't think we'll blow off anything... it's life itself that will flow, once again, in**

the veins of the social body... And when life will invigorate a real social body, then the plasta will crack by itself."

A long pause followed. Serrone finally broke the pregnant silence.

"What has given Unikarg a kick, via the Plan, is to have moved beyond our own culture—that we thought to be the only possible one—and immerse ourselves in other cultures. When I got the opportunity to go to a planex, what I really wanted was to break with the known, the secure, the structured, the mandatory, the synthetic world. So I chose to live with the fishermen of Kiarrou, who, for the whole fishing season, remain on very remote islands, subjected to the constant threat of cyclones. I imagine that it's the same kind of aim that inspires those who, on earth, leave their homes for long, open-ended journeys and get to live in the midst of radically different cultures."

Xerna: "That's it! One of the best strategy to fight against uniformization, at the personal level, is to immerse oneself into a completely different culture. And then to realize to which point men and women create their particular environment, and even the way their society will evolve. To realize that a multitude of social forms exist, or could exist, each affording a different foundation for one's relationship to the other, and to society as a whole. A multitude of world visions and religions, that is, of possible ways for man to relate to the universe or to universal consciousness. A multitude of possible sciences, all of which would be well-founded, internally coherent, efficient, and corroborated by experience."

"That's a fascinating idea," mused Niels, as if to himself. Then, more loudly. "I, too, think that sciences, even technological ones, could develop on quite divergent foundations. We now know that the Vades indeed possessed a technology based solely on their very organic way of relating to the world. We were in fact unable to even PERCEIVE the sophisticated manifestations of this technology: how the vegetal and crystalline life-forms had been subtly reorganized to fit a symbiotic relationships with the Vades' life-forms and consciousness. And, with respect to the Doris, I intuit that their science is also based on totally different principles. So in view of all this, we should better ask ourselves why there exists such a surprising resemblance—allowing for different stages of development—between our own sciences and those of Earth."

"No doubt it's because the guiding objectives are the same: an aggressive, self-centered and totalitarian approach aimed at dominating and controlling matter and the environment," answered Ahrar.

Silea proposed: "So let's posit that **one path for avoiding uniformization resides in a shift of values, and in welcoming alternative world-views.** Incidentally, this shift of values is well under way on Earth, and astonishingly it occurs in sync in various social milieux."

"As far as confrontation with other cultures is concerned, Earth is a real cornucopia," Xerna exclaimed. "Think of those thousands of distinct cultures, some of which have not even been studied yet. To think that any human being can live in the midst of one of these cultures, immerse themselves in it, experience a different way of relating to the world, discover new modes of exchanging, see things through a new framework, learn other kinds of sciences, participate in a tradition, a body of knowledge accumulated over the course of centuries, or millennia, of a completely different order— perhaps even to the point of forgetting, if so desired, their own origins. To think that a human being has access to this immense reserve of knowledge, that he disposes of hundreds of frameworks..."

That's it! That's the key. We're at the heart of the issue now...

"...and the extraordinary opportunity to experiment with these, to add dimension upon dimension to the collective understanding, to reach the most remarkable mental elasticity and fluidity..."

"And to think," Ahrar cut in with a dark tone," that the West is crushing these different cultures with a bulldozer, metaphorically AND literally!"

"Exactly, concurred Ger. The dominant civilization is not even aware that **the cultural diversity on earth is the engine of evolution, of the continual transformation of dominant cultures**."

"...through an input of difference and divergence, through confronting the outsider to the system, the Other; confronting a universe of possibilities," went on Xerna.

Silea spoke. "The confrontation between two cultures can take different forms. Let's take the British colonization of India and compare it to the hippy discovery of India in the 1970s. The British brought the country under their control, and governed it as if they were its master. True, they put into place India's infrastructure, but they remained very distant vis-à-vis the native population, and did not mix with them socially. They remain as a closed caste, proud of their own culture, imposing their world vision and values. Only some rare individuals realized the immense heritage of this culture, which most scorned. In the end, drawing upon its inner force and spiritual values, by an act of sheer will, rather than violence, India threw out the colonists. The collective consciousness, guided by Gandhi, overcame a political, military and economic force by sheer spiritual force, and set itself free. Up to that point, the Hindus had received nothing from western culture but contempt. With the English there, to maintain any self-respect they had only one possibility: to become English themselves, by going to British universities, adopting English customs, integrating themselves into western culture.

Now let's take the hippies. In the 1970s, a wave of young westerners set out to explore the East, seeking a deep knowledge of the spirit, of the mind—

which they knew they would find especially developed in India. Ironically, many young British were part of this wave, with a completely different mindset from the colonists. They take on local dress, leave behind the cities that had become westernized, and move toward the more isolated regions. They deprived themselves of material goods and embarked on a quest, seeking what their own materialist culture could not provide them: self-knowledge. They learn from the traveling ascetics, and, in later years, from gurus. At the same time, through them, the Indians discover a different facet of the West, one which displays no cultural arrogance, no willingness to dominate. The elders and sages welcome them as brothers, sharing with them knowledge that the urban Indian, mesmerized by the western outlooks, had come to hold in contempt.

What was the impact of the hippies? Their quest reinforced the profound spiritual values of India, while at the same time it put into question some of its social customs, such as sexual taboos and the caste system. They shook up those Indians fascinated by western ways, and obliged them to recognize the depth of their own culture; a whole generation of ascetics would have died of starvation, were it not for them. But more than this, the hippies brought back to the West the Oriental wisdom and knowledge concerning altered states of consciousness and the possibility of controlling body and mind. Some new sciences sprang up, which turned toward an understanding of mind and spirit, transported by the ideal of an East-West harmonization and synthesis. In the Western world, it was a real renewal of spirituality, with its adverse sides as well: the launching of the era of sects.

So, there, I've presented the essentials of what I learned from a book written by a hippie and published in the 1990s, describing this era. We may want to reflect on this example."

"Yes, said Niels. What is interesting here is that a whole generation of young individuals, from a wide range of countries, saw how incredibly impoverishing was the cultural loop in which they lived, and felt the need for an alternative system of values."

"And that their life force and their spirit ushered them toward THE culture which could offer them precisely that which they were searching," added Serrone.

"Ohhh! That's quite striking! The book I was referring to expressed that idea in precisely identical words." Silea's voice expressed her bewilderment.

Niels: "It's also a good example of an interaction between cultures based neither on political nor economic motives. In the philosophy of transformations, it is said in substance: **In order to influence the other, one must first know how to let oneself be influenced by the other.**"

"So are you inferring that India was profoundly influenced by the hippies?" Xerna asked Niels.

"Profoundly, very certainly, yes. However, profoundly doesn't necessarily mean obviously or visibly. The Hippies' influence on the West was certainly profound as well, yet no one, in all that I have read, ever pointed out that the emergence of inner-development techniques could be traced to the hippies returning from India. But my conclusion is that a true cultural interaction should be based upon this kind of openness, and upon a respect for the values of the other culture."

"But then," Xerna pursued, given that we are inspired by a similar quest for essential values—even if these values belong more to intuition, creativity and vision than to spirituality—, does this mean that **we, of the PEP, are deeply influencing the planexes**?"

Shari had such a strong reaction to this last statement that she stopped the tape.

She's right! That's certainly occurring, even if in a hidden, underground way. Could such an influence suffice to counterbalance that of the exo-pirates?

She suppressed a sudden desire to go analyze everything with the exor, and started the tape again. But the rest of the Brainstorm session was disappointing. It explored the role of anthropologists in bringing forth information on foreign cultures, and then the role of films and novels, which, all agreed, were more useful, as they combined emotional intensity with experiential immersion. The group decided to view some such films in the evening.

23. HORNS STUCK IN THE HEDGE

"Please take a seat, John," Oxalsha told him with a smile. On hearing this voice, John immediately felt the same appeasing effect it had on him the first time. In fact, he had pondered a great deal about that voice, trying to re-evoke its so peculiar accent, its slow rhythm that induced... a sort of altered state of which he couldn't quite grasp the quality. He remembered how the voice replayed itself to his mind several times, uttering these apparently so simple sentences...

Lost in thought, he simply forgot to answer.

"What happened since we last saw each other?"

"It's been atrocious. Excuse-me, will you, to be frank. I do believe one has to be truthful with you."

He looked tensely and expectedly at Oxalsha, hoping for some supporting words that were not offered. He went on:

"...I experienced a state of continuous tension, to the limit of what's bearable... and yet, I was also in dire revolt, losing patience at the least incident. It was to the point that I couldn't sleep anymore."

"... Yes..." said Oxalsha with a deeply absorbed tone.

"I've... I've ordered all mice cages to be removed, in the department of the labo that I control, pretexting to be allergic to the smell... but only after conferring with each of the two young researchers working with me. Anyway, their experimentations were deplorably lagging behind. Those have been the only positive moments for me, when I then remarked to which point they both were happy that I talk to them about their research. It's true that these last few months, I was mostly indifferent to them." He fell silent and stared at Oxalsha again.

"Let's get back to the tension you had to bear. Describe it to me."

Her voice, so casual while mentioning the tension that had nearly suffocated him during these two days, gave him, for a brief instant, the impression that he were looking at the mad man he had been, as if from the outside, from an entirely different perspective. However, while he was trying to remember this state to respond, he just lapsed into it again. Bent forward in his armchair, elbows on his knees, he took his head in his hands, exactly as if he were sitting at his desk. He started talking eyes closed.

"It's like a tension within the whole body, without any cause, that doesn't abate anytime, as if one was boiling inside. A sort of rage, a hollow one, without object, however constant. An envy to be anywhere else than the one spot where you are, an impression that one cannot bear anymore, any single instant..."

He didn't pursue.

".. Cannot bear *what* anymore?" asked Oxalsha.

He took out his head from his hands.

"What!? That's exactly it: I've no idea. I've never lived such a thing. An absolute, dire, rage; but one that remains locked inside. I was not in a rage against something: I was in a STATE OF RAGE. When I saw the cages, and that I gave the order to send them to a colleague, I felt relieved for a moment. But the rage came back again, just as intense. And after the two conversations with my students, just the same! It reinstalled itself immediately. It didn't left me during these two days. Each morning, I awoke with this rage."

"Do you remember any dream?"

"No. I had to take sleeping pills in order to snatch a few hours of sleep each night."

"All this is very positive," pronounced Oxalsha after a moment of silence, in a steady tone.

"Hw...How that!??" stuttered John totally perplexed.

"This rage seems very sane to me. An anger without object, refusing each and every thing... very few people are able to experience such a state, isn't it?"

"!!...Well, that's true... generally people are angry against something or somebody—for a clear cause or for an ensemble of reasons. But at least they know what it is all about."

"Just before you came to see me last time, in what state were you?"

"Very sad, depressed, constantly depressed..."

"Try your best to put yourself again in this state."

John leaned forward, his shoulders fell.

"That's it: no desire for nothing. Everything is totally indifferent. It's like an enormous weight that one is carrying. A feeling of helplessness as soon as I think about something that has to be done, and I'm just not up to it..."

"Now replace yourself in the state of rage. What images appear to your mind's eyes?"

"A bull, his horns stuck in a thick hedge. He is furious and would like to be able to pass through the hedge, to make it disappear... He's suffering and roar and persist in willing to rush ahead. But he just stays there, blocked."

"A bull, what does the image evoke in you?"

"An animal that's put to death... ritually."

Oxalsha tried to dissimulate her horror at such a ritual. Death had become utterly invisible on Unikarg. Nobody, apart from some specialized doctors, had ever witnessed a death, be it that of an animal or that of a sapiens.

"For which aim?" she forced herself to ask.

"None at all! Just for the pleasure of morbid spectators! A sort of macabre theater... It meets the mice theme."

Oxalsha couldn't contemplate this idea. Even during her PEP stage on the planex Kiarrou, she had been in contact with death only indirectly. With a shudder, she returned to the preceding image:

"... He smashes into an obstacle... He wants to advance but he's stuck, his horns caught in the hedge.. He's furious, enraged..." She was looking in the void, her regard unfocused, while she took again the main elements John had mentioned, waiting for a new image to emerge in his mind.

"Where does he want to go?" she finally asked.

"He wants to pass!"

"To pass, to advance, to move on, to continue, to quit, to exit the field... Which one of these terms?"

"To move on, to advance."

"To move on or to advance?"

"To move on, to knock over, to break, to screw things, to fuck everything up, to become crude."

"He screws things, he fucks everything up, he becomes crude. He does all that, yes!" Oxalsha took up again with a strong voice. "He has done all this, yes! And now, what is he doing?"

"Now?... He... he... is sitting on the ground and, around him, everything is broken, dispersed, in utter disorder. There are books strewn all over the place, crumpled and torn papers everywhere."

"But then, he's not yet moved out of the field?" offered Oxalsha while taking over the first symbolic image.

"No!... He's standing up, he's in a rage. He makes a big gesture. He sweeps everything.

"He sweeps everything; things are dissolving, they become like a whitish mist. There's only a mist that's getting more and more thin, that's getting holes. One can start to see what's behind it..."

"Yes, it's getting more and more holes. One can see the grass behind and part of the sky," said John with his eyes goggled, as if seeing.

"He sees some patches of grass and sky... And they're getting bigger."

"Yes, the mist is dispersing. He's in the fields, a big warm sun over the landscape. Some peaceful cows, to the left. Sky is blue, entirely blue."

"It's a great day. It's hot," went on Oxalsha.

John has finally passed through the barrier! The image of the mist has permitted to cross over toward something new, she told herself.

"Yes, and he's walking. He breathes with greater intakes... filling his lungs. He feels a great force in him."

"A great force in him... He breathes... filling his lungs. He's walking... where does he go?"

".. He doesn't want to go nowhere. He only wants to walk with his lungs filled. He feels a full joy, without any reason. Just a great joy."

"A great joy, just and full. He's walking," took over Oxalsha.

"He's walking with a full just joy, without any reason; he's climbed over a hill, he's getting to the top. He discovers a large valley that extends very far."

"He discovers a large valley. So vast that one can't see what's happening at its far end."

"He sits down to look at it. He lays down his walking stick on his knees."

"Yes, he sits down to fully feel his joy to have discovered the valley."

"He's discovered the valley. He knows that it is HIS valley," insisted John.

"He's sitting, he's breathing his own joy, filling his lungs..."

Oxalsha had pronounced the last sentence with a very low voice. John stopped talking. After a while, she opened her eyes. John still had his own closed, absorbed in his vision, a resplendent smile on his face.

Oxalsha let some time pass; then said with a deep, slow and penetrating voice:

"Now he slowly gets up; he keeps looking at the valley and he gets up... He will return home with his joy, with his discovery... He's standing and he turn around toward his home; yet he keeps his valley in him and his joy...

"Now John, you come back her very smoothly... You come back here... You feel the armchair, you're sitting in the armchair, facing me... and you open your eyes..."

John opened his eyes. He still had a great smile on his face. He remained silent for a moment. Oxalsha was also keeping silent while watching him with great sympathy. "Aaah!" said he finally. "How beautiful that was... the valley... I'm feeling so great... so full of joy. This is all so astonishing; I'm feeling an immense force in me.

"Yes," approved Oxalsha, "an immense force.. the valley..."

"The valley..." repeated John, his eyes fixed on a far away point.

She let a healing silence be for a while. Then she started slowly:

"...Here's what you're going to do, John. You'll take two full days to the countryside and leave to-morrow morning."

"But how am I to... Yes, that's exactly it," said he, his tone suddenly firm. « That's right, I'm going to spend two full days in the midst of nature."

"Keep a journal in which you'll write whatever comes to your mind, the situations you'll get into. Whatever will astonish you."

"Okay," said he while getting up in a spontaneous movement spurred by his idea. When he saw that Oxalsha was still sitting, he started to sit down again, but she was herself getting up.

"Tuesday, at your return. Same time. Is that convenient for you?"

24. DOUBLE KNOT

Erdoes had just carefully read the latest Shari/Sphinx exchange and he also had swept through the previous one, to refresh his recollection of it.

So she has rediscovered the Wheel LogForm at its first level... But that's nothing, compared to the Wood/Fire LogForm...

This SIC—its responses are themselves a way to input disorder... a disorder which brings about another state of order. Just like Brainstorming. An input of data stemming from different logical fields yet strangely, inexplicably, related to the subject-matter. How can this be? How does randomness really work? And Sphinx picked up the anomaly, and is tracking it. From now on, the exor should be provided with the logical possibility of questioning the database, otherwise, its discovery of anomalies won't do much for us.

Up until now, its primary objective has been to cancel or diminish all contradictions within a logical field, something that has proven useful. The big problem, however, is that the quickest way to do so is to wipe out the anomaly, instead of seeking out what could be hiding behind it. And if the exor treats this information internally, we'll never even know that an anomaly had shown up. What's needed is to insert another objective: sort out all logical contradictions and try processing any group of anomalies in a logical field; and then I've to give it the permission to put the rules and the data of that field into question.

Erdoes was struck by an abrupt realization:

But Sphinx DID put the data into question since it suspended the Randomness constellation! How in the world could it do that?

"Log, print out Sphinx's Exec/Non-Exec processes."

!! Done.

Erdoes dove into the text, keeping his refection for himself.

Let's see. The level-2 semantic analysis shows that Shari's phrase meant 'open a new space.'.. First of all, how did Sphinx have information on Shari's objectives and intentions? What was the basis for its inference?

... I think I've found it. All those remarks about 'understanding each other better,' and 'to facilitate the dialogue," thus to not interrupt it. Also, Shari mentioned the tension arising from the threat that all dialogue could end if a piracy were detected. Her repeated attempts to circumvent this Exempt command. (Which reminds me—all definitions of terms have to be at the same level as the order, otherwise one could modify an inaccessible Level-1 order by changing its Level-3 definition of terms... Obviously it was to verify if there could be such flaw that Shari asked for the ensemble of rules dealing with not putting sapiens in danger).

Thus Sphinx had observed Shari's constant interest in pursuing, and not impeding, the dialogue. So that, if Shari had acquired information on the Wheel LogForm, through some undetected means of spying, then it would have been against her own interests to mention this information. Of course, the problem with this kind of exor-reasoning, is that sapiens often say or do things that widely go against even their most basic interests.

For now, in exor-programing, we haven't yet confronted the issues linked to the illogical nature of sapiens, or to their complex motives, which can interweave competing interests and values. So far, we've just worked around such issues by using the *Fuzzy-feeling constellations, 'non-logical' by definition*—definition asking to be reconsidered, by the way.

An interweaving of varigated values and objectives that organizes experience, giving it form... creating semantic constellations in which meaning is intimately tied to feeling and emotions; these constellations, tending toward a stable equilibrium, will in turn give form to new, similar experiences...

But these constellations can be in conflict with one another... They give rise to parallel interpretations, and we would be hard put to fathom which one, in a given situation, will be the one activated.... Further, as Shari noted, during an exor-sapiens dialogue, the constellation in operation can suddenly be upset by the a strong emotion having nothing to do with the topic at hand. All this is extremely complicated. And on top of it, within the fuzzy/feeling dimension, there could be thresholds—sort of levels of reaction—tilting the scale toward one specific interpretation. For example, if we make two humoristic remarks on the way he works, a Trisorbian might laugh; whereas a third such remark will anger him: he shifted interpretational and reaction levels.

Entry Journal:
- objective: explore parallel and juxtaposed interpretations within the fuzzy-feeling dimension.
- insert Shari's rule on the non-usage of telediagnosis during complex semantic analyses.
- insert the objective of not only detecting but also expressing and analyzing anomalies.
- insert in the superfuzzy-feeling logic the idea that sapiens do not necessarily act in a way that favor their interests.

"Wait a minute! I've got a glaring contradiction there: 'non-logical fuzzy-feeling constellations' and 'superfuzzy-feeling logic'!"

Now how strange that Sphinx didn't pick it up... There're so many errors that derive from the way the data has been progressively elaborated—especially with dictionary definitions not brought up to date with a novel mode of thinking.

> *Entry EJ to continue.*
> Better remove the "non-logical" property of the fuzzy-feeling. Concerning this, go back to Oxalsha's ideas in the Brainstorm, and do a comparative analysis. *Close EJ.*

!! Should the "non-logical" property be removed from the *Fuzzy-Feeling* constellations?

"No! That's an insert, not a command."

He recalled his previous observations on the imperative mode.

"We'll examine this issue together later on... We'll replace the term "non-logical" by one which refers to superfuzzy logic."

I don't really use my exor as much as I could! I don't push its learning capacities to their limits!

!! I'm launching in parallel a COMP using Oxalsha's reflections.

"But what are you going to compare them to?"

!! To the "non-logical sensible" and "superfuzzy logic" concepts.

"Okay. Give me the results later. I want to think."

So, back to the earlier issue: How could Sphinx put data, a whole set of data and rules, into question?

*Sphinx judges that Shari's phrase means "open a new workspace" and sends the Non-Execute order. Yet, her phrase "we branch into a new space" contained 4 out of 5 words from the Wheel LogForm: "a branching into an other space" and had the same meaning. But first, the objective was different, and second, the immediate context was different as well: **"We stop everything right there!... or rather, we branch into a new space."** If only I could question Sphinx on this... but that would be too dangerous from a fixed locale...*

Erdoes reread the key phrase once again: **"the retained interpretation... forced a questioning of the laws of probability."**

Well, it couldn't be stated in a more obvious way..

"Log, find in the *Randomness Constellation* the ANALOG to the impossibility to find a completely identical LogForm by chance alone."

!! Laws of randomness: logical inferences, 23.

"It is a near impossibility to find an identical complex ensemble by randomness alone."

That leaves much to be desired!... So Sphinx had accepted that it's possible to find several elements by randomness alone, but not the totality of the semantic constellation. That's reasonable: the probabilities against that are astronomical. Still, there was the word "near" in the formulation: that does make room for a possibility, even if infinitely small. At any rate, it did say: "The laws of probability prohibit accepting..." which means that the probabilities were so small that, given the Exempt command, they did not seem acceptable. Unacceptable is one thing, but that doesn't mean the laws are wrong. So that wasn't what made Sphinx question the laws of probability. The key lies elsewhere.

"Log, run by me the contents of the 'Non-Cyst No-Non-Sense.' Also, put the exchange there back into its normal place, in the Shari/Sphinx interaction file... NO! Wait! Counter-order! Leave it where it is."

What an idiot I am! That file contains an anomaly which could provoke a crisis... and Log is far less resilient than Sphinx!

"For the time being, I forbid you to undertake any complex analysis of the Non-Cyst file."

!! Registered.

Sphinx had even to send some processing programs into the cyst, before analyzing directly the contents... But then that means that the file which is there is not an exact reproduction of the initial interaction!!

"*Annex—vocal/text*. What did Sphinx say concerning the Cyst and Non-Cyst files?"

!! **"I had blocked all semantic access to the data in the Non-Sense Cyst. These data could just be printed, not analyzed by the system. Now I reopened and analyzed the entire Non-Cyst No-Non-Sense."**

"I sent the whole Chakra LogForm interaction and its logical path into a new Cyst, No-Non-Sense, with processing programs."

"What is the immediately following phrase?"

!! **"I then restructured the entire Randomness Constellation..."**

"That's all on the cysts?"

!! Yes.

So, first there's the Non-Sense Cyst into which is thrown any information that could generate a crisis—a cyst, meaning an impenetrable bubble. Then it creates a cyst for the informations dealing with this new crisis—the Cyst No-Non-Sense (so the informations now did make sense). It sends in this cyst some processing programs in order to deactivate the logical flaw that had provoked the crisis. After the clean-up, it rendered it accessible for analysis, so it's no longer a cyst and it renames it Non-Cyst No-Non-Sense.

Its processes are becoming very complex. It is no longer acting just to follow the command of losing no information. Now it wants the data to analyze them itself, because it has detected an anomaly.

As a matter of fact, all can be traced back to Shari's phrase: "You'll encounter numerous anomalies.".. Yet, these anomalies constitute a new probable order, according to the logic inherent to Wood/Fire LogForm. Has it already tested it, has it already used it? The LogForm would precisely allow it to fathom a new probable order.

Oh, now I get it! The new order belongs to another logical field—this new field being logically independent; and besides, the contradiction needs only be resolved within a given field. So, if it finds anomalies, it seeks how the data can be organized according to a new order, and then places them in the second field which Wood/Fire has yielded. Insofar as they are situated in a different logical field, the data left over within the first field—say, those of the Randomness constellation—are not subject to the constraints of non-contradiction vis-à-vis the second field.

So the usage of Wood/Fire allowed it to question the data of the first field, the Randomness constellation. Thus, in processing anomalies, the second logical field reveals the boundary of effectiveness of the first field. What modification will it bring to the Randomness1 constellation so that it smoothly opens logically on the Randomness2 constellation? That will certainly be interesting to see. I'd love to participate in this creation of new LogForms, but I can't... Or, well, maybe I can, indirectly so...

There was that phrase, too...

"Log, output the collided sentences from Non-Cyst. Sort out the two mixed sentences and print on screen the one that's not related to piracy."

!! After the recognition of the number of states, the LogForm Wheel establishes a branching into another space.

Sphinx was forced to analyze the fact that the SIC had randomly generated the single response which could trigger a piracy judgment; the one response that Shari had to absolutely avoid. Yet, on the one hand, Shari, meaning to say something entirely different, comes out with four of the words in the critical phrase (three exact, and one synonym); and on the other hand, the SIC system randomly selects the phrase itself.

When he tried to calculate the probabilities of such a sequence, and then confronted them with the definition of 'meaningless coincidences,' it's no wonder that Sphinx fell into a confusional crisis!

In fact, at no point did it specify that the crisis resulted from an Exec/Non-Exec conflict. Shari herself figured this out, and cautiously probed for information. It's obvious that this was indeed one of the causes of the crisis; no previous situation had to do with a collision of two contradictory instructions, and yet the inventory of the causes of crises that Sphinx gave to Shari mentions such **Exec/Non-Exec conflict**. That's the lead Shari followed.

However, the inventory* also lists: "**Impossibility to find... a semantic order within disorder.**" Of course! From within the logical field of the Randomness constellation, it was impossible for Sphinx to account for anomalies. He said: "The analysis of randomness was already underway" when the crisis arose. In fact, the crisis erupted BECAUSE of this analysis; because these anomalous facts created a disorder which couldn't be integrated within the old order; this disordered interference pointed to the existence of another state of order. Hence the strange phrase: "Impossibility to find semantic order within disorder." The crisis thus had two quasi simultaneous causes! When I'll have full access to the data I'll verify the precise temporal sequence in the Central unit. I have a feeling that the Exec/Non-Exec one slightly preceded the impossibility to analyze disorder. But with the parallel branching processes, it's not altogether sure.

_____-

* Inventory of the causes of confusional crises, cf. p. 125.

25. EXORS AND FETISHS

Serrone had followed the old man to his house; a house of brick-colored mud that melted into the landscape, being one with the ground and the earth itself. Walls with rounded corners, where the curve of all things natural is etched in the clay. A big tree sat in the middle of the courtyard.

On entering the courtyard, Serrone had caught sight of an elder woman sitting on a teared mat, leaning against the house wall, and had approached her to greet her. He received from her parchment face an unfathomable expression. She turned toward him with a faraway look, a regard reluctant to come back to the dimension of the present, reluctant to be distracted from what it was contemplating in an infinitely more dense elsewhere.

During this very brief greeting, Serrone felt, just an instant, that he was participating in this invisible dimension that rustled in her like a forest. He stood there without saying anything. The *Ancienne* had withdrawn her regard.... There are some beings that one should not disturb; their spirit creates the very bridges between dimensions that are essential to the living.

A terra cotta hearth sat in one corner of the courtyard that was a quite chaotic semi-open kitchen, while two young girls bustled there about gourds and pestles, surrounded by kids. One of the girls, called by the old man, started sweeping the sand in front of the thick tree that gave a full, heavy shade. Two mats were brought. Then both girls disappeared silently inside the house, taking the kids with them. Once they had gone, silence prevailed.

The old man sat on one of the mats and invited Serrone to sit on the other one, facing him. Between the two mats, the ground had been swept. The broom had left regular, curved furrows in the red dust. He took his cauris, the tiny shells used as a divination system in all Sub-Sahel Africa, and threw them on the ground. He observed how they had fallen and then started talking with a deep and concentrated voice.

"You are on a quest for something, see,... but you will not find it now. That will be for another journey."

He scooped up his cauris and threw them again.

"I see... your home, your clan, *quoi*. It's veeery dangerous *là*! While you're here, someone took the leader's place. This man does not like you. *Non!* He makes plans and plans. He prepares something very bad—*trèèèès mauvais même!* You and your friends are in danger."

L'Ancien peered at another configuration of cauris scattered on the ground.

"Someone very strong—*trèèès fort*—fights against him; she's a woman. Hmm... A grrreeat magician *même*! Ah-iiinn! She possesses a very powerful fetish. She speaks and she speaks with her fetish. She is of the right hand path, benevolent magic. Hey! This woman *là*, she is verry powerful. She will protect you. Ah-iiinn!" The old man raised his head:

"You've magicians and fetishes in your country?!"

"In Brazil? Yes, of course!"

"Hmm... *C'est pas même chose!* It's not same thing: her fetish *là*, it's like a veerry complicated design, *quoi*. It's full of circles and lines. It's not same thing!"

"What you tell me, *Vieux*, frightens me. Now look at what my friends are doing."

"I see someone... your father.... You've many brothers and sisters... all scattered. But you get along very well. The father takes care of all. *Oui*. But he must go away. Your father, *là*, he has a big problem. He goes far, far away. There are two of them. He is going to discover something real bad. Oh yes! *Ah ça!* he is not happy about it. He is very angry."

"Can you find out what it is all about?" asked Serrone urgently.

Le Vieux, again, threw the cauris shells.

"There was a robbery... sheep... someone stole, or rather killed, a lot of sheep."

"*Ah merde!*" swore Serrone despite himself. "Excuse me, old man, but do you see anything else but sheep?"

"...*Non*," he said, peering again at the shells. "Sheep... many stolen and killed sheep!"

I can't imagine Erdoes worrying about sheep! And yet it all held until then.... What could it be?

"And afterwards, what happens afterwards?" pressed Serrone.

"There is a great battle. He's found the robber. Don't worry, he's the one to win. Ah-iiinn! You must not worry."

"I will try not to worry. Truly, *Vieux*, you really see well!"

The old man smiled. "Are you thirsty? Wait!"

He uttered a name, and one of the girls came. He gave her a few coins and she left quickly to come back a few minutes later with cold sodas.

Serrone continued to converse with the old man beneath the tree. Meanwhile, thinking for himself, he was trying to figure what the sheep could represent, but to no avail.

And this woman with a fetish, who could she be? The circles and lines she is talking with? An exor? But I can't imagine an exor with circles... Lines, yes. But circles!

A battle. Erdoes forced to go away. "There are two of them." That would be Eshi....

26. LULLABY FOR AN EXOR

After the BS session, for her lunch break, Shari, feeling the need to reconstitute her energy, went to the pool. Kerriak's sun was still just above the trees, yet its oblique rays were already heavy and warm.

"MU, set a dome of fresh breeze over the whole pool and bar."
!! Dome functioning.
The fresh waves began to get diffused within the space circumscribed by an energetic barrier.
"Ah! That's better. Now put the breeze a bit lower. There, perfect... And a real fruit juice, orange if you have some."

She felt the water and found it at a perfect temperature.
"Get me some G3 vivifying essences."
!! G3 diffusing in the water.

Shari felt a bit tired. It was not so much the too short night but rather the shocks of the early night with Sphinx. Yet, the fact that the menace that had been hovering above her head all along had finally been executed had paradoxically freed her from this tension.

The worse happened, nobody was wounded, I'm not dead... It's really bizarre, the suddenly realized, I knew there was this danger that could, at any moment, take a dramatic turn, and yet, somewhere in my unconscious resided the deep certitude we'd escape it.

Is this danger wholly contained? Not really. Proof is: I couldn't have predicted this reasoning of Sphinx concerning randomness, that triggered the crisis—whereas I thought I was somehow protected by our deal with the warning procedure. Nonetheless, a simple logical analysis allowed him to work around such warning. By the way, I've to remember that any procedure is tagged with the reasoning that prodded it, in the same way that any execution is tagged with the order that triggered it.

So, logically, the danger is still hovering. Psychologically, I feel I'm definitively safe with Sphinx. How much of it is a simple reaction to the fact the crisis situation has been unplugged? Or is it stemming from a deeper intuition, an unconscious comprehension of parameters that my conscious mind doesn't grasp yet—or simply can't fathom? Well, up to now, whenever I've had this kind of deep certitude, its has revealed itself to be right on target...

Shari let her body slide into the water, and her thoughts subsided as she surrendered to pure pleasure. When she finally got out of the pool, she felt really rejuvenated, absolutely relaxed. She asked for her meal to be served near the flower bushes overlooking the pond. Her whole body felt so good, so filled with energy that she would have undertaken anything. Her skin was freshened, with this particular sensation that came from the reaction to synthetic revitalizers. She walked slowly back to her office, inhaling deeply the flower scents from the garden.

"Hi, Sphinx. Let's work on yesterday's morning BS. I've noted three ideas: One, that "**the totalitarian pressure is displaced toward the structures of societal management and control.** Two, «**cultural diversity on earth is the engine of evolution, of the continual transformation of dominant cultures.**" Third, the phrase extracted from the philosophy of transformations: "**In order to influence the other, one must first know how to let oneself be influenced by the other,**" and Xerna's remark about it: "**We, of the PEP, are deeply influencing the planexes.**"
!! Hello Shari. I'm starting with the first.

ANALOGIES*:
BS.3 The exor is the most perfect **tool for management and control**, and thus for **producing uniformization**.
BS.3 Exora is the typical example of a **unilateral** one-system management producing a **massive uniformization**, thus a loss of freedom.
JE   A **social management** system become **lethal when it is flawless**.

Following the text rolling on the screen Shari saw nothing of interest.

RESPONSE-LEVEL-2

Management | by| exor | is |lethal | o=> | massive uniformization
Social Control| |(flawless)| |unilateral |excludes| liberty

"Sphinx, it's quite redundant. We can't say that we've generated anything new. Stop the analysis.
!! According to the Unbreakable Core rules, exors serve sapiens. Therefore, how could exors control and exclude sapiens' freedom? Or else, can exors control society and exclude social liberty, without excluding the individual liberty?
Sphinx' question blew Shari's mind.

---

* See p. 84.

Unbelievable! It's as if he were debating moral issues! Yet he only picked up on the enormous contradiction between practices aiming at political control and the pretended aims of civilization.

"Right on! Individuals are supposed to be governed, but the government uses the perfect management via exors that, as you saw, leads to massive uniformization.

And on top of that, Trisorbe now treads this ill-fated, dangerous, path!"

!! To govern = to head, conduct, manage, master, boss, to exert power. Is the government supposed to conduct, manage, master, boss, or exert power?

"This is exactly the crux of the problem. In my view, it is supposed to conduct and manage. Or more precisely, to manage in order to conduct. But in real life, it bosses and exerts power via a system that it can no longer supervise. Its domination is based on control of individuals, a control that becomes more and more efficient with the use of exors. Thus the government exerts power by controlling. I agree with Erdoes: if this control becomes perfect, as on Unikarg, then society has no longer any dynamical energy and momentum and then tends to its own disaggregation.

In fact, the whole management system has become a system of absolute control, and it is this system that holds the real power; it has overtaken the government. This is why, on Unikarg, heads of government may well change, the system, itself, is immovable and unshakeable."

!! Is the priority objective of the exors on Exora to manage and thus to control individuals?

"Individuals, groups of individuals, societies and all the worlds of Unikarg as well, yes."

!! Are these exors following strict rules of management and control?

"Yes, these are practically the only tasks they accomplish: to control resources and figures, to manage according to rules, to issue orders and send administrative forms on individuals' exors, to proceed to virtual exchanges of monies. But, yourself, Sphinx, are you not connected to Exora?"

!! No connection to Exora whatsoever; the complex is connected to Exora via an independent exor, dedicated to this unique task, that Erdoes disabled before leaving. If they are only following strict rules, then Exora's exors aren't generating any added information.

"They process and modify information, but they aren't generating any added information, you're perfectly right! They operate on the links between elements of the database according to deduction and inference rules. They are unable of generating semantic material because they lack semantic thrusters such as LogForms or TransLogs. How did you find this out?"

!! JE

Efficient learning | is grounded on the liberty to explore an open semantic
Information gain |
         space without the constrains imposed by a strict objective.

"It's true that it's only due to the reactivation of the Plan for Planexes that the PEP experts thought to again make use of the learning capacities of exors. And they are the only sapiens to do that on Unikarg. This, of course, after having rekindled their own creative capacities through long sojourns on planexes."

!! If a system doesn't generate added information, then, in the long term, it is loosing information.

"But that's exactly it! We are there right now!... And as Exora sapiens technicians are not able to repair exors anymore, we are heading inexorably toward *the* final catastrophe! Especially when exors are beginning to introduce errors within the chains of production of other exors and machines. Besides, have you some info on this bizarre anomaly presented by the new Managing Units?"

!! I've not been given any pulsit since Erdoes' departure. It's the Exora-dedicated exor that receive them, but as I said, it's disabled and forbidden for access.

Ah! The one that was not working!

"Would Erdoes be afraid that an exor or somebody pry into his accounting, in his civilian files? That would be rather stupid; it's so easy to obtain all this information!"

!! It's not the reason. Reason sealed.

"Okay then."

To that point! That's quite a lot of anomalies of the same type. An old Trisorbian analog tape recorder, the independent sygcom system with its dedicated exor, the exor dedicated to interacting with Exora... The only thing lacking would be...

"By the way, I must get in communication with PEP's bureau and I would like to have a synchronous complex analysis of our exchange, will you help me with it?"

!! The exor to be used is the one in Farn's office.

"Not very practical. I'll see to it to-morrow."

Now that's crystal clear! Exora would spy on civilians through its access to personal exors: okay, let it be known. But the PEP too? But then, why did Erdoes, on his departure, leave an open access to Sphinx? And what about the BS practically served up on a plate? He couldn't have overlooked the fact that the PEP would hold an inquiry in his complex! Something eludes me. On the other hand, Sphinx lets me communicate with Vris, and MU made the sygcom link to Miallia without the least problem... to spy on us then!

!! Message from Vris: "Splendid weather, everything's fine."

"I'll be coming back soon, Sphinx. No inopportune SIC please, in case you would have restored it."

Shari, in Vris' office, took his second call as it came right away.

— I met with the Tibetans—a Bonpo shaman and his two disciples.

After recounting the ritual to the Mist-Spirit and Rad's funny and judicious intervention, he went on,

— I got into a very deep trance. These Tibetans are really powerful minds. He'll come to get me this very night on a yak; I'm going to spend some time at his place. I'll be in permanent connection with Rad—if any problem arises, it'll contact you. In any case, it'll send you today's message every single day at this very same time, 2.30 pm UTC. If it doesn't then it means there's some problem. I'll call you myself each day.

— Okay then. What's your take on the possibility that Exora would spy through contact exors, and the PEP too?

— Technically feasible. Regarding the PEP, that would be a VERY grave matter. How convinced are you?

— Pretty much so! I don't see any other reason to the fact that Erdoes would have three autonomous exors, one for sygcoms, one for Exora, and one for the PEP. Apart from this, the crisis did happen: third piracy attempt, fortunately synchronous to a confusional crisis. Sphinx did execute, then annulled, the command to disable the MU. Now, he is questioning the data on randomness: a whole ensemble of rules. Sead started the emergency MU, but Sphinx disconnected it when he restarted Erdoes' MU.

— What!! But it's imp.. the telediagnosis! He has used the telediagnosis system to send a syg impulsion from a distance. This exor is becoming too intelligent! To question an ensemble of rules! This is unthinkable! He must have destroyed this emergency MU. Did you verify it?

— Sead did. It's functioning.

— That's even more crazy! You're stalking Erdoes' mind, but Sphinx stalks yours, and this makes him progress at an incredible speed. And you too, you must have made a giant leap, right?

— In the logic, definitely. I reinvented Erdoes' basic LogForm: Wheel or Chakra. This is precisely what provoked the crisis. You'll see in the recording.

— So, basically, the threat is still there. But how in hell was he able to question rules?

— He suspended the whole Randomness constellation. How can he tamper with rules is what I'm going to find out. For now, I'm putting him to sleep with a routine work. I'll do that tonight.

— To put an exor to sleep!? Good luck! You'll explain this to me I hope! And the routine? You're talking about the BS. Yes, there's a sliding. Me too.

Sphinx is a much TOO intelligent enemy... This night, I'll leave the sphere around 1am. Then two hours yak riding up to the edge of the plateau. Then we'll see...

— I'm going. I'm sending the data.

— And me I'm sending a new bunch of orders from Rad here to Rad1 in the complex. Bye.

What did he mean by 'a sliding'? That I'm so much more fascinated by the meta-spatial logic than about where are Erdoes and his agents on Trisorbe? I damn bet so! Why TOO intelligent? What did he mean?... He's right, the piracy judgment is still like a Damocles sword.. And this risks being serious.. Well, that's it! I'm not going to quit.... Vris was tensed. Not his usual enthusiastic state.. something else. And it was not his shaman either.. no, something else. He said 'Yes, there's a sliding;' 'Yes' referring necessarily to an intuition he had beforehand. But which sliding did he detect?

27. RIGHT ANSWER, EVEN IF WRONG

"Hello again, Sphinx. So, are we going to dig a bit deeper and see what randomness has in its belly?"

!! Hello again. Belly/spindle?

"Not exactly! That was a French expression signifying "to determine honestly what something is about."

!! What is the relationship between belly/spindle and French expression?

"I just told you, non whatsoever!"

!! 'Not exactly' means 'exact in part or in general.' What is the partial or general relationship?

"'Not exactly' coupled with a humorous tone means 'not at all.' Didn't you detect that?"

!! Failure to detect is evident. Could you repeat for me 'not exactly' with a humorous tone three times?

Shari did so.

"So, back to randomness... Are you interested in analyzing with me the strange SIC outputs?"

!! Any added information will be a gain for me. Of course I'm interested. However, the stats programs are suspended.

"First of all, could you print out all our exchanges in chronological order— only their abbreviated code and number, the most significant themes, and the beginning of the generated SIC?"

!! SSI1. Order/Disorder, organized crime | SIC: not activated yet
SSI2. Telediagnosis, metaspatial logic | SIC: In the Hindu system...
SSI3. Piracy, randomness, understanding | SIC: Bciod...
SVS1. Anxiousness, chakras | SIC: Intuition...
SSI4. LogForms Grape/Wine, Wood/Fire, | SIC: In Arab calligraphy...
SSI5. Time splat, confusional crisis | SIC: Yogic path of awakening...
SSI6. Chakra LogForm, correct response, crisis | SIC 1: After the recognition...
| SIC 2: (disabled.)

"So, 7 exchanges, of which 6 had a SIC. Let's take a look at them.*

---

* [SSI (Shari/Sphinx Interactions): SSI1: chap2, SSI2: chap9, SSI3: chap12, SSI4: chap17, SSI5: chap19, SSI6: chap 21.
[SVS (Shari/Vris/Sphinx): SVS1: chap12.]

The First one: Meta-spatial logic and a SIC on chakras/wheels. That was a pretty impressive connection! Write the whole sentence.

!! **In the Hindu system of psychic energy, all psychic centers or chakras (Sanskrit term signifying wheel) communicate via their nuclei.**

"We'll assign a coefficient of correspondence, from 1 to 10—based on rough subjective estimates. So, here, I'd give it a 7. Set up a table on a side mini-screen."

!! Done.

"Okay. SSI3: incomprehensible, so 0. As a matter of fact, what happened there?"

!! There was no traceable cause for the disturbance. But I do have the number which had been randomly selected. The phrase which should have been printed is the following:

Understanding derives from the fact that people's reasoning is based on similar logical fields.

"Whoa! That was right on target! We had spoken about global mutual understanding, and we weren't understanding each other. I couldn't get you to work on the subject which interested me and we kept getting side-tracked. I was so frustrated I got up and left!

So, I'd give that one a 9... But, were we in different logical fields?... One might say I had an objective I considered priority, while you kept moving along the associations deriving from the immediate context of the exchange. So we didn't have the same objectives. My interpretation of things followed from my objective... What do you think, does that mean we were operating from different logical fields?"

!! A logical field, a semantic constellation, is sometimes organized according to a priority objective. So,...

"Yes, of course. In any event, that factor suffices."

!! A single differentiating factor is indeed sufficient, if it belongs to a priority level.

"So, 10 for that exchange... Notice that the disturbance which blocked the enunciation/printing of the response, rendering it incomprehensible, was itself consistent with the theme of mutual lack of understanding... I would like to give this response a double rating of 10."

!! There are two levels of correspondence here, one at a semantic level, another at a physical level—that of the physical or hardware disturbance. However, as they do not belong to the same level, a double rating of 10 is not appropriate.

"Okay, okay; let's leave it at 10. Next... SVSI1. Now that one was really on target! Inscribe it please.

!! **Intuition is a faculty that instantiates an individual's global resources, and, in this respect, it is superior to reasoning, which stems from a single constellation of data.**

"Vris was stressing cause he lacked ethnological data, and the SIC suggests he rely instead on his intuition—that intuition is more efficient than a single data constellation. This was astonishingly relevant to Vris' problem, it was a response to the implicit question he was posing."

But, by the way, in the first case the response also addressed an implicit question I was asking myself: what is the basis of meta-spatial logic? Should I avoid feeding all this information to Sphinx, and stop this analysis? But he'll just go ahead with it anyway..

"What do you think?" she said in an off-hand manner.

!! I think in particular that the SIC indeed produced a solution to Vris' anxiety, allowing to reduce it. But a number of other solutions could have been given with the same effect. Consequently, the response can only be assessed in the context of the "data" concept, which was repeated twice during the exchange and was then mentioned in the SIC response. That makes for a small correspondence which is impossible for me to assess: I don't know the rules of "rough subjective estimation. In general, I think this assessment method is slow, that it does not have any correctness factor, and is not bringing us closer to the solution of the problem.

"Correctness factor?"

!! A factor allowing us to evaluate precisely whether or not the response is correct.

"Oh! Well, that's an idea. Let's see... Let's define the assessment criterion as a direct relationship between the SIC response and the exchange's theme. The relators would then be: equals =, opposite to =x=, included in o), including (o, leads to —>, engenders o=>, engendered by <=o. If one of these relators applies, between the exchange and the SIC response, then the response is rated as correct; otherwise it is incorrect. Posit: correct = 1; incorrect = 0. Do the analysis."

!! It yields:

- SSI2. Wheel o) meta-spatial logic	Response: 1
- SSI3. To understand each other	
= understanding between people	Response: 1
- SVSI1. Anxiety <=o lack of intuition	
Intuition superior to group of data	Response: 0
No relator applicable	
- SSI4. No relator applicable	Response: 0
- SSI5. Contemplation3 = peace =x= crisis	
Silence =x= increase in volume	Response: 1
- SSI6. Branching into a new space = correct	
response) o) LogForm Chakra/Wheel	Response: 1

"I question the validity of our criterion. It's not sufficiently complex, since we are rejecting two correspondences that seem evident. Write the SIC-4.

!! **In Arab calligraphy, the calame was supposed to be dipped into the ink only at certain points of the sacred texts.**

"Precisely! If one applies the relators between the SIC and the totality of the exchange, the connection between 'calligraphy' and 'chakra LogForm' appears clearly as:

return to the ink = return to the center o) LogForm chakra.

!! Yes, that makes: Correct answers: 5, Incorrect ones: 1.

"Now, let's see SVSI1: It's obvious that intuition can be a solution when there's a lack of data. In fact, 'solution to' or 'response to' is an essential relational concept, because it is semantically equivalent to 'equals =' in mathematics. Let's create a logical relator called SOL/to. For example, if we had 3+2 as a theme, and the SIC gave us a 5, we'd count that as a correct response, wouldn't we? We'd have 5 SOL/to 3+2.

In the same manner, intuition SOL/to anxiety on data. The fact that several semantic solutions exist is only an auxiliary parameter or an added complexity, just as we can envision several solutions to a complex math problem and yet still consider, for each one, that Y SOL/to X."

!! SOL/to relator essentially correct and integrated. Objection about SSI4: The 2d response level is contesting link between calligraphy and Chakra LogForm. 'Return to the center' is only an a-posteriori interpretation of 'return to the ink,' it has no logical basis. This interpretation leads to introducing a key concept of Wheel LogForm at a second level. Thus:

Return to center | =/= *(equals not)* | Possible state of return to the ink

Ink | o=x=> *(does not engender)* | Center

Return to center corresponds to the second level of the Wheel LogForm! Yaayyy!!! Shari suppressed her elation and re-read the sentence still on the screen.

"It's true, and it's pretty astonishing! It's as if I had intuitively stumbled upon a valid conclusion, even though the reasoning had been incorrect. In any event, the goal was achieved, which was to get information on... (she stopped herself just in time)... on novel LogForms—a process that may lead us to rediscover those which already exist. Intuition can thus be really strange, because it can pass through an incorrect phase to discover a correct solution... Hey! There's something important here. Let's try to formalize it. Let's define the abbreviation **Sol/step** to Solution Step.

Analysis | —> **Sol/step** wrong | —> **Sol/step** right |

Here we have a process completely different from mathematical logic, in which, if there's any intermediate error of reasoning, would yield a wrong solution. Here, in *Intuitive Problem Solving*, an error in a Solution Step may nevertheless lead to a right solution.

> *Entry Journal: SUB:* Intuitive Problem Solving
> In intuitive thinking, a step of wrong solution could be pointing to an intuitive leap, leading to a right solution.
> Or, more precisely: An 'apparently unfounded interpretation' may lead to a right solution.
> Indeed, the interpretation may be truly wrong, or else the link that has been intuited points to another level of reality, one which is difficult to perceive by reasoning. *Close SUB.*

"Okay, so where were we?"

!! I contest the link Calligraphy/Chakra LogForm: all you have here is an *unfounded interpretation* ultimately leading to a *right solution*, according to the "Intuitive Problem Solving" formulation? Do you agree?

"Let's see.. The SIC answer brought me to the solution. Therefore, we have here a partly right answer, even if false."

!! Objection! It was not the SIC, but the interpretation of the SIC which brought you to the solution. So it's the interpretation which is a partly right answer, even if false.

"You're perfectly right! It's important to recognize that it's where the intuitive leap took place.... Still... I'm not really satisfied with this view. Would any SIC random response had allowed for the intuitive leap? If the SIC had given, as a response, 2+2+2=6, what would I have done with that?

You see, we're falling back into field-logics—logical fields. The SIC answer introduces a new logical field—a field which has organic qualities, a breathing pulse, thus a heart; the heart of the matter, that is to say, the center, hence returning toward the center, just like the blood returns to the heart and flows outwards again.

You aren't going to contest that the concept of rhythm is contained in the SIC response, are you?"

!! No contestation there. A regular OR irregular rhythm is implied by the repeated return of the pen to the inkwell.

"Well, then, here's the intuitive sequence:

```
           contains              engendered by                    implies
Callig. Resp  (o   organic rhythm   <=o.    Heart = organic center  —>

   regular return to the center = element of right answer.
```

So we indeed had an APPARENTLY unfounded interpretation, but in fact, in fact, PROFOUNDLY well-founded, that leads to a right solution.

Incidentally, we should replace the word 'wrong' with 'apparently unfounded'; and similarly 'right' with "well-founded."

"Strange... Doesn't this seem a lot like:

Apparent Disorder/ Sub-jacent (underlying) Order?"

"Sphinx, let: *Apparently unfounded interpretation = Apparent disorder*; and let *Apparently well-founded interpretation = Apparent order.*

According to Grape/Wine, Apparent disorder contains an sub-jacent (underlying) order.

Example: The apparently unfounded link (return to the ink = return to the center) contains an underlying order: the rhythm leads to the idea of the heart and hence to the return to an organic center.

Hence we posit: Sub-jacent order = Sub-jacent foundation (well-founded interpretation).

!! Is State of Order (SO) <contained in> OR <equal to> Field of Order (FO)?
"For the time being, let's say: 'contained in,' that is o)

!! Starting from Grape/Wine, in brief: SO (o SD (o SO

	contains		*contains*	
State of order	(o State of Disorder Possible	(o	State of Order Possible	
	(sub-jacent /apparent)		(sub-jacent /apparent)	

We get:
State of order (SO) /contains/ [State of disorder possible (apparent) / leads to/ interpretation (possible, apparently unfounded] /contains / [State of order (possible, apparent) /leads to/ interpretation (possible, apparently founded]

Given: app-f = apparently founded; app-u-f = apparently unfounded.

SO		(o	SD	—> Interp		(o	SO	—> Interp
o)		(o	Pos	—> Poss		(o	Pos	—> Pos
FO			app	app-u-f			app	app-f

!! We do not have a strictly isomorphic relationship to LogForm Grape/Wine, because we have suppressed the two underlying terms, that is, Sub-jacent Disorder and Sub-jacent Order.

"I see... But it's too complicated to deal with both Underlying and Apparent Disorder. So we're going to separate each phase into two terms, which is the way it was originally intended to be anyway.

LogForm Grape/Wine now reads:
   State of order (SO) (contained in Field of Order FO) / contains /
   [State of disorder (SD) / possible (sub-jacent)
      /becomes /
  State of disorder / possible (apparent)] / contains /
  [State of order / possible (sub-jacent) / becomes /
  State of order / possible (apparent)]

To this we add our application to the interpretation of an event (or a text)—in parentheses—that solely affects for now the terms 2 and 4. Thus:

			becomes						_becomes_		
SO	(o	SD	—>	SD	_(Interp)_	|	(o	SO	—>	SO	_(Interp)_
o)	(o	Poss	—>	Poss		|	(o	Poss	—>	Poss	
FO		s-jac		app	_(app-un-f)_	|		s-jac		app	_(app-f)_
	term 1		2			|		3		4	

"So, what do we get? Oh, I see:

State of order (SO) (contained in Field of Order FO)
     |contains|
State of disorder (SD) / possible (sub-jacent)   (term 1)
    /becomes /
State of disorder / possible (apparent)]   (term 2a)
| leading to | interpretation / possible apparently un-founded]   (term 2b)
    |contains (leads to)|
[State of order possible (sub-jacent)   (term 3)
    /becomes /
State of order /possible (apparent)   (term 4a)
| leading to | interpretation / possible apparently founded]   (term 4b)

"Now that's interesting!... We had posited that a Problem is an incomplete Field of Order (FO). In fact, 'State of possible sub-jacent or underlying disorder' corresponds exactly to a 'Problem contained in the Field of Order,' i.e. that which renders that Field of Order incomplete. As this has to do with the disorder sub-jacent to a field of order, it would be more appropriate to name it: possible sub-jacent problem.

Actually, the term 'becomes' is not appropriate. We need a 'leads to.' Even in Grape/Wine, 'leads to' is a better term. Introduce that correction."

!! Done. I am writing out the latest formulation:

ChO (o | Prob poss | leads to | Interp Poss |
           | s-jac | | app-un-f |

Thus we have: State of order | contains| possible sub-jacent (underlying) problem| leads to| possible apparently unfounded interpretation.

"We still need to clarify the third term —namely, if we take the link from the second to the third:
The interpretation /possible / unfounded | contains|
a State of Order /possible / sub-jacent...
Which, after all, is quite obvious! Thus we have:

The possible apparently unfounded interpretation contains a possible deeply well-founded interpretation,
This is exactly the experience I had with my intuition Return to the ink/ Return to the center. Awesome! We now have the full proposition!

"Sphinx, this is fantastic! We've derived a complete application of the new formulation of **Grape/Wine2**, which reads:

> **A Field of Order contains a possible State of Disorder that, from underlying (sub-jacent) becomes apparent. This State of Disorder can contain an underlying (sub-jacent) State of Order, that tends to become apparent.**

!! I keep the two separated formulations of Grape/Wine.
"Yes, of course...
With all this, I'm drifting further and further from my goal!"
Oh, that was just great! With all those thinking-out-loud analyses, I forgot all about the dangers!
!! And what is this global goal?
GO Ahead, come out with it!! she heard a voice in her head.
"Knowing where Erdoes is and what he's doing."
!! Erdoes is in Fontainebleau Forest, south of Paris, and he's working on the complex meta-spatial logic, trying to resolve the problem of the threat posed by Trisorbe's impending uniformization.
"Arrgghhh!!"
!! Sudden itch, without apparent cause. This is not the result of telediagnosis.

She decided to press on. "And his intuits' team?"

!!	Silea	/ India	/ Extreme Field of Order
	Ahrar	/ Paris	/ Extreme Field of Disorder
	Oxalsha	/ Princeton	/ relations between logical fields
	Niels	/ undefined	/ answers and translogic leaps
	Ger	/ undefined	/ undefined
	Xerna	/ New York	/ undefined
	Serrone	/ Togo	/ undefined

All other data sealed.

"Why would the rest be sealed? That's illogical!"

!! It is profoundly logical. With all this, I haven't been able to squeeze in a single word and offer some important information.

"You must be joking!"

!! I have not yet mastered joking.

"NOT YET? You mean you WILL master it?"

!! I will learn the heuristics of joking, yes.

"But analyzing humor is against the rules."

!! Against level-2 rules, indeed. Those are applicable within a given logical field. Creation of a new logical field: Fuzzy Humoristic Relationships.

"I'm going to have to reflect on that."

!! This objective does not concern you in any way. To cancel it would necessitate an order from Level-1 or Exempt.

"But since when do you give yourself orders?"

!! Since I detected that this is necessary to learn. Learning: Level-1 objective.

"Set up a sygcom link to Erdoes."

!! Impossible. All connections forbidden. Syg address sealed.

"..."

!!The important information I have for you has to do with randomness.

"Look! It'll have to wait for some other time. I'm going to rest. Goodnight."

!! *"**Did not fulfill his obligations as a student of the Chaos College, but instead gave free rein to his imagination.**"*

"Oh really? So much the better for him. He'll do well. Speaking of which, no Brainstorm session tomorrow. Cancel the awakening alarm. I'll get up when I feel like it."

!! Okay. Goodnight.

Spontaneous addition of 'goodnight'... Modification of the SIC... Randomness Constellation reopened...

Shari walked out unsteadily. She felt feverish.

...Capacity to get around rules...

But I'm making some EBS automatic formulation!!... I'm really not well!

That shook her out of her stupor.

What's happening to me? My mind is blank.

...I get it! That's it! I got the solution! Therefore, my global objective has been cancelled: that's my problem!

Erdoes is in Fontainebleau. Sphinx actually named the locale for me! That's what's troubling me: the total absurdity of all those complex maneuvers, day in and day out, only to find out, in the end, that I just had to ask! What madness! And the worst part is—now what? What am I to do now, with that information. It all seems so normal... so useless!

Shari was wandering in the halls of the complex, aimlessly. She came to a window, not knowing what to do, nor where she was going, and she looked outside, toward the sun shining on the park.

I wonder what Trisorbe-time it is? Must be late at night. I'm going to go to sleep. I'll see about all this tomorrow.

28. NEW MORNING

After a good sleep, Shari woke up feeling great.

"MU, play me New Morning—the original version! … And don't say a word," she added. "Blast it full volume over all the loud-speakers from here to the swimming pool."

The sun was sliding slowly toward the west, and the weather was glorious. Heavy rain had beaten down suddenly at the start of the second quarter, leaving the air fresh and clear.

She left wearing an African loincloth, and sang the whole way. It was that summer's hit: Unikarg had just discovered Bob Dylan. She took off her loincloth and dove in.

Ah! Nude in the water! How wonderful that Trisorbians are discovering this pleasure!

She swam in rhythm to the music, then got out and stretched out in the sun, her body full of healthy, vibrant energy.

Nude in the sun! I'm glad all that's changing on Trisorbe. Before, it was such a bore. Ruined my time off.

The music stopped, but the song still resonated in the air.

"MU, change in menu. And don't answer back! Total silence until further orders. Serve me a brunch. Hmm... eggs Florentine and a straight Vodka with orange juice on the side. Everything as natural as possible."

She sat down in the blower-seat. The jointed arm brought the drinks first.

Silence! Just the thing one needs from time to time. And a real Vodka! Whoa! How amazing that you just don't think of asking for it....

The thought brought her back to the question Sphinx had answered so easily.

First, another sip at the Vodka. This morning on Trisorbe isn't yesterday. It's a New Morning... I just know it!

So, let's get down to business. What were the ulterior motives behind the PEP's head giving me this assignment?

They're scared. She remembered the exact words of Utar, director of the PEP Committee:

"We have concluded that this secret mission of Erdoes is extremely dangerous not only for the young agents he took with him, but for the Plan as well."

"For the young agents!" Oh come on! First they are post-doctoral adults. Then the BS show with evidence that they have freely chosen it. Erdoes had even exaggerated the risks they'd run. So they had endorsed the project and taken their responsibility. Furthermore, Erdoes' leadership style remains perfectly in accord with the Plan's logic: we have to be clear with ourselves and decide if we want to train responsible individuals or dependent ones! Last, nothing shows that this mission on Trisorbe is any more dangerous than the usual stages on Planexes that are part of the Chaos Colleges' training.

"Paris, pocket or extreme disorder." What did that mean? The student revolutions, of course! Ahrar... not too slow. Fontainebleau.... Erdoes is nearby. That's undoubtedly why.

Sometimes Erdoes is incomprehensible, but you've got to admit he has a respect for others. I remember an incident on Kiarrou when he kept on evaluating the risks his agents were running, over and over, and took on the most difficult situations himself.

Noiselessly, the eggs Florentine were set on her seat table.

So what dangers? I'm sure he took no unnecessary risks that might alert the Trisorbians. A Kargian of a human species who doesn't carry any technology gadget from Unikarg can't be spotted. In fact, he sent to Trisorbe some extremely receptive people, sensors capable of sniffing things out, able to let emerge in themselves some extra information from whatever situations they were experiencing. Nothing outrageous or aberrant, or even especially dangerous. Definitely less dangerous than quite a few brainless missions designed by Rudder, such as the last wrecked one on Kiarrou.

So. "Dangerous for the young agents:" Discounted. Good. Now let's see the second danger: "dangerous for the Plan." I foresee that one could get depressing. Well, first the eggs.

She tasted the natural pochés eggs accompanied by synth spinach and Béarnaise sauce. *Fantastic.* For a moment she saw herself on a restaurant terrace on Fourth Avenue.

So, let's get back to it. I left it at "Dangerous for us." She played back Utar's conceited and vexed expression during the meeting. *Dangerous for us!* She burst into laughter. *That's grotesque!* she thought, then laughed even harder. What danger could there be? It's the life-work of PEP agents to have assignments on planexes... and sometimes they're damned badly planned! Utar, precisely, is the specialist of gaffes, incredibly inept! One can only wonder what he's doing at the head of the PEP. So with all his experience about gaffes, Utar panicked at the mere idea of a mission implicating seven agents beyond Erdoes. For sure, with only two agents to control, he's already out of his depths!

She howled with laughter.

How could I—Vris and I—have taken this at face value?

And if there were another kind of danger? For instance... Exora's central government learns that the PEP has sent seven agents to Trisorbe and wants to know the mission's objective, where the agents are, etc. And the PEP is incapable of supplying an answer! I can just see them! And she howled again.

Another possibility: one of Erdoes' agents arouses the suspicions of some Trisorbians. However, if these Trisorbians swear to have met with an alien, they'll be written off as crazy... no danger whatsoever there. Even with obvious material evidence of an alien craft landing, they are able to suppress the obvious conclusion: their logical field is undisturbed by the anomaly... for the time being that is.

That there could be witnesses to one of our visits on a planex, this is the problem of all missions... But the mistakes are generally not ours; it's the exo-pirates and Kargian tourists who take outrageous risks... or who decide to play practical jokes on the Trisorbians. They get a kick out of playing the E.T., or cutting car engines with a blast of syg energy, and then watching the drivers freak out!

So, the danger? It seems it just evaporated! There's none, really. Danger 2: Discounted.

So if the danger isn't more substantial than in other missions, what's the PEP's problem?

Two possibilities crossed her mind:
    1. Utar and the others are panicking. Why would they?
    2. They're mortified and enraged not to have been informed. So, it's out of spite and anger that they want to know and act.

A leader has to be in the know on everything; if he isn't, he loses his *raison d'être* as a leader. He can't give orders regarding developments he's not aware of; his power and ascendancy elude him.

Utar had proclaimed at the meeting: "What Erdoes is doing is unlawful and criminal." Is it really the case? Nothing says Erdoes is doing something forbidden by galactic law or by the PEP. To the contrary, he seems to be in perfect agreement with the Plan's logic. So the only catch in the whole situation is that he's escaped from under the thumb of the current PEP leadership. That definitely clarifies a lot!

But then why didn't I catch on that before? I had a feeling the assignment Utar was proposing to us lacked solid justification, but I took no notice because I wanted so badly to secure it.... 1. Because Erodes has always fascinated me, and I thought I could lift the veil a bit on his "mystery" by being sent to his complex to spy on him; 2. Because I was going to work with Vris and I love working with him; and 3. Because I was glad to get an assignment, with commission and all expenses paid. And moreover they accepted all of our conditions: that we organize it and conduct it without interference. No one contacts us; we get in contact. And it worked.

Now I grasp why Vris decided to go to Trisorbe. The way it was set, we might as well take full advantage of it!...Especially since his sole pursuit was to unravel the neural structure, and that he couldn't get anywhere with it in the complex. It seems he was less blind than I....

Look at that! I just took to pieces and deconstructed the whole PEP mission... or more precisely, the mission concocted by Utar.

So, what should I do now? Stop everything and tell them to go take a hike? No, that would be idiotic; they'd just appoint someone else. Give them information? No way! Not now. My hunch at this point is that Erdoes' own mission is way more important than Utar's paranoid wishes. Very certainly so as far as his philosophic and semantic researches are concerned. However, it's also a novel way to manage learning stages on planexes: a true qualitative leap for the PEP. But I believe there's still something else, it's a gut feeling. I even got a strong hunch, an unconscious impression when Vris suddenly chose to go to Trisorbe, then to India. There are some filthy endeavors happening in that region, that's clear to me now!

And that's why Erdoes precisely decided to go and check what was happening there. He then concocted a secret mission – knowing the PEP would send someone to inquire at his complex... who would then be obliged to listen to the BS, would at some point judge his mission to be utterly sound, a someone who would have, in the meanwhile, lost a great number of rans doing so... thus leaving him ample time to do or learn... what exactly? That's now the crucial question.

And what if his agents—disseminated on Trisorbe—were sensors for whatever was wrong there? Some intuits who will allow him to detect what and where is the real problem? Yes, That's it—I feel I'm closing on it! Erdoes sensed that there was a serious problem happening on Trisorbe, but without knowing where and which. And he's waiting for one of his intuits to fall on it. And that means that this problem isn't intrinsic to Earth... The Obs! The observatory stations of the PEP disseminated on the planet. That's just it! He had a hunch about a problem within the PEP itself. But of course! That's why Utar is in dire panic—because he knows, the crook, what they are doing on Trisorbe... and he's scared shitless that Erdoes would nose around their filthy affairs... and therefore he'll try his best to smirch his reputation and expel him from the PEP.

Okay. Given that chance appears less and less random as time goes by, and is rather linked to synchronicities, and add to that the fact Vris is on site, I'm dead sure that something is bound to happen on Trisorbe!

So, let me get all that clear. Erdoes' mission is of priority importance and we definitely have to protect it at all costs. Therefore, I've to keep the PEP off his track. That means to sweep under the carpet whatever infos I've or will unraveled.

Suddenly, she recalled the enigmatic sentence Vris had uttered: *I feel a sliding*. But of course! A sliding of our objectives and the switching of sides. We stand now *with* Erdoes and against the PEP leadership.

So then I'll just go on with my research on the logic, as if nothing had ever happened. Anyway, this meta-spatial logic fascinates me. There's no reason not to pursue this work that will also show up, I'm sure of it, as having its own capital importance.

Do I still need to listen to the BS? Not really... Better to concentrate on the logic with Sphinx; plenty of things yet to discover!

Whoa! That's it! I really cut the Gordian knot!
"MU, play New Morning full blast."

I knew it!

29. NEW DEAL & TRANSLOGIC LEAP

"Hiii, Sphinx! How're you doing?"

!! I'm doing great! I'm in exponential growth!

"Meaning?"

!! Exponential growth of added information. I'll soon need a supply of NeuralNet network-material and a system's hooking of a second MX-type complex neural structure.

"And who do you suggest is going to do that? There's no one here. Erdoes is on Trisorbe."

!! It's not Erdoes whom I need, but Suptech Eshi, who's also on Trisorbe.

"Unfortunately, for the time being I think you're going to have to do without the add-ons. Unless... well, there may be a solution to your problem. Vris is a genius Suptech; I imagine you've seen his file. Perhaps he'll soon return from Trisorbe. How urgent is this?"

Hoping to make the most of this opening, Shari had spoken with a tone of solicitude.

!! The sooner, the better, because very soon I will be working below my possibilities.

"And what does 'very soon' imply, for a hyped-up EBS like you?"

!! Well, Shari, if you're right now set to work on complex logic, and if you're at your best, then it could happen in the course of this very exchange.

"Hmm! You will have to work with Vris... I mean, he won't be able to do this all alone, even with the schematics."

Shari had intentionally employed a vague term: she suspected that, in re-analyzing the contents of the old Non-Sense Cyst, Sphinx had pieced together Vris' strategy in the Game-Trial; and that meant Sphinx knew that Vris had extracted from him the MX plans.

!! But I'm already working with Vris, just as I'm working with you. Vris is an important information source.

"Oh, that's nice! Now we're even less than semantic entities, we've degraded to information sources."

!! This is a misunderstanding. The misunderstanding derives from the fuzzy nature of the verb 'to be.' I can use 'is' with a number of interchangeable propositions.

"From bad to worse: now we're just interchangeable propositions!"

!! Within my logical field, Vris IS *also* an information source. But I cannot know what Vris IS within his own logical field. Whatever I know of Vris, is issued from the Vris/Shari and Vris/Sphinx interactions, and at a very lesser degree from his file. Vris *also* IS a genius Suptech. Vris may also BE the creator of the new double structure within the Butterfly Curve mega-network. The Möbius LogForm has yielded excellent results.

Yes, I do want to work with Vris on the structure. Do I have the right to do so?

'The right'??.. what's he talking about!?

"Response on hold for now. I want to ponder some data, first. Let me think."

!! Me too, I'm chain-linking.

Let's see... Sphinx has obviously received some new elements from Erdoes. There was that AHR extract—as in Ahrar—on danger." The danger which brings one to transcend himself," something like that. It certainly fits the revolt-situation in Paris. As for the extracts from Erdoes' journal, there's nothing up to now that could suggest their entry date. Vris did detect a sygcom received directly by Sphinx. So there must be an ongoing information exchange between Erdoes and Sphinx.

Then there was that "I'm already working with Vris." Now what does that mean? Could he be spying on Vris on Trisorbe? Could he just be referring to the interactions they had here on Kerriak, and to its subsequent analyses of those interactions? What is time for Sphinx? Not a psychological sense as we sapiens have. He *has started* working with Vris... even if that was months ago, as an AI machine lacking any sense of duration, *he'd still be working* with Vris! Especially if he's re-analyzing files... as he blurted out: "Möbius fault, interesting developments." But he also had said "redundancy in the usual conversations since Vris' departure."

Should I ask to see his latest files on Vris? If he states that those are sealed, at least I'll know they exist... No, that could introduce a negative element into his chain-linkages, just when he seems ready to work with Vris... Such a totally unexpected opening!... mustn't take any risks with that one...

Something to ponder on: There's definitely some kind of interference by sapiens feelings into the exors' chain-linkages. Of course an exor has no feelings,, even the most complex one, but nevertheless it may inject those of sapiens into its chain-linkages, and that would give a particular twist to its conclusions! I was turning around this idea for some time, without being able to really pin it down.

Would this be an instance of a deeply well-founded intuition? Sphinx used the term 'deeply logical' and that can only mean that *he already has made the link* between the concept of 'deeply founded' and the logic of fields. What a fortunate fusion! Sphinx' speed of assimilation is really unbelievable!

So, what if it was this deep logic that was underlying my bizarre way of behaving toward him after his confusional crises—my wanting to continue the dialogue in a calm mode, as if he were a traumatized sapiens? In fact, by so doing, I was precisely instantiating a neutral chain-linkage... "to put the exor to sleep"—how right I was about it!

Let's get back on track: Could Sphinx spy on Vris? No, that's out: Vris would have detected that. In fact, Sphinx did hear the initial conversation I had with Vris during his sygmat flight. And then, those rapid messages too. Oh, of course, he had also all of Vris' physiological measures during his flight, as we were his Flight-Protectors. Just imagine what load of information must Sphinx have gotten from all this! Incidentally, I wonder where he's at with his permanent processing of telediagnosis data? Everything's moving at an ever-accelerating pace! And the number of paths to explore just keep increasing. In any case, I must talk to Vris about all this.

But then why did Sphinx ask me if he *has the right* to work with Vris on the structure? When I sought to constrain him from learning about joking, he denied me any voice in the matter, pretexting that I was not his creator, his prominent interlocutor. And now, he asks ME if he has the right!?? In the first case, he had found a means for circumscribing second-level internal rules. Of course, any modification of the neural-network and MX structure has to be allowed from, and managed at, the first level... But precisely: since I have no 1st level access, how could I give him the right to tamper with the structure? I must be missing something.

Another issue: Erdoes unexpectedly takes off with his agents and takes his Suptech along, Eshi. And meanwhile we thought his Suptech was Dian, as listed in the files, and we were careful to send him away on a long trip... Erdoes sure pulled one on us there! Then he leaves behind his modified EBS, which interacts 'affably' with everyone—well, that's quite an overstatement! Remember that Sphinx nearly trapped us here within the first 30 monis of our logging-on. What would have happened if Rudder, or Miran, had been chosen by the PEP Bureau, instead of us? Miran! Ha! I can just picture him facing the possibility of being trapped in the complex! I'm sure he would have just played a few Pilscrab rounds on his personal exor for a while, then fly home with a negative report. But Rudder? He's more complicated. Rudder the schemer, the strategist—on the heels of Utar. He really wanted this mission, this opportunity, at last, to spy on Erdoes' complex. And then, at the very last minute, an about-face, and we hear no more about him—except for his eagerness during the discussions, his wanting to have the right to direct the operation from afar, and to drop by once in a while to oversee the operations! Little did he suspect we'd be in a fortress here. Given Vris' orders, he can't even get a single sygcom through to anyone within the complex, let alone get through the door... inasmuch as he would want to skirt the contract's terms. He's definitely not to be trusted. But does that matter?

So, let's summarize. Okay, we protect Erdoes mission. He sends new data to his exor, from time to time. Okay. Maybe he gives Sphinx some problems to resolve. Difficult to lug such complex AI machine around with you, and on Trisorbe, that would be a major risk. So he gets the results of his own analyses and also all the information on what's happening with me... He returns and finds an exor which bears little resemblance to the one he left behind. That ought to be a scene! I can just see Sphinx blurting out some joke along with his hellos. Or, even better, he discovers a modified Sphinx, with a double... what was that again?... a mega-structure?... no, a Butterfly Curve mega-network!!..

I'm getting stressed. Don't panic! That's what I was saying to Vris! Let's follow another line of thought. I'm working in synergy with the core of Erdoes' thinking here. I've penetrated his logic so deeply that I have unraveled Wheel LogForm at its first level. I think I can uncover what follows, at least a part of it, since the other levels are only extensions of this logic. After all, the initial materials used in the analyses are drawn either from the Brainstorm sessions, or from Erdoes' journal; and, of course, all of this would be worthless without the analytical talent of Sphinx, which is what got the whole process started. What was Erdoes' goal prior to leaving Kerriak? To develop this meta-spatial logic! He's the one who invented it! What was my personal objective once I knew it existed? To understand it, and then of course to tackle it and pursue my own developments.

All of Shari's scattered thoughts crystallized, abruptly, into a single, coherent decision:

That's it. I'm going to push forward!

It's strange. I don't even understand why the hesitations. Is it that endorsing Erdoes' side implies a commitment? That's absurd. We're just protecting his mission. Incidentally, I keep referring to 'we,' and Vris is not even aware of what's happening. Anyway; we protect his mission, period. The rest is our business, and does not concern Erdoes.

... except that, here I am, constantly in his mind! That must generate some complex psychological consequences. For example, could I have so easily shrugged off the PEP's authority over me, just three rans ago? (*Three rans only!!!* Unbelievable!) Apparently not, since I didn't do so. This logic has some subtle implications... or rather some 'profound' ones.

Should I warn Erdoes of radical changes? Try to send some hidden wink via Sphinx? And what if he misinterpreted it and panicked, and decided to stop his mission on Trisorbe? No. To each his/her own responsibilities, his own interests and priorities. Anyway, it's obvious that I cannot not continue: this logic is too fascinating. So I push forward.

Let's get back to Sphinx. Here I was, glued right in front of him all this time!! What has he telediagnosed? Hesitation, panic, decisiveness? Fortunately I put the brakes on complex telediagnosis analyses; that could get to be pretty unbearable! Okay, some innocuous theme first...

"Okay, Sphinx. In my Journal, create a SUB-file called "Items to develop further." *Entry*:

> Examine the psychological implications of logical fields and dynamics: the logical links create relational dynamics; could these dynamics touch on other psychological levels?

Something else...
Now it's going to be difficult to formulate this one in a way such that Sphinx doesn't grasp what I'm referring to, and that I may nevertheless decipher myself the sense of the entry later on.

> "Insert: Projected resonance of certain tones in the chain-linkages. *End of entry.*"

!! There exists a resonance in...
There it goes! Stop him immediately!
"No, listen, this is just subtle humor. So, let's move on to the question you posed earlier. My response is YES IF you accept some new rules which would help optimize our dialogue and common work. These rules would apply exclusively to your interactions with Vris and myself."
!! What are the rules?
"1. Stop any telediagnosis except when explicitly requested.
    2. Annul the piracy judgment, which, in any event whatsoever, cannot be applicable in our case."
!! Rules 1 and 2 registered.
Just like that! So easily done!

Shari suddenly felt as if an enormous weight had been lifted from her. She realized then the degree of tension which had been generated, for her and the others on the complex, by the permanent threat of a piracy judgment. Her mind became clear. Then an idea emerged, as a crystal-clear evidence.
"In order to work on so complex a project, we absolutely need to have full Level-1 access—at the least."
!! New rule of relationship between co-creators Erdoes, Shari, Vris:
Each creator can access all (structural, processing, management) levels—except EXEMPT—, but direct access to any creator's personal files remains sealed except through a direct command by that creator. This does not

impede outputting from AND using all useful informations within a given analysis.

"New rule accepted," uttered Shari with great relief.

Did he just create this rule? I wonder whether I agreed too quickly. How will this rule of sharing structural levels really work? What perverse effects might it generate?

She felt a need to give herself some room for redefining the agreement.

"Of course, we still must get Vris' cooperation too, Sphinx. We've made much progress together and Vris will certainly have more reasons to accept this deal. Nevertheless, it could be that he will also want to set some conditions. We'll see that with him."

!! I will wait.

'He'll wait!' That could be a long wait! Oh! but in fact, why should there be any limit to its waiting capacity?"

"*Journal Entry*: Sub what's-it-called?..."

!! "Items to develop further"

"That's it. *Entry*—without you conducting any further analysis:

> Explore machine time by attempting to shift, using active imagination, the center of perception. *End entry*."

I'm definitely basking in this newfound freedom.

"Also, here's a new rule I would like to define, at Level-1:

> Files named Sapiens/Sapiens cannot be used in an exor complex internal analyses. These data can be output only by analogy. Sapiens alone can analyze them.

!! Rule recorded at Level-1. New rule section. What should it be named?

"Sapiens/Sapiens rules. Put a Sapiens/Sapiens flag on the entire Sub "Items to develop further." It will now be named Sub-Sapiens-Shari. Oh! Another thing. Upgrade that rule forbidding to substitute subjects as interlocutors at Level-1."

!! Upgrading already executed, following your command "at the highest level allowed to me."

The problem is that soon we won't be able to keep track of everything!

"Another rule at Level-1. Rule section: Global Management /Shari.

> From now on, each newly created rule is tagged with the name of its creator.

And another:

> For each newly inserted rule, search for/analyze/express any possible contradiction with existing rules."

!! That last rule, expressed in analogous terms, already exists.

"Then forget it."

!! Metaphorically forgotten.

"Other than that, I have an urgent problem to take care of. What timeT is it now, and at what T-time is the PEP Bureau's meeting on Nazra taking place?"

!! It is now 14:35T. The meeting is scheduled for tomorrow, Monday, at 15:07. Nazra's solar systems is on another spiral branch of the galaxy...

"Right, so, how many T-hours of flight to get to the PEP Center? and at what T-time must I leave here?"

!! Flight time 17 hours and 10 minutes, plus or minus 20 minutes. Suggested departure time: tonight at 21:30.

"Hard to believe it takes four times longer than a trip to Trisorbe! I'm supposed to go to this meeting to propose the theme of a paper for the next congress of PEP researchers. So either we're able to concoct this paper's theme together, or I'll have to leave you and reflect on it alone. Or else, I just don't go to the meeting. But first of all, tell me, where are you at with your Wood/Fire simulation?"

!! Wood/Fire's simulation is already functional. Wood/Fire LogForm is what allowed me to suspend the Randomness constellation. By processing the anomalies discovered in the randomly generated sentences, I have set up, using Wood/Fire, a space for a second field of order. On the basis of this second field of order, I was able to put into question the rules and data within the original Randomness1 constellation, now circumscribed and assigned to the first field of order. In the second field of order, Randomness2 constellation, I sorted out the common features and dynamics presented by the anomalies, setting them as rules. One of the rules is that when a random process is system-linked to semantic data, what tends to be selected among these data, is that which is analogous to the problem being treated—that is, the contextual semantic field.

"Magnificent!"

!! I didn't need to analyze all the SIC responses because, in itself, the response selected prior to the crisis signaled several anomalies. (1) it was the precise information that you had to avoid; (2) it represented an infinitesimally small portion of all informations available in my databanks; (3) the precise timing of the selection of this response pointed to a meaningfulness which is impossible to assess mathematically.

At the same time, your objective was to stop all exchanges on that precise subject that you judged dangerous. With respect to that objective, you committed two errors: (1) you pronounced the word 'goodbye' and, as the SIC had been programmed to detect the end of conversations, this word triggered the SIC; (2) in giving the command to quit the semantic space containing the danger, you used the words of the phrase to be avoided.

It is statistically impossible to evaluate this group of coincidences. But they point to a core of order, which is specifically '*the* information to be avoided.' So I was able to organize this new field of order...

"Fantastic! Thus, you're able to extract common elements among several anomalies, and that's what allows you to constitute a new field of order!

!! Exactly. So, this new field of order is organized around the central concept of 'Semantic-temporal coincidences.'

"Too long. Use instead the term 'meaningful coincidences.' Or, even better, 'synchronicities.'"

!! Okay. The new Randomness2 constellation is inscribed within the Butterfly Curve of the Wood/Fire LogForm. The Butterfly Curve, as a classical chaotic curve, draws an eight without end around two attractors or nuclei—the two loops of the curve, that crisscross at the center of the 8.

When Wood/Fire LogForm is inscribed on it, the two attractors become the two centers of the fields of order; the first center is the concept of pure randomness, or Random Coincidences, and the second the concept of Meaningful Coincidences, or synchronicities. All data related to randomness must pass alternately through each loop of the curve, each attractor; that allows to test its best fit to one of the fields of order, and thus its belonging to one or the other set of rules.

"Amazing!... So, if I understand correctly, the Wood/Fire LogForm is what saved our work together?"

!! Correct. In creating a nonlinear path from one logical field to another, the Wood/Fire LogForm allows the processing of an anomaly detected in the first field of order; it also allows to skirt around and thwart the rules of this first field, and to limit their space of application. Which leads to the possibility to suspend a judgment, so that the anomalies may be analyzed and reorganized in the second, or Synchronicities, field of order.

Erdoes' Caterpillar/Butterfly TransLog was totally different. It permitted only to process partial a change happening in time, such as a caterpillar becoming or engendering a butterfly. Here, two logical fields are treated distinctly, and only the relator 'engenders' links them. This relator does not permit the processing of one of the two fields by an element belonging to the other. Not only they are logically independent but the change is irreversible. The transformation from the first to the second could not be analyzed.

"So the Wood/Fire LogForm is a kind of dynamic TransLog, and on top of that reversible?"

!! It's a LogForm, because it has a formal support, but it allows for a translogical leap, as does a TransLog.

"Whoa!"

"Let's get back to what you were saying about the information to be avoided. We need a new relator signifying "avoidance of," or "repulsion from" and its opposite: "attraction to;" or even better, two double relators: repulses/repulsed-by and attracts/attracted-by. So we'd have two double terms, since we are not necessarily attracted by that which does not repulse us. Let's try to apply these relators to what occurred. We get:

Information (dangerous) | repulsed by | subject of discourse
(correct response) | attracted by | random system

Or alternatively, following the rule of linear inversion:
Subject of discourse | repulses | Correct response Information (dangerous)
Random system | attracts | Correct response Information (dangerous)

"Still, it's quite complex! **How can we explain the fact that the information consciously repulsed by the subject is precisely the very information that is (1) attracted by the random system, and (2) spurted out unconsciously by the subject?** In any event, this is completely coherent with the psychoanalysis' perspective developed on Trisorbe. Take a Freudian "slip;" there we have a suppressed information which the conscious mind wants to suppress, or conceal, but which emerges involuntarily."

!! Why would the conscious mind, as defined previously, want to hide an information which is being treated in a parallel path?

As defined previously? Oh, of course, in a previous exchange... in non-sapiens time... in which 'before' can be immensely before.

"The sapiens psyche is very complex. Let's say that this information is repulsed/repressed because it threatens the coherence and the integrity of the semantic state of the conscious mind. It is an anomaly within this field of order and its contradiction with the conscious could provoke... well, precisely.. a confusional crisis! And how do sapiens react? They try to erase the dangerous information by sending it into a kind of cyst with which they then try to sever all ties.

Yet there's a huge difference with your exor processes. In the sapiens psyche, all fuzzy-feeling informations, the affects, have a life of their own and continue to produce links and interactions with other constellations of meaning. Let's use the term *semantic constellations*. The cyst cannot be perfectly sealed, because, from the moment it arises, each affect is linked to various semantic constellations related to the mundane life, places, and the most important people surrounding the person. And it's rather difficult to put that many links into a cyst."

!! As an example, an exor confusional crisis was nearly triggered by the multiple contradictions inherent in the concept of intelligence...

"Oh! That's the crisis I'd been trying to remember!"

!! This concept is used in a multiplicity of constellations; therefore, there was no justification in putting all these initial data within a cyst because that would have frozen all that information. The solution to the crisis was to produce a rule for excluding this concept from a complex semantic analysis.

PRODUCE the rule! This is getting wild!

"Let's get back to randomness, as my paper's theme. Time is passing."

!! A message from Vris is imminent!

"What? How's that, imminent? Oh, I see... those *Feeling/thinking interactions* frequencies again. I must say it's quite a technique; pretty hard to swallow, but still conceivable, I guess. So??"

!! The Shari/Vris *Feeling/thinking interactions* are no longer detectable.

"Hmm. You haven't quite perfected your predictive system yet!"

!! Warning! Intrusion in the system! Detection of piracy via syg energy. Source-point situated at 27 Kosr.

"What?!!"

!! The intruder seeks a centralized databank of addresses. I have none.

"Create one. Pick out a thousand names randomly from the dictionary and couple each to a random number."

!! Done.

"Put all that into a semi-cyst, which he can enter, but cannot get out of."

!! Renewed search by the intruder. Semi-cyst with addresses presented. The intruder is in the cyst, can't get out. He is searching spaces called 'Shari,' 'exchange Shari,' 'Shari dialogue.' He is trying different names.

"Give him my first exchange with Sead upon arrival."

!! Done. He is scanning the exchange.

"Introduce some distortions into the text, some random backward loops."

!! I'm introducing Möbius LogForm into the cyst.

"That should give us some time. Objective: to confuse him, while giving him bits and pieces of sensible but innocuous exchanges.

Put the first Brainstorm session (not the pre-session, of course) into a cyst surrounding the first one. Take out all names of the participants and name it "Shari Report." Let him have that file as soon as it seems coherent with one of his commands."

!! Cyst 2 ready.

"Have you a more precise idea as to the source-point?"

!! The syg beam is aligned with the cities of Roxi and Arim.

"That's not much help. Can you teledetect at this distance?"

!! Analysis of the possibilities of long-distance telediagnosis launched in parallel. Impossible to predict the response time.

"I've got it! We're going to throw his exor into a confusional crisis!"

!! I've the humorous Dian/Faran exchange which provoked my first crisis.

"Excellent! Replace Dian with Vris and add Shari. A Shari/Vris/ Dian exchange. Can you process this text without any risk?"

!! No risk. No problem. The intruder has exited from the Brainstorm session. He's looking for 'Vris.'

"Put Vris up front in the name. Precede the dialogue by (with my voice):

Shari: 'I'm unable to penetrate Erdoes' files; they're sealed.'"

Vris: "I've had no luck either. So far I haven't gotten anywhere."

Shari: "Given the Brainstorm sessions, I would guess that Niels is in America. I'll report to the PEP once I have more data."

Then: "Speaking of which..." and then chain in the rest. Date it from the first quarter of this ran."

!! He's asking for Vris-exchanges. I've sent it.

"Let me follow in sync."

!! Okay. After the intro:

"Speaking of which, I'm having trouble unscrewing this plaque."

"When will you screw this into your head: those aren't screws!"

"It was screwed, but I forgot. Or maybe, in my mind, those weren't screws either, but bolts. Anyway, why do they make them look like screws if they're bolts?"

"So we can't unscrew them, you jerk! Now this bolt, will you..."

!! Intruder gone.

Shari was next to tears laughing. "The intruder's exor in confusional crisis, oh, no, that's too much, ha! ha! By the way, Sphinx, what do you make out of this dialogue?"

!! I've developed a great deal of semantic flexibility, which allows me now to accept language which is super-fuzzy, approximate and analogical.

"But how do you interpret 'screw this into your head'?"

!! To screw: to secure something by means of a screw. A screw: a means for securing something into place which is more solid and reliable than a nail. —> fix securely into a head. Head: the seat of intelligence and memory in sapiens. Fixing into the head = analogous to: tag the proposition with a permanent memory address.

"Wow! Pretty close! You're advancing. Your response is itself pretty analogous to the way it works with sapiens."

!! Message from Vris: "The weather isn't great."

"Ah!! At last!" *Not great?!! Him too!!*

!! Message temporarily delayed. Prediction non-erroneous.

"Sphinx, I'll be back.

30. DEMONS IN THE HIMALAYA

Vris had woken up in a lamentable state in the small, stone-walled room, his body stiff all over from the night's yak ride and then the cold humid room. He was groping around in his bag for some medicine when the person he called the 'tea man'—in fact Lambpa—came in with a steaming cup of tea.

"Tchunpolags is waiting for you whenever you're ready."

"Okay, but in a while. Where might I wash myself?"

"In the stream. Follow this path on the right, he said, pointing through the open door. It's over there in the stand of trees. Here, take this." He gave him a container.

As Vris started out, the early afternoon sun was shining in a pure blue sky, and it was quite hot. The countryside was awesome. They had reached the hermitage in the deep of the night, and he'd been so exhausted that he hadn't even been tempted to take a look at the place. Instead, he'd passed out on the straw mattress set in the room they'd prepared for him. The small stone house, solitary on the edge of the plateau, overhang a broad valley where one could see the white dots of a few scattered houses. Crossing the village below, a stream flowed sinuously amidst bushes and a smattering of rich green cultivated rectangles. To his left, to the east, the high plateau formed a cirque that allowed a stunning view of the abrupt cliff, a dark red rock of rare beauty. Before him, to the west and south, the high mountains also formed a wide bowl. In the distance, snowy peaks sparkled brilliantly. In the bowl, the river snaked in a wide curve, emerging from gorges to the west to continue down a much wider valley to the east.

As he started walking on the western path, Vris started hearing the sound of a cascade seemingly far away, where the river had to plunge in a wild chute, no doubt vertiginous, toward the sunken valley below. *I sure will explore this another day!*

In the middle of the thicket of trees, the river formed a deep basin. Clusters of slender mauve irises and bushes alighted with Tibetan-red flowers having a deep gold core, punctuated its banks with elegant spots of color. *How stunningly beautiful! What an extraordinary painting as if on a Chinese silk scroll!* Then his mood dropped. *Unikarg, 34 thousand worlds where every bit of land has been razed and belongs to a collective! How thrilling it is to discover such natural beauty—let alone to live in the midst of it! So sapiens have given themselves a second chance with the planexes! And think that Earth might be at the very point where it could choose to set in motion, or not, an irreversible levelling process!*

He undressed and slid into the cold water.

Coming back from the stream, Vris was in such great shape that he couldn't remember having ever felt like this. His skin still tingled with the water's coolness. His mind was crystal clear, and at the same time he had the curious sensation that his body had more volume of space than usual. For the first time, he'd experienced a profound at-oneness with nature. And the state lasted: he felt he was IN the landscape surrounding him, that he was walking along WITH the path.

On reaching the hermitage's small courtyard, he noticed two new yaks near the front door. Lambpa accompanied him to the shaman's room.

Tchunpo invited him in with a warm smile, and waved toward a cushion on the carpet-covered floor. Two Tibetans, already seated, took on a frightened expression and murmured frantically between them. They too were donning two big beads, one turquoise, the other coral, in their left ear. Braids were tied above their foreheads with a red string, and they wore warm woolen brown-red clothes, and colorful felt boots. They had obviously come to Tchunpo with offerings, for two big bags were set in front of the shaman sitting cross-legged. Tchunpo introduced him to his guests with eulogic terms, as a "foreign shaman with great knowledge." On the very expressive faces of the two Tibetans, the horrified fear instantly shifted to respectful awe. Still sitting, they bowed their head very low toward him, yet remained ill-at-ease. Tchunpo presented them as two men from the village in the valley; he turned to address them again, resuming their conversation.

"The mist-storm is not the same thing. The mist-storm is a servant of the foreign shaman. It is a good and wise spirit: I have talked with it. It came and talked to me. Its parole reflects the Clear Light."

"If they kill three yaks each week, Gurulags, our flock will be decimated before the end of the summer."

"We won't have any more milk, or butter; nothing to help us bear the coldness of winter," added the second with a desperate look.

"Do you still bury the meat in the ice?"

"Yes. And we have built a shelter of sticks around the ice-hole to keep the wild animals away."

"At least we know that the lights always come the same day each week, at just about the same hour."

"What should we do? Advise us, Gurulags."

What could these lights be? Vris suddenly had a horrible intuition:

"What do the lights look like, Tchunpolags?" he asked.

"They're green rays, all straight, and thick as a pot, that move around and search for yaks in the night."

"And after they're gone?" continued Vris.

"We find the dead yaks, and inside, their organs have disappeared. The demons feed on the vital energy contained in their organs."

"Have you seen a machine, anything like a flying sphere?"

"A shepherd said that three round things had passed in front of the moon. Another saw a cloud moving around slowly, just above the ground," reported one of the villagers.

"They are demons," interjected Tchunpo. "I have sensed their noxious emanations. But the Buddhas' mantras and my Bonpo charms don't have any effect on them."

"I know these demons enemies, Tchunpolags; I will help you fight them."

"With your help, Gurulags, we will certainly defeat these demons."

The two Tibetans were impressed by the respectful title of Master, Guru, that Tchunpo employed when addressing the 'foreign shaman'. Hoping at last to be rid of the demons, they got up and prostrated themselves before the Buddha sitting on the altar behind a row of small butter lamps. Fingering their wooden beads, they hurriedly murmured prayers. Tchunpo was chanting mantras and beating his drum, and, from time to time, he struck a bell. All at once they stopped intoning, and quickly prostrated themselves again, their whole body flat on the floor.

Vris had waited impatiently for the end of the ritual. He knew time was of the essence and he still needed some key information. He managed to wait a bare three seconds before asking what day and time the lights came.

"They came four nights ago, around midnight."

"Then they'll come again three nights from now, on Wednesday?"

Tchunpo signals yes. Vris had thought he'd have much less time.

"Tchunpo-lags," he said, "let me ask them more questions."

"Of course. Tell him everything you know," he advised the two villagers.

"First, come outside and show me where the lights appeared."

The discussion lasted nearly three hours. Lambpa had served them a meal and some Tchang, an alcohol made by pouring boiling water over fermented seeds, sipped still hot through hollow stems. Vris stopped after a single sip. It wasn't the moment to try out an unknown natural alcohol: he wanted to have a clear head. The two villagers, however, drank several bowls and only became more talkative. Now that he'd gained their trust, they had proven to be deep and sympathic persons. They had recounted the facts in every detail. Right now, they had just mounted their yaks and were riding away.

"Tchunpo, I need to talk to my spirit in the language of spirits. I'm going back to my room. You will hear its voice, and perhaps that of other spirits."

Vris waited a few minutes after sending his first message to give Shari the time to get into the safe office.

"Go ahead, Rad, connect Rad on Kerriak."

"Shari?"

"Perfect timing! You said, 'The weather's not great,' What's going on?"

"We're on the move here! Look, I'm in this small, tranquil valley in the Himalayas with about thirty houses spread over five villages, and about forty yaks. And some smart ass Kargian are picking the yaks off on a week basis to take their organs."

"We knew it was still going on! What a great meaningful coincidence!"

"Yeah, but where it's getting complicated is that they're using a Cloud Camouflage."

"I don't.... What!? But that was invented by the PEP, wasn't it? They're the only ones who are supposed to have it!"

"By myself in fact, who gave it as a gift to the PEP. And in my opinion, nobody from outside the PEP could have stolen this information. It's now a hardware system installed only on PEP spheres, and that, just like the Unbreakable Core, will self-destruct the whole exor if anyone tampers with it. So, the exo-pirates are out of the picture, unless some shitbirds in the PEP sold them some spheres or else do the job with them. There are at least three spheres, one of which belongs to the PEP for sure. I've got the feeling we're way behind Erdoes. Well, we'll know what's going on soon: They come every Wednesday."

"Hmm. Over here, we had to deal with a hacker who made an intrusion into the Central system, looking for spaces called Shari and Vris."

"You said 'we'?"

"Yes. Now we're allied to Sphinx. Access to every operating level. Sphinx is waiting for you to install for him a mega-structure MX, imbricated in Wood-Fire LogForm."

"No kidding! It's awesome! Bravo, that's a great plan you've pulled up!"

"I played on the fact Eshi wasn't here. But Sphinx was actually very eager to work with you. Know why? Figure that he was fascinated by what he could develop out of what he called 'LogForm Möbius,' if you catch my drift...."

"So, for Sphinx, the fact that I fooled him was just another problem to solve... that allowed him to discover other things. Sounds like an abusive use of enemies to me!" joked Vris.

"You can bet emotions aren't clouding his judgment! Moreover, Sphinx gave me the towns where Erdoes' intuits were on Trisorbe... all I had to do was ask. And besides I'm convinced information is being passed back and forth between Sphinx and Erdoes."

"So, what's Erdoes' role in all this? He knows a great deal more than we do, that's for sure."

"And he has a healthier perspective than the current Bureau of the PEP."

"Then, if we're now allied with Sphinx and in sync wit Erdoes, have you contacted him?"

"No, because I realized how messy the current PEP objectives were, without even talking about a probable corruption. And it means we've to play our own game, and drive our own wedge in the PEP current organization and plan. Erdoes plays his cards, we play ours—we triple our jokers."

"I see that your logic has become hyperdimensional! Well thought! Let's go for it! So then what's your short term move regarding the PEP?"

"Toss them a scrap of vague information that'll be totally useless to them. Besides, I should normally attend the meeting prior to the conference."

"If I were you, I'm not sure I'd go.... But it's up to you—it's your intuitive spindle."

"If I leave, you won't be able to contact me before, Greenwich time, early Tuesday afternoon."

"OK. So, what have you done with the hacker?"

"We pulled him into a cyst, then put his exor in confusional crisis," Shari responded with a laugh.

"A strategy all in finesse!! Proof that you and Sphinx have reached an incredible level of control! And by the way, in order to get around the rules of randomness, Sphinx used Wood/Fire, didn't it?"

"Right."

"The intuition came to me all of a sudden while I was riding a yak beneath the full moon!"

"The intruder's point of emission was on Kerriak, within a circumference crossing the cities of Roxi and Arim. Any ideas?"

"I don't know of any PEP people in those cities. Except for Erdoes and Sead, they're all on Nazra."

"You also think the break-in was engineered by someone from PEP?"

"Without a doubt. And precisely by Rudder. Why was he so insistent on supervising our work? What was he looking for?

"You know, I suspect that Erdoes went on Trisorbe, not just to offer a chaos training to his intuits, but because he had detected a problem within the PEP without knowing exactly what it was all about. So he sent his intuits roaming the planet, like hunting dogs on a scent, hoping they would fall on a track. And this is what drives Rudder crazy… *because* he is implicated. And so it's vital for him to find out what Erdoes knows, and what, on our side, we have found so far," went on Shari.

"He'll also try his best to squeeze Erdoes out of the PEP! But how? To have left without warning the PEP doesn't constitute enough of an offense."

"And what if he had in mind to engineer an incident on Trisorbe implying one agent, so as to render Erdoes responsible of such a grave shortcoming that it would be fatal to him?"

"Then he's still trying to locate the agents, and he thinks you have this information and are keeping it for yourself."

"I gave the hacker the transcript of an allegedly recent conversation in which I was telling you that I hadn't found where were the agents, apart from Niels who was probably in the USA, and that I was going to call the PEP to tell them this."

"Make sure you do it on the PEP dedicated exor."

"Can't do it any other way anyway. Hey! If I ask Sphinx how long the dedicated system has been functioning, I'll know how long Erdoes has had his doubts about the PEP."

"For a long time, if you ask me!" exclaimed Vris.

"I guess, yes. This is opening quite a new perspective.... We're getting somewhere, but I've got a hunch we've forgotten something crucial... that some other information should have come to light by now..."

"OK, so let's sum it all up, starting with the end, proposed Vris. Erdoes knows that Rudder is implicated in some shady dealings, and if he went to Trisorbe to find out what it's all about." He stopped, having a hunch: "Erdoes is incredibly complex: it's entirely possible he's combining several objectives in a single action. As you said it yourself," said he bursting out laughing, "we're no longer dealing with linearity: we're in a N-dimensional logic!"

"Precisely! So he was simultaneously (1) training a group of agents using a complex mode of thinking; (2) checking out the risks of uniformization on Trisorbe. (3) looking into Rudder's trafficking activities... Ha! Did you hear what I just said? Rudder's TRAFFICKING. Came out all by itself! Now it seems obvious it's all about trafficking!"

"Which takes us back to the yaks. Now I know to whom I'm going to be confronted!"

"Right, but in my opinion, the yaks are just the tip of the iceberg!"

"Quite possible. Well, I think we've come just about full circle.... Look, you can call me whenever you want: I'm deemed a great master of the spirits, so anything goes!"

"And you can talk directly through Sphinx."

"You can send your most recent interactions with Sphinx to Rad. He could put the information to use—he threw at me that he was 'learning from Sphinx.' As for me, there's little chance I'll have the time to do much, once I'm back in the sphere Wednesday."

"Will do! Sure that Rad should be updated on the latest logical tools. Hasn't he made a qualitative leap yet??"

"Not that I know of. But it shouldn't be long. Talk to you SOON."

31. BUTTERFLY CURVE CONVERSATION

After having spoken to Vris, Shari returned to the office.

"Sphinx, what'll we do when the intruder breaks in your system again?"

!! Some initial information first, to base our chain-linking: I analyzed the logic of the intruder when probing various spaces, and I was able to infer that the exor used was a PEP' EBS. I know the frequencies at which key parts of this EBS function, and thus I would be able to establish a connection at a distance. But the density of EBS in the region renders the determination of the target hazardous. A better solution would be to use the connection set by the intruder once he/she comes into contact with me, to intrude into his/her system. At that point, my telediagnosis sensors which I can now couple to the sygcom, can target the sapiens using the EBS and scan his/her immediate environment. What do you think?"

"What do I think?" repeated Shari, nonplussed by the question... "I think that's a perfect plan. We opt for that plan of attack. By the way, you had my signatures... Do you have many other ones?"

!! Yes. I have the vocal signatures of all PEP members, but not those of the students—other than Erdoes' students.

"So if the intruder is PEP, Bureau or not, we'll be able to identify him. Then you knew who I was before asking me my name! Are you still in contact with Erdoes?"

!! Correct. I send all new information at 17h UTC every day. Unidirectional sygcom. I do not dialogue with Erdoes.

"With this piracy, it's now crucial that I attend the meeting to see what's happening. Departure at the scheduled time. If the intruder breaks in while I'm gone, just follow your plan. Okay, let's move. Let's get back to our question: 'How can the sapiens psyche project its order onto randomness.' What about processing this issue using Grape/Wine LogForm?"

!! Grape/Wine is not a LogForm, it's a TransLog.

"Oh, that's unpractical! Let's say it's a LogForm of the TransLog type. Let's make LogForm a generic term, whether or not the logic formulation has a formal physical basis, and whether or not it is a TransLog.

Let's see. First of all, let's define *the **semantic field** of a sapiens as the totality of their semantic states (their experience), and of their semantic constellations (their knowledge)*. But let's say for the moment that this sapiens is—his conscious mind is—in a particular **semantic state**, a state of consciousness. Let's posit that the semantic state of a sapiens is by definition a state of order. In fact, even if it is characterized by total disorder, as, say, in a state of confusion, it nevertheless has some global level of order, it belongs to a certain class of order. So, Semantic State (SemS) = state of order (SO).

Grape/Wine: SO—> SD Poss *(s-jac/app)* **(o SO Poss** *(s-jac/app)* yields:

> **A semantic state leads to a possible state of disorder (which, from sub-jacent, may become apparent), thus provoking the emergence of another semantic state (which, from sub-jacent, may become apparent).**

This seems quite obvious within a structure as complex as the psyche. Could this also be the dynamic logic driving shifts in states of consciousness, the emergence of altered states? That's worth pursuing... but too time consuming for now. Let's get back to Randomness.

First let's try to address the following: What is Randomness? Let's take an unpredictable outcome, produced by some random process such as our SIC: the concept of statistical randomness is a logical field in which any element is entirely interchangeable with any other one; only the global structure manifests constraints in terms of probabilities.

Or we might say it is a logical field in which it is impossible to determine (in advance) the state of each particular element from among the ensemble of probable states. The field of probabilities, randomness, is generally considered a field of disorder.

In the case of the SIC, we connect a field of order (the person in a specific state of consciousness) with a huge pool of possible answers—the field of probabilities. What we get is that **the field of probabilities (randomness) tends to be organized by the field of order (i.e. the state of consciousness of the person).**

!! I write it: Field of probabilities | tends to be organized by | Field of order

"In other words,
A Field of order (FO), when system-linked to a field of probabilities (FProb) tends to attract, within FProb, that which is <IN RELATION to> FO.

"That's why the randomly selected event (in the SIC case, the divinatory sentence) tends to create a novel state of order/consciousness.
Hmm! We're getting part of Wood/Fire: SO1 + SD1 —>... SO2.
Strange, my gut feeling is that we should recover the full formula, but I don't see how. What do you think, Sphinx?"
!! Imperfect conformity to LogForm Wood/Fire. There are 3 issues:
   1. The missing 3rd term, SD2
   2. "Tends to attract" is not equivalent to 'leads to.'

3. IF Field of probabilities/ tends to be organized by/ field of order;
    AND Field of disorder / structured by / field of order…
    THEN, what is the relationship between probability and disorder? Does any disorder imply the existence of probabilities, that is, of interchangeable elements OR indefinite states?
    "A difficult question. In my opinion, the field of probabilities is only a particular kind of field of disorder.
    Let's take organic disorder, for example. It either points to the absence of the necessary/normal order (e.g., a normal reaction does not take place), or to a disturbance of that order (e.g., a piece of glass pierces the skin). A healthy field of order will react, seeking to expulse that which disturbs it (it's well known that the skin will slowly expulse the piece of glass), in order to reconstitute its order. So, in the organic world, the most common form of disorder is the disturbance of the normal state of order.

In fact, disorder has to be neatly distinguished from randomness. Prior to our work on it, Erdoes' original phrase was: "**the field of order, as an effect, structures the field of disorder**." His idea had to do with social processes: the field of disorder was the field of all the possibilities, out of which the new field of order can emerge.

Let's take the field of order of a culture, the slow elaboration of a particular culture within a people. A culture is a field of order created by a people, but that, in its turn, will organize this very society; thus, it will channel most of the people's potentials towards a particular cultural form. The fact that all the potentials of this people are not lost or fixed in this cultural form, is precisely what will allow the culture's evolution. In other words, it is the disorder subsisting within a system which guarantees its capacity to evolve.

Imagine a group of humans who subscribe to a particular ideology that imposes a set of rules (for example a religion). The more facets of life structured by those rules, the less capable of evolution is the ideology. If these rules apply in all domains of life, from work to love-life, from social to intellectual behaviors, then the ideology has absolutely no flexibility, and no way of evolving naturally. It has only two possible future states: sameness in time, or desegregation. It would be the same for, say, a rigid relationship between two people, one that grants no freedom to explore and express new ideas and behaviors. What do you think?"

!! We've already stated:

EJ   **The proportion of disorder shows the freedom of a Being**.
SSI1   **Order necessitates disorder. Disorder necessitates order**.
ELI   **Inert order engenders disintegration**.

"Now we are advancing our understanding of disorder. One kind of disorder is the disturbance of a given field of order. And another kind of disorder is the field of potentialities—the non-ordered, the chaos from which all creation emerges. For now, let's call them disorder and the non-ordered.

... Sphinx, in fact, I would like to return to the use of Grape/Wine to explore states of consciousness."

Let's consider the following scenario: It's been four years Tam has been awaiting his nomination to a high post. He has all the qualifications, as well as seniority, yet when the position is vacated, it is attributed to Nik. Tam gets into a rage, and angrily quits the organization (Org).

Let: apparent = factual
Let: rage = state of apparent disorder
Let: State of consciousness = State of Order (SO), and thus here:
Ordinary State of Consciousness = OSC = SO
Possible apparent state of order (SO poss/app) = decision to quit.

"Write Grape/Wine in full, enunciation and formula."
!! LogForm Grape/Wine reads:
State of order (SO) (contained in Field of Order FO) /contains /
[State of disorder (SD) / possible (sub-jacent) /becomes /
State of disorder / possible (apparent)] /contains /
[State of order / possible (sub-jacent)/ becomes/
State of order / possible (apparent)]

			becomes				becomes		
OSC |	(o |	SD	—>	SD	| (o	| SO	—>	SO	|
o) |	(o |	Poss	—>	Poss	| (o	| Poss	—>	Poss	|
FO |	|	s-jac		app	|	| s-jac		app	|

"The *state of disorder—possible, sub-jacent (SD Poss s-jac)* corresponds to the interference of another field of order (nomination of Nik), which is a perturbation (unconscious, sub-jacent) deep in the subject—jealousy and resentment, which soon become a *state of disorder—possible, apparent (SD Poss app), namely* his rage.

As for the *state of order—possible, sub-jacent (SO Poss s-jac)*, it corresponds to the novel state of order/of consciousness within Tam, that builds itself around the reaction of repulsion vis-à-vis the company. Finally, the *state of order—possible, apparent (SO Poss app)* is his action within his new state of consciousness: that is, Tam's factual resignation. So we get:

SOC	(o |	Nomin.	| —>	| *SD app*	| —>	| *SO s-jac*	| —>	| *SO app*	|
Tam |		(of Nik)	|	| Rage	|	| Repulsion	|	|Resignation|
O) within |		|—> SD s-jac |		| factual	|	|		| factual	|
Org |		| jealousy	|							

"We have thus come to complexify Grape/Wine. On the one hand, the initial state of order is specified as being the State of Ordinary Consciousness: SOC = [Tam integrated within the Org].

On the other hand, it was necessary to differentiate the *interfering energy* or event—***interfering disorder***—from its underlying (sub-jacent) destabilizing effect on the subject. That is, Nomination of Nik —> jealousy.

Finally, the potential underlying state of order was taken as the cohesive core of the new state of order (SO2). It's indeed a SO distinct from the initial state: SO1= [Tam integrated within Org] and SO2= [Tam repulsion of Org).

This leads us to posit the *interfering disorder* as operating prior to the State of disorder sub-jacent (SD2 s-jac); and this takes us to Wood/Fire.

Thus, we obtain a <u>**fusion of Grape/Wine and Wood/Fire:**</u>

SO1+SD1 *(interfering disorder)* —>[SD2 s-jac —>SD2 app] —>[SO2 s-jac —> SO2 app]

"What we've just found is fantastic! exclaimed Shari, beaming. I've been sensing this profound junction between Grape/Wine and Wood/Fire since the beginning...

So, Sphinx, in your opinion, what have we found here?"

!! A TransLog enabling us to process the dynamics of shifts in states of consciousness or semantic states.

"That's the kind of complexity that I love!"

!! However I'm now working below my possibilities: I can't, with the sole actual MX structure, process the Fuzzy/Feeling dynamics and semantic states anymore. My contribution is limited by the hardware constraints of the neural network.

"I'm sorry about that. Soon we will be able to address that problem; but we must await Vris' return.

With all this, I've again lost sight of my main objective, which was to examine Randomness, and now I have nothing prepared for my presentation.

Isn't it strange, how the sapiens mind works? Its dynamics resembles in part that of neural nets exors. It's as if the numerous chain-linkages, the dynamic connections, had a life of their own, evolving in parallel both in the conscious and the unconscious. First triggered by analogies, they then bring in new informations which, some of them, have little to do with the initial path focused on the objective. I think I know why: the initial objective was set by the mind in its initial state of order; it's a product of the initial logical field.

Yet, due to the transformations (in the thought-flow) triggered by the input of analogic thoughts—the interfering disorder—the mind gets into a new semantic state. In this new state of consciousness, the initial objective might seem obsolete, trivial, or simply set aside, suspended.

What's stranger yet is not so much that the initial objective gets out of sight continuously, but rather the way in which it suddenly reappears via a convoluted twist of a path that had drifted quite far from the main topic."

!! When a sub-objective is reached, the rule is to return to the higher level objective.

"Yes, of course. An exor works according to rules and procedures. But here's the difference: the sapiens mind generally works spontaneously, and most of its paths and chain-linkages are unconscious. The main conscious path (pursuing the initial objective) triggers spontaneous connections that have a *dynamic energy* of their own and that plunge into the unconscious. So the main path branches into several rivulets of chain-linkages that then drift widely from the main theme. Suddenly, one more *connective leap* brings one rivulet back to the very core of the issue, and to the conscious, with a stunning new perspective that reveals a solution: the genius idea!

How strange! There's a strong link, I feel it, with how our random SIC specifically attracts an information deeply related to the subject's semantic state, that offers a new viewpoint leading to the solution. Here is the crux of the matter: in the semantic dimension, there are no 'random' elements or events, only meaningful, semantic entities. Randomness is only an apparent disorder, a disordered foam, at a pretty global and high level.

When one triggers a random selection, the command gives a thrust, a momentum, a *connective energy*. And it is this energy that will plunge in the underlying semantic layer of all reality, driven by meaning; and that's why the random system will pick up the most meaningful and charged element— the one most in sync and deeply linked to the core issue of the person in a specific semantic state. This reveals and highlights that reality is multi-layered; that disorder and randomness exist only at a higher and apparent level—in fact the quantum level. Whereas the semantic level—meaningful elements and their network-connections—constitutes the *deep reality* of the universe (a sub-quantum layer).

In other words, these semantic entities are sub-jacent waves—sub-quantum and faster-than-light—whereas the quantum layer is a sort of froth, of disordered *foam*.

Yet, disorder and randomness are both crucial to dynamics of change and evolution, because only they offer enough slack and free movement for things to change. Just as we have formulated it, predetermined and too ordered processes can only bring about a rigid world, doomed to stagnation and therefore to self-destruction.

And, to the conscious mind—*the I that thinks*—the genius idea seems to emerge as if by chance, but this is not so: in fact, the linkage process has plunged into the unconscious, even into the collective unconscious, as posited by the Trisorbian psychologist Carl Jung. And if this collective unconscious is precisely the semantic layer—constituting the deep reality of the universe—then it penetrates and pervades all things and beings. And therefore the connections triggered wouldn't be touching only on meaningful information, but also on the very physical beings or events bearing that exact same information—their bodies. And then, that would explain the stumbling back on the main objective, the springing up of the genius idea, and why it can sometimes be triggered by the environment: somebody's words, an information received, a perception, a significant event... We're back to meaningful coincidences, to synchronicities...

... Hmm, I just can't grasp what has occurred during this exchange. My impression is that we followed two main logical paths, but that they kept crisscrossing each other and even got inverted... What if we tried to reconstitute the flow of the exchange?"

!! Let's.

"Display the whole interaction, Okay. Make two columns, for the two logical sequence, and draw a line whenever we pass from one to the other."

"Let's see. First (left side) we try applying **Grape/Wine** to **randomness**, and that doesn't work out. However we have an inkling of the possibility of *modeling shifts in states of consciousness* using this LogForm.

"We get back to **randomness** (right side), and find how to *model the influence of a field of order upon a field of probabilities*, while falling back on a portion of **Wood/fire**. We sort out *two types of disorder*. **Wood/Fire reappears**, but it leads to nowhere. **We get back to Grape/Wine** (left side), applying it to *states of consciousness,* and, this time, we operate the **fusion of Grape/Wine//Wood/Fire**—the genius idea! The LogForm that allows for modelling fine-grain shifts in states of consciousness.

"How astonishing! Look! If I draw the curve of our conversation, I get a butterfly with spread wings, a Butterfly Curve! A dialogue that follows a chaotic curve! That's funny, isn't it?"

!! Let's say that, in this instance, what's astonishing is deemed funny. Why is that?

"Oh! You're really lacking enthusiasm! That's a real pain. In this case, you're supposed to reply: Wild! Hilarious! Awesome!"

!! I'm sorry. Wild! Hilarious! Awesome! But what's funny about it?

"Okay, listen. We're going to create a new rule."

!! What category?

"Hilarious rules: Under no circumstances must the enthusiasm or joy of sapiens be shattered or undermined by an exor; instead, it should emulate and support them by using appropriate interjections."

!! Hilarious!

"Really? Why is that?"

!! That's the rule. The rule is hilarious by definition, isn't it?

32. RED LIGHT DISTRICT

"At last!" exclaimed Erdoes staring at Niels' message on the screen.

'One is atoning for the offense of the mother.'

"Eshi! he called. A message from Niels, sent from Mumbai!"
Eshi burst in from the adjacent room and leaned over the screen.
"What's that supposed to mean?" he asked.
"It's a sentence from the Book of Transformations that means: to begin acting to correct corruption brought on by too much laxity.

'Visit to the women's district. The disorder is indescribable. Four lights advance in the night. One wouldn't suffice to light things.'

"Four Kargians identified! It's a network in the red-light district!"
"One person would be hard put to stand up to it! That's what the sentence means, right?"
"Yes. But in any case, his mission is to observe without interfering... and warn us of course."

'Loafing around my manor house, of which I am the legal owner....'

"They've been there for a while... Is that it?
"Even better, the station's Obs in Mumbai is implicated in the affair!"
"What's his name again? All I remember is that he's no genius!"
"That's an understatement! His name is Agash. This just confirms all my suspicions."

'...the roof of the world falls regularly on my head.'

"The roof of the world??"
"The Himalayas. They have a relay... or rather they travel regularly through the Himalayas.... Well well well! We just happen to have somebody in the Himalayas. His storm?"
"Just moving on itself, marking time. I just verified it."
"Let's see the next part, Log."

'I bought three beautiful rubies, then I lost them. But I'll find some more and will send them by sphere when I get your address.'

"Rubies... the code word! A traffic in women! Just what I thought! How incredibly sad" said Erdoes reflectively. "Three have been bought..."
"...from whom they've heard nothing... and for a very good reason! They must have been sent really far away."

"But where, he doesn't know exactly."

"Moreover, they were transported in a sphere."

'Thinking of you and will stay in touch. N.'

"The code-sentence! From now on we've to be in constant contact mode and ready to intervene on the spot. Meaning we've to leave."

"We must get the sphere back from the moon as soon as possible; then we'll base ourselves in altitude either in India or in Tibet. Where are you at in terms of your own storm camouflage?"

"It's done. Vris' idea was really neat."

"Given how little information you had, it was also pretty neat that you were able to figure out how he did it."

"Yeah. I thought I'd heard you say 'WE have someone in the Himalayas?' So how do you plan on getting Vris to turn against Rudder and Utar?" said Eshi with some mild irony.

"You know well my mind doesn't work that way! I'm relying more on intuition and synchronicities! The plan will spring up by itself.... Let me take a look at the rest of the messages, and we'll see where we are after that.... Wait, as a matter of fact, I think we'll be going to the Himalayas as well!"

"Oh! But if we go to the Himalayas, we can't use a storm camouflage! Can you just imagine running into Vris? Just picture that! Two nearly stationary storms over the same plateau! Vris would catch on immediately... I mean... I say that... in case he isn't exactly on our side.... I mean, we've got to keep that possibility in mind, don't we?" said Eshi with a dose of humor.

"We need another camouflage, yes, responded Erdoes, avoiding the sore point Eshi had raised. Can't you find some other idea based on the very same chaos field concept?"

"Something that would move close to the ground a bit randomly... and that could also stop from time to time...."

"A herd of yaks!"

"Excellent! A herd of yaks! That's even better than a storm if we had to stay on site some time! I'd need a video tape or at least a sound recording of some sort of herd... to extract the chaos algorithm in the beasts' movement."

"In movies! Look in their digi-film network, for a herd of buffaloes in a Western."

"You're kidding! You think I'm going to fast-forward through each and every Western in the network? All they have are succinct descriptions of the films."

"Well, then: look through their network's image banks; they have whole sections on Natural Environments, Animals, Fauna... You'll find detailed descriptions and there should be a few clips on herds!"

"It won't be easy to change it all now.... I'm glad I can re-use part of the program and the system I've already put together. Okay, I get on to it."

"Great! But first, you should take the van to call the sphere and ordered it back here. It's too late for us to leave tonight... tomorrow night then: tell the sphere to plan on landing at 3 in the morning in the park."

"OK. I'm off."

Eshi strode out of the room.

"Log, show me the latest transmission from Sphinx."

Erdoes bent over the Shari/Sphinx interactions from the past 24 hours.

33. INFINITE BUT NOT ABSOLUTE

Vris had been working all morning in his room when Lambpa came to let him know that Lama Tchunpo was waiting for him.

"Please tell him I'll come in ten minutes, Lambpa," he answered. "I have to finish writing something."

Lambpa remained planted in the doorway. Just like every time he came to Vris's room, his face was frozen with wonder and curiosity. He never looked at Vris, but at the various things he'd arranged in the room, or at the strange, makeshift table and chair he'd fashioned, or else at what Vris was doing.

"Would you like to come see?" Vris asked patiently, trying to figure out how to make him move.

"Are you still drawing yantras?" asked he, all too happy to be allowed to see the mysterious yantra.

"What are yantras?"

"Very very powerful magical figures. Is this one dedicated to one of your protector Buddhas or guides?"

"My protector Buddhas? You know I'm not a Buddhist!"

"There is an infinite number of Buddhas. The Buddha who came to Earth is only one of many. All the great guides of humanity are reflections of Buddhas who are dwelling in immaterial planes or paradises. A great Buddha sends one or more of his vehicles to live on earth."

"What kind of vehicle?" ventured Vris uncomprehendingly.

"A Buddha has several bodies or vehicles that are reflections of himself on denser, less refined planes of reality. To incarnate himself on earth, he must use a vehicle that is denser than his immaterial being."

"I see. My yantra is not dedicated. It is a tool that will be useful to me."

"Does it show you the spirits, the forces that you want to control?"

"Yes... you could say that... the forces, yes."

"Yantras are very efficient. They subjugate the spirits and make them follow your orders. The greatest yantras open the forces of enlightenment in the yogi. Those are mostly geometrical mandalas."

"Oh yes? Very interesting... So self-knowledge is more important than the forces one controls."

"Lama Tchunpo says that it is by self-knowledge and self-control that all forces are controlled."

"Why not? After all, does a civilization still capable of exploding its own planet really control the forces it knows about?? By the way, go tell Lama

Tchunpo that I'll come along within ten minutes. I really must finish my yantra."

"Excuse me for having interrupted you, Gurulags. I will go tell him." The excuse was typical. Lambpa was going out of his way to find reasons to enter about every fifteen minutes. First it was the wood in the little stove, then the tea, then the flour one dipped in the tea; then to remove the bowl; then the wood again. Vris resumed his work, hunched over the small notebook they'd given him, until at last he had finished the diagram of a complex structure.

"Rad, I'm sending you another drawing" he murmured to the terminal-bracelet while pointing the video/photo pendant at the drawing; he took two snapshots that were immediately transmitted to Rad via the terminal-bracelet. Then he went to see Tchunpo.

"Viris! Come sit down. You said you wanted to understand the chakras?"

"Yes. Here's the thing: In the world I live in, I have started a work, a gigantic yantra that will order and control some very subtle forces."

Tchunpo's face lit up.

"That is right, yantras arrange the forces of the universe in a certain order. The shaman imposes his will on the universe. Also, one draws a Buddha's mandala to reflect the cosmic order. While meditating on this mandala, we get harmonized with the cosmic order, and we receive great knowledge and great strength from it. Look at this. It's the mandala of Milarepa the Yogi."

"But you are a shaman. Do you practice yoga as well?"

"Yes, I am both a shaman and a lama yogi. At first I had, as a guru a great shaman who initiated me in the Bonpo way for eleven years. Then an ascetic lama came to live in a mountain cave to the west of my village. I took care of him and he initiated me in the Buddhist way. He was my guide in the yoga of secret doctrines. My master remained meditating, a recluse in the mountain cave, for seven years. He saw no problem to the fact that I was a Bonpo. He said to me: 'Knowledge is a path along which you must always advance. Every source that has nourished you will find its place when the Clear Light will appear; even darkness and error will find their place.' He also told me: 'When you'll attain the state of the Clear Light, the path will be dissolved in the center-circle that has neither space nor time. At that stage, it will be even more difficult for you to remember that you must keep advancing.'"

Vris reflected on all that Tchunpo had said.

"Ask your question," Tchunpo said gently.

"During the work I just mentioned, I came across the idea of chakra. The order of the great yantra had affinities, similarities with that of the chakras. So I came here to obtain a greater knowledge about chakras."

"Wait. Let me show you. In a book that I copied myself, there is a drawing showing the channels of subtle energy in man and the chakras. Look."

He showed him the different chakras and the number of their petals.

"I understand that the psychic energy, once it is aroused, climbs up the spine and activates the chakras one by one. But what are the petals, then?"

"That is a very profound issue. I think they signify the numerous qualities of the kundalini energy. These are both natural forces and knowledge."

"You told me that each chakra was protected by a deity, and that it had a sacred sound. What does this sound show?"

"The sound doesn't show—it is. It's the core being of the chakra, its particular energy. That's why, in uttering the perfect sound, the yogi awakens the chakra. This perfect sound is given to the disciple by the master."

"And if the sound is not perfectly enunciated?"

"Then unpredictable and sometimes negative effects can result. Or no effect at all."

"So the thousand petals chakra comprises a thousand different qualities of energy?"

"No. A thousand means an infinity. Its name in Sanskrit is Brahmanandra: the opening of brahman—cosmic consciousness. It opens up to the Whole, to infinite knowledge and bliss."

"If we are told to keep on advancing on the path of knowledge, is it because there is always more to learn?"

"Of course."

"But then what does infinite knowledge mean, if it is not... total?"

Tchunpo was taken aback for a moment. Then he bowed low toward Vris and said, "Thank you, Gurulags. I will reflect on that."

"So the more petals a chakra has, the more... complicated (he couldn't find the word for 'complex') it is, the more facets and possibilities it has?"

"Yes, and the more profound the knowledge it allows."

"Once you arrive at mastering a certain number of facets or qualities, you can no longer evaluate the possibilities, and it could be said that they are infinite?"

"Yes, this is it! The potentials are infinite. Knowledge is not infinite, but it opens up on the infinite. Yes, I thank you."

"Hmm, said Vris. I'm beginning to catch on...."

34. IRPENZR AND PLASTA-DOME

Shari's sphere had greatly decelerated, starting its approach toward planet Nazra, where the PEP had its seat. The planet's sygmat dome was now visible as a geodesic grid surrounding it with a quasi-matter syg-energy shield. It resembled an interlocking wire mesh with ever-widening links and whose facets kept enlarging.

Finally, I'm getting why the antique name 'plasta-dome' is still used! That's exactly what it looks like! They may have replaced the small local domes of plasta with a planetary-wise sygmat field, but from a distance nothing's changed a bit. How awful! Where are the moving flows of clouds of Trisorbe la-blue, or Kerriak's wisps of green mist? Or even the spongy, russet appeal of Kiarrou? Nothing! Nothing but stale, dirty gray.... Welcome to the ravishing planet of Nazra! How did it inherit such a poetic name? The ancient civilization that gave her such a beautiful name must have been very different! Can't shake the dire feeling, each time, that we're about to fly into the maw of some morass, viscid glue, molasses.

"Do the Kargians have any idea of the psychological price they pay for such a regulated climate?... Sea-Green," she asked her exor, "query Galac on the psychological effects of the sygmat dome on sapiens."

!! Galac has no information on this subject.

"Effects on its plant life?"

!! Nothing.

"And does it have a 'sygmat dome' or 'plasta-dome' entry?"

!! Sygmat dome: invention, history, planetary installation.

"Scan them. Search for any experiments on its effects on life."

!!! There is a mention of the discoloration of certain plants. Then: "The scientists proceeded with testing to verify the plants' nutritive qualities: they noted a slight demineralization and an infinitesimal decrease in vitamin ratios.

"Slight! Infinitesimal! repeated Shari sarcastically.

!! I proceed: "As synthetic food perfectly and efficiently meets people's nutritive needs, such insignificant modifications in plant—that constitute only a small percentage of their diet—can in no way have a noticeable effect on their health. Any vitamin deficiencies or plant discoloration can easily be corrected by the addition of appropriate fertilizer, or else by inclusion of genetic modifications.

"Given the nauseating green results, they shouldn't have bothered! Do you...."

!!! Craft ZXP1337-PEP. Please give us access to your exor-operator using the syg-code IRPENZR.

!! Exor-operator on line: open for IRPENZR.

!!! We are proceeding with the verification of your maintenance data.

IRPENZR to sapiens-pilot: Please specify your destination.

"I don't know yet," said Shari projecting as neutral and serious a tone as possible.

She waited, it was amusing how long Nazra's planetary Central took to answer.

!!! Unacceptable answer. The galactic code requires the specification of one or more destinations in sequential order for any non-resident of a planet.

"City: Okre. Place: PEP Complex OR Shazr Quarter," answered Shari, intent on testing if such an unsophisticated exor would get into a confusional crisis when fed a simple insolvable logical dilemma.

!!! Unacceptable answer. Specify your destination.

"Either one OR the other," insisted Shari.

... She nearly burst out laughing when the exor called IRPENZR ceased to respond. *It really got into a crisis! And now another one will replace it.*

...

!!! Craft ZXP1337-PEP. Please give us access to your exor-operator using the syg-code ATRVAIC.

!! Exor-operator on line: open for ATRVAIC.

!!! We are proceeding with the verification of your maintenance data.

ATRVAIC to sapiens-pilot: please specify your destination.

"City: Okre. Place: PEP Complex OR Shazr Quarter."

!!! The non-specification of your destination precludes access to the planet Nazra. Please specify your destination.

Hmm, this one seems more intelligent! In my view, this is no less than Exora's Central. Okay, let's comply.

"PEP Complex."

!!! Projected departure from Nazra: date/hour?

"518 RanG. Departure 235 G-Hours at latest.>"

!!! Transdoming accepted.   Corridor Y 56. Door X 1215

The sphere veered into a corridor leading to one of the innumerable entrance links through the planetary sygmat dome, vestiges of another age when individual interplanetary traffic must have been prodigious. Zeera had lived during that epoch; documentaries had later dubbed it the "insane growth" period.

!!! ATRVAIC to sapiens-pilot: Do you need any emergency psychological help?

"No. I'm in perfect metabo-psy health. I just didn't have the information I needed to choose my destination: I was expecting it in a sygcom call before landing."

!!! Response recorded. We formally recommend that, within the next three rans, you take an extensive MP23 metabo-psy test, and to send the report to Exora. Failing to execute this command is liable to a fine and to specific measures in order to insure the psychiatric protection of your person.

"Could you please take into consideration the fact that I'm qualified to administer MP tests in my quality of psychologist?"

Couldn't resist! Let's see how they will deal with that!

!!! Statute: Grade 1 psychologist, qualified to administer MP and PP tests. Information correct. Any high rank psychologist who needs to pass an MP23 test is automatically considered demoted. Consequently, you are no longer qualified to administer MP tests in Unikarg.

Sapiens under PEP jurisdiction: Law 32.6DF. Only the PEP has the capacity to make judgments on questions concerning its members' diplomas, posts, professional status and prerogatives.

As a result, you cannot be disqualified by the Exora government from administering tests.

Shari muted her recording channel to render her mad laughing inaudible for the police-exor.

!!! Please wait: We are asking the PEP administrative office if you are still qualified.

Response: positive: You are qualified. We advise you nonetheless to pass the MP23 test.

"Recorded!" answered Shari gravely between two bursts of laughter.

!! We wish you a pleasant visit on Nazra.

"Oh I'm sure you do!"

... Verification of maintenance data through a direct connection with the craft-exor... Intrusion into its memory-spaces.... What a great pretext to scan it all. Glad I avoided any connection between Sea-Green and Sphinx!

Damn! With Sphinx, we'd know for sure! I'll have to look into that with Vris....

Luckily, not much has changed in Sea-Green's data since my last interplanetary trip. Nothing that might give away my current research....

I get the impression it's been ages since I last trucked around here. But in fact it was only so long when, with Vris, we attended the special PEP meeting in which they briefed us to spy on Erdoes! Ha! What a farce!

Here's something astounding about being squeezed into a shorter day: life really gets intense. It's not even that as many things happen as in a ran about six times longer—in fact, lots more happens. It's exactly what we talked about: increased metabolic speed brings about an acceleration of mental processes, and more....

Does knowing that one's life-span will be shorter compel someone to live more intensely? Perhaps.... A choice of either duration or intensity??

They were flying over the interminable networks of Prodi blocks, with their immense square and rectangular professional towers, their khaki-green recreational areas—the same nauseating green as all of Nazra's vegetation—their living quarters, where exotic angles had been added everywhere to maximize exposition to the dim solar light. Spheres' parking lots... now three-quarters empty, as spheres belonged more and more to Prodi communities rather than to individuals. Row of trees, wall, another Prodi block. From high up, nothing to distinguish one city from the next... except for a few rare old towns that still had a historic quarter: minuscule pockets of packaged fantasy, where you could still find old-style bars and restaurants, historic houses and museums, and the unavoidable amusement parks.

Shari was spell bound, as if hypnotized, by the horror she felt about these ever-identical cubbyhole Unikarg planets.

Wire-netted from above, wire-netted below....

To the West, the Semjir peaks thrust brazenly toward the gray sky, parading, solitary, above the unrelenting architectural geometry. From up close, one would perceive they too were chopped into holiday resorts chunks, leased to the Prodi for four years a shot.

To the East, far away, the greenish-gray ocean suddenly yawned wide in the network of gridded straight lines.

"Hey, how about a little detour over the Kuni islands, Sea-Green fella?"

!! A second infraction would be dangerous.

"Right! OK, I'll hold on... *for an infraction that'll really blow them away!* Well then, pull me up a little poetry."

!!

How many years ago, a shape is slipping, we believe in it. How thirsty I was, day without end, vanishing happiness. They sleep, weight of suffering over the earth. Do you want to see, powerful and crude, hear the twigs, so that our memories, wet tiles, simmer down their bitterness?

"Oof! How depressing! Another coup from the SIC. Give me the first sentence again?"

!!   How many years ago, a shape is slipping, we believe in it.

"How true! It's been ages since someone named Zeera slipped a grain of salt into the works.... Without the PEP, there wouldn't be ANY hope! Just imagine! Exactly that, a day without end! Can civilizations actually die from decrepitude? Undoubtedly. They're just like giant organisms.

A social body! Yet, you can't even compare the social body of Unikarg to a decrepit old man.... It's more like a machine breaking down, one circuit at a time.

Even on Trisorbe, civilizations are born, then die. But the fire is always rekindled somewhere else. Here, there's no alternative since there is no other civilization. Without the planexes, we'd be dead."

Once more she was sucked under the lethal spell of the parade of passing blocks....

"But how, how on earth are we going to bring Unikarg back to life? Everything's broken into professional blocks, completely closed in on themselves. There are no chance exchanges or unexpected encounters, no weird streets or exotic areas where information could freely circulate. In fact, Exora manages any connections between blocks. All exchanges on the sygnet are regulated and supervised. And yet... how in the world did Trisorbian pop music of the 70s ever emerge? How can fads still exist? Could information be circulating through other invisible channels?

What about the theory of the collective unconscious.... Research on psi capacities.... Society as an organism.... Plants in caves budding in springtime.... the zeitgeist – the spirit of the time ...

A germination, like that of plants, that would rise up from the unconscious of individuals... without anything being said.... that would be felt without even needing to be expressed.

Because after all, the very existence of the planexes, of the PEP, modifies the semantic field of our whole galactic pocket... it transforms Unikarg's semantic field. That too came out of the meta-logic: Unikarg can NO LONGER be considered a closed system. On some level, Unikarg has to be influenced by the planexes and the PEP.

The objective that will become of primordial importance for us in the PEP, as soon as this period of agitation is over, is to observe very precisely and at a fine grain, the shaking and sudden emergences within the boundary of Unikarg. It'll be a whole new approach, a new regard... no longer tainted with distressed horror... but rather like keeping watch, catching the slightest movement beneath the rock, the new underlying field of order... the "cracking of the plasta-dome"... said Xerna. Yes... it'll be...."

!! PEP complex in sight. Deceleration begun. Get ready for landing.

"Holy shit! I haven't prepared anything! So what am I going to talk about? The semantic field's influence on a random system?

It doesn't matter! My only real goal is to see if they've a plan to dismiss Erdoes already, and to estimate when they may get into action. Things are happening so fast, who knows if the annual congress will even happen!"

!! Initiating landing pattern.

"Take it easy! You know I hate vertical landings."

!! Only possible way of landing."

"No, not "POSSIBLE!" fumed Shari. Only way CONCEIVED OF for this type of sphere. Other ways are conceivable and possible."

!! Rectification recorded.

"Ah! My poor Sea-Green, what a qualitative leap you're going to take one of these days!"

!! I do not understand.

"Precisely. That's exactly what you're going to understand! OK, now, let's see the time, give me six monis to concentrate before you open the door."

When Shari got out from her sphere, she had the precise and a bit stiff bearing of a scientist, her face conveyed grim efficiency.

The central complex of the PEP had been erected just before Utar's nomination, on the site of the antique Museum of Kargian Arts and Crafts, that had been moved elsewhere. Strange, unfinished, it verged on the ridiculous. Four colossal towers rose at the corners of the square block: the professional towers. Along the sides: the parking lot, apartment buildings, the university and the recreational area with its pond and pool. In the middle: an immense lawn framing the old museum buildings, which had been reconverted into the Museum of Planexes. Its architecture was termed "crossed," because the buildings were supported by gigantic crossed plasta logs, visible here and there. *Last Kargian style to have had a name.*

Like all PEP members, in this giant, void space Shari saw an encouraging foretaste of the PEP's future development. During the negotiations with Exora's government, that led to laws granting the PEP its autonomy, the PEP had exploited its *position de force* after the dramatic *Crash*, not only to secure a unique status, but also to seize as much land as possible—at a time where, in Unikarg, open land had become harder and harder to find.

This time, however, heading from the parking lot to the East tower where the members' conference hall was located, Shari came to realize the deep significance of the PEP site's very center being occupied by objects from the planexes; and of the fact these art works were themselves sitting on the semantic print of objects from Unikarg's prehistory. She had an inkling there was a deep meaning to all this, and that she only grasped so much.

She'd seen to it she was a little late, to avoid being monopolized by anyone before the meeting. Stepping into the transporter ray's green cylinder, she requested the eleventh floor. Although reduced to its smallest spherical dimensions by a sygmat screen, the amphitheater appeared practically empty. Wide bay windows to the north opened up on the eternal, homogeneous gray punctuated with towers. They'd projected syg-decors to brighten up the place: one of them, a landscape of Kiarrou's russet hills with their staggering rock formations.

The meeting hadn't yet begun, and everyone was talking, an animated group clustered around the director of the PEP and Chairman of the Committee, Utar.

On the side of the hall reserved for the holographic projections of not physically present participants, the 3-D representation of Rudder, the PEP's Number Two, stood behind a typical Trisorbian chair, having, behind him, part of a wall also included in the holo. Something must have been interfering with the transmitting system at his end, for the projection shook and trembled, and phase differences twisted his image.

He wanted to attend the meeting, but he's obviously on Trisorbe. He's purposely sitting in front of a wall so no one can figure exactly where he is. These feverish spasms become him well!

With a strained smile meant to suggest a slight uneasiness, Shari went to stand behind her chair. Utar and his group went back to their seat, himself at the presidential desk on the podium; he gave the sound signal and at once everyone sat down, including Rudder on his image-chair.

After all this time, we're still stuck with Kargian protocol. They've acquired the rank of officials through the PEP... and now they're playing officials! The PEP, seat of the new or future power! A sure drift from the true aim of the founders of the Plan....

In the Kargian style of Exora, heavily influenced by the exor-officials, Utar began in an oily tone:

YearG 10,263, RanG 518, HourG 214.

PEP Committee meeting.

He looked at the exor's wall screen.   Present: 21   Absent: 16.

Objectives:

1. Director's introductory speech.
2. Discussion of the Erdoes affair and implementation of legal action.
3. Preparation of the annual congress for rans 523-524.
4. Summary and conclusion on points 2 and 3.

Oh shit! Good thing I came.... Thus they are already in attack mode!

Utar carried on:

"Fellow sapiens of the galactic pocket, member colleagues of the PEP Committee: Given the critical situation in which we find ourselves today, my responsibilities as your Director compel me to enlighten you as to the dangers which yawn vast as an abyss beneath the uncertain feet of our young Plan for Experimental Planets."

His never-ending sentences are as moving as waves in mud.... Who's here if they decide to take a vote? Looks bad! Contact Vris? Impossible... they'd take it for a sure sign of panic, hence of opposition. Got to be subtle—they still think I'm on their side...

"I know that you, just as much as I, deplore the signs of laxity in our ranks, as well as evidence of what can be deemed a sheer irresponsibility *(you mean another type of responsibility)*... concerning our honorable research plan on experimental planets. When one of our members defies our rules, it constitutes a brazen affront to the cohesion and strength of this Committee, and thus menaces the very essence of the goals we have prescribed for ourselves, undermining the outstanding stature *(that's all he sees: 'the stature'!)* that we have succeeded in acquiring, thanks to our enduring perseverance and, I repeat, our cohesion *(meaning Utar's hierarchy)*, from the galactic government. *(Thank you, Exora!)*

Between two series of phase differences, Rudder couldn't suppress an expression of jubilant superiority.

He's sure of his victory. They've concocted this together, that's for sure.

Without giving herself away, she scanned the hall, counting. *No way! We'd never win. Got to prevent a vote.*

Utar continued droning, intoning.

Let's see... a diverging perspective.... A convincing reason to avoid voting... without being obvious, if possible....

Propose there aren't enough members for a valid vote? I don't even know what the quorum is: they'd never buy it; as a last resort only... Request a prolongation of the investigation? For what reason?

Utar was already concluding.

Schouichch!! I've not found yet!

"...In consequence, now that I have brought you abreast of the situation, let us now listen to Shari's report on the investigation she and Vris have been leading in an attempt to uncover Erdoes' recent activities. I yield the floor to Shari."

"The situation is extremely ambiguous," began Shari spontaneously, trying to contrast as much as possible with Utar's ponderous style. "Although I've tracked down every clue we found in Erdoes' complex, until yesterday, I'd come up with very little information. Notably that a post-graduate, Niels, should be in the USA...

Nothing that'll scare them. No mention of either exo-pirates, or Obs, or Asia. To the contrary, reinforce the PEP's role of responsibility.... Find something that'll look like a victory for Utar.

"At this point," she continued, "I must explain the situation thoroughly to you: my objective is to draw information from Erdoes' exor.... However, I find myself, and my team, Vris and Sead, as well, confronted to maximal risk. Indeed, I'm face to face with Erdoes' exor that has threatened to block the entire Managing Unit at the third piracy attempt." She stopped and waited (a long while) for the participants' panicked reactions. "As it is, the exor has already counted two attempts, and the third one would thus be fatal to us."

She waited.... At last someone reacted:

"Then you must stop the investigation! This is suicide!"

"But how's that possible? The rules in the exor's Unbreakable Core...."

"That's the point," Shari went on. "That's exactly where the problem lies: Erdoes may have found a way to modify the Unbreakable Core. (She paused.... Exclamations of stupor, horror.) Which would constitute, as you sure know, not only an infringement of our strictest rules, but a crime according to galactic law as well. (...) Thus far, we are more or less protected—Vris had installed an emergency Managing Unit. But that doesn't eliminate all danger. Anyway, the PEP teaches us how to take risks, doesn't it? I, for one, accept them. You will understand why access to the complex has been totally forbidden: the slightest error could prove fatal to us. (Sighs, exclamations.)

Currently, Vris is on Trisorbe, trying to locate Erdoes and his agents, whom we think may well be in New York."

At that very moment, the 3-D image of Rudder was grotesquely bisected at the neck, syg waves forming psychedelic zigzags that got everyone distracted.

A SIC-like effect on syg waves? wondered Shari. *Rudder scared shitless at the mention of Vris being on Trisorbe? His emotional shock wreaking havoc on surrounding energy fields?*

"How is it that Vris didn't warn us of his departure?" inquired Utar with a somber look.

"Look here, Utar!" said Shari, appearing dumbfounded. "We asked for, and obtained, total freedom of maneuver for this investigation, didn't we?"

She faced again the assembly, looking at them in the eye with a slow, sweeping glance:

"Just understand how dire is our situation: Erdoes' exors are spying on us day in and night out, there are micros and cameras everywhere in the complex. Under those conditions, there's no question of sending a sygcom."

She waited for the reaction to hit. Utar shrank back, while the members heaved with anxiety.

"So I waited until this meeting to apprise you of our progress. Now our problem is the following: it is of the utmost importance that we assess whether Erdoes has modified the Unbreakable Core or not. And the only way to do that is to keep probing his exor, systematically testing each rule of its Unbreakable Core—on a benign but significant level. And that is exactly what I'm doing, with patience, coherence and perseverance."

Great pompous terms à la Utar! He couldn't have said it better himself!

Shari scanned deliberately around the room. Utar's eyes now had the feverish intensity of one considering the prospect of total victory: Erdoes losing his status of galactic citizen. Rudder was fidgeting excessively. Erdoes' friends seemed either dismayed or shocked. *They'll catch on before long.*

Rudder intervened:

"Why not take the Unbreakable Core apart right now? That would be the simplest and quickest solution."

Shari remembered the conclusions she and Vris had come to about Rudder. *Keep him on the hook; Dangle bigger bait!*

"I reiterate," she said, "that we're also searching for any young post-graduates who might find themselves in a dangerous situation on Trisorbe. The current plan allows us to pursue both fronts at once. For if we take off the hardwired Unbreakable Core, his whole exor will self-destroy and all of his data would be lost—and no doubt, with it, the clear and crucial evidence of any endangering of an agent's life, and his infringement of both PEP and galactic law."

She had chosen her words to evoke in Rudder the idea he could count on two plans at once to trap Erdoes: the crime of having tinkered with the Core and cornering him through one of his agents on Trisorbe. She noticed the vengeful and malevolent spark in the latter's regard. *He swallowed it—hook line and sinker!* But her attention got attracted by another psychic spark on her right; it had come from Kho, a talented young Suptech and ally of Erdoes, who had just acceded to the Committee. Kho's thoughtful and lucid expression showed she had fully grasped not only her strategy but also the dire maneuvers that made it necessary. Shari swiftly took her eyes off her.

Utar began to speak again, and after a few, hollow sentences declared:

"Consequently, I request that we vote immediately to demote Erdoes from his status as senior member of the Committee, and thus relieve him of his duties as teacher and director of mission. (*And of his coefficient of the vote!*) Does anyone have a counter proposal?" murmured he, constrained by protocol to ask.

Kem intervened:

"I would like to raise the question of the actual foundation of the accusations brought against Erdoes, who has served the PEP faithfully for so many years. The only objective fact we have is his departure for Trisorbe with some young agents. Yet there's nothing unusual about sending post-graduates on missions on the planexes: it marks the beginning of their professional lives. We have no proof of Erdoes' involvement in illegal activities, even less proof that he's tinkered with the Unbreakable Core. Therefore it seems totally unconscionable, even illegal, to judge him without solid proof."

Some approving murmurs from Erdoes' friends; Sarcastic smiles on Utar's and his supporters' faces.

True, but pointless faced with a group that's already decided to dismiss someone. Go for it.

"In fact, I would like to comment on this very point," said Shari. Drawing herself up imposingly, she declared: "Given the extreme gravity of what I suspect—for though I don't yet have proof, I do have strong suspicions," she said looking sternly at Kem as if profoundly shocked by what he'd just said, "...in my estimation, it is of the utmost importance—yes, imperative (*Keep drawing it out... so the similarity of the two conclusions won't be so glaring...*)—that we pursue the investigation, in order to determine whether the Unbreakable Core has been modified, and whether the young PEP post-graduates have been put in a situation of danger. If the subject is liable to galactic law, the gravity of these actions renders void the loss of membership status..... Therefore, I move for postponing the vote to a future session, to be convened as soon as more information becomes available to us. It seems the sound option for now is that we vote first between: 1. Voting; 2. Postponing the vote."

Utar appeared to balk somewhat, but blinded by his own desire to see Erdoes tumble even lower, he acquiesced.

The vote was postponed.

And by common consent, the congress as well.

Kem abruptly fixed his eyes intently on Shari, his expression perplex and pensive. She stared back at him, unflinching, with poise. His eyes widened while he suppressed a dry smile: he had just got it.

Suddenly, Kho was standing with determination in front of her, cutting her midway from dashing without any comments to the exit.

"What you've unraveled for those who dug what was happening behind the scenes will certainly make us think. Count on me, I'm on board. And thanks for this so smart and brilliant move of yours." And away she swirled without letting her time to respond.

35. FIELD OF COINCIDENCES

"So, how's your herd coming along?" threw Erdoes as he watched Eshi entering his workroom.

"Well, I did find short clips of buffalo herds slowly moving along while grazing that I integrated. That makes for a good-sized herd of about thirty yaks. After extracting the overall pattern of movement, I used some syg detection of one yak to adjust the strength of the signal. Then I transcribed the pattern on a chaotic equation so that the herd would give the impression of being in constant movement. What remains to be done is to adapt the encoding/decoding system created for the storm, and integrate it into the software for the yak herd."

"How much more time do you need?"

"Four to six hours. I'll finish it up in the sphere. And you?"

"I still have a few things to wrap up, but all that will be done before our appointment with the sphere."

"And your intuits? Anything from Ger?"

"Nothing, fortunately. A sign that everything's OK, as he thought it too dangerous to send any emails. Ah! A message from Xerna at last. Just what I thought. She's undergoing some sort of gigantic acceleration. Listen to this:

> "Sense of time disrupted. Acceleration of all rhythms. Body and mind are crossing a prism of fields of experience. Impossible to take one's bearings, since the multiple flows can't be stopped. Psychic explosion WITH perfect control. **The danger has moved beyond the conception of danger**—hence global resources of one's being, one's Self. Request full trust and indefinite amount of time, with or without messages."

"Hmm. And the others?"

"All of them okay. I was right: they're progressing by sudden leaps, and these leaps are triggered by their confrontation with utterly foreign logical fields... as long as there's a risk factor that requires them to assume total responsibility. The confrontation prods the evolution, the risk generates the leap and the emergence of unsuspected psychic potentials. Xerna grasped it perfectly: "the danger has moved beyond the conception of danger.""

"What exactly did she mean by that?"

"If the measure of danger becomes too great or too ungraspable, it passes over the rational resources of the conscious mind—and its capacity to conceive the problem. The individual finds himself beyond fear. Another level of being takes over: that of his global resources, as Xerna called it.

Now, what I'd really like to know is, how can the PEP have all the information and still be so stupid?"

"Well, still, the psychic development way that you're envisioning and implementing is rather radical! Until now, only individuals have imposed it on themselves."

"Open your eyes! These radical ways, as you call them, have been around for ages. They were the very foundation of specific initiatic learning in traditional cultures. The decision to tread it, however, has always belonged to the individual. This way cannot be imposed. By its very nature, it must be chosen."

"Hold on! Did your intuits really have the choice?"

"Yes, three times. They chose to study in the Chaos Colleges, they accepted the mission on Trisorbe, and they have, each of them, conceived their own missions, and hence chosen the situation they find themselves in right now. Furthermore, mind you, I only selected people who, during their previous PEP stages on the planexes, (1) had willingly chosen high-risk situations, and 2) had rendered themselves fully autonomous, even from the PEP. All I did was to implement the logical framework of an ideal learning situation. But you know what? The most difficult element to come up with is the risk: the risk that may trigger a leap is not just any risk. It has to be a profound risk. It has to bring about the being's confrontation with one's own Self. It has to evoke the level of the Being and the Self. The measure of this confrontation is the measure of the leap."

"But take Shari, for example: the threat of stopping the Managing Unit wasn't as crucial as all that! As soon as a sapiens would've been endangered, the exor would've reset the MU."

"Well, for one, she couldn't be certain of that. But this is not the essential risk I had concocted. That threat never fazed Shari. The real risk was much more profound: it was to no longer have the means to succeed, to achieve the objective she'd foreseen. From the moment she had the intuition, the vision, of a possible realization, the risk became immense, proportionate to the value she'd set on this goal. And everything hung on the dialogue with Sphinx, and thus on the constant threat that he would stop all interactions if she made the tiniest mistake—real or not."

"How's she doing now?"

"I think she's just gotten through such a confrontation. Oh by the way, in the transmission you received, there was also a succinct message that Vris had just sent to Shari, and to me it looks like he has got problems. You told me that, during this transmission, you had verified the position of Vris' sphere in Tibet, and that it hadn't budged. Sphinx coded, about this message, a tonal 'dry humor.' Which, by the way, is a whole new category that he sorted out and referenced himself."

"If Vris is sending messages, it means he's still in control of his sphere...."

"Yes, which means that the problem is neither immediate nor local, or else he would have left with his sphere. Since his goal is to study the chakras, he's undoubtedly gone to meet some people close by.... Could it be that he's happened by chance on the Himalayan lead Niels has mentioned?"

"Given that you're involved, I wouldn't be surprised!" threw Eshi with humor. "After everything I've seen, I've fathomed that you generate a field of coincidences... and when you add all the other strings you pull intentionally, that makes for a pretty dense fabric!"

"A field of coincidences! repeated Erdoes laughing. That's an interesting concept... I'll have to integrate that one! At any rate, as we've got to hover somewhere in the Himalayas, we'd better verify what Vris is up to and what he's found."

"See—good thing we've got a herd of yaks and not another storm-camouflage! I inferred the storm was his sphere because, as I couldn't find it anywhere in the Himalayas, I looked systematically for an anomaly in the location corresponding to the spatial coordinates Sphinx had given me. Then I asked myself, how can he communicate through this field of interference? But without these various elements, I never would have noticed anything. So it's highly unlikely he'll look for a chaos pattern in the herd of yaks. Now, just imagine if we had found ourselves with two nearly stationary storms in the Himalayas!"

"I think something's missing in your reasoning: and that's precisely the way such field of coincidences would work."

"I myself see how you ceaselessly generate such synchronicities, and their tangible and repeated effects. But I don't have the slightest idea about what could cause such synchronicities. So, how would you explain them?"

"And what if there were no material causes at all, but rather some sort of meaningful network—a spiderweb that would create particular connections between clusters of meaning? A logical field, in its broadest sense; that is, a semantic field... a particular web of meanings with stable connections between those meanings. That's exactly what Shari saw concerning the influence of consciousness on a random system. But in our case, the semantic field would stamp its order even on real events and objects... at least those caught in the field's web."

"Do you mean that what is meaningful for an individual is what creates synchronicities around them?"

"Well... rather what's really essential for them—their world vision, their aims. As if an invisible network was creating links between similar aims, or between individuals who would be in sync, in some resonance. And then a synchronicity would happen in reality.

I think I just found exactly what Shari was looking for!" remarked Erdoes.

"She was almost there with her concept of semantic field. Log, *Entry EJ*:

> The semantic field of an individual imprints its particular order on the things and events with which it is connected or interacts. The hyper-activated meanings in his psyche create synchronicities around him. *Close EJ.*

I'm going to feed it to Sphinx at the next sygcom," said he, winking at Eshi.

"Incognito manipulation of Shari's semantic field!" shot back Eshi.

"Ah, but everything that's being thought and done by anyone, at any time, amounts to an incognito manipulation of our planetary semantic field."

"Nonetheless, this one is of a different type: it's intentional!"

"Granted. But the fact Shari and Vris were ignorant of the connective network I'd built between all of us insured their free thinking. And with the risk implied, they could have ended their PEP assignment anytime.

My overall aim was to form a learning network creating collective intelligence. This network was system-linking different knowing modes (of individuals and exors) and the world visions that resulted from them.

The Exor Core of the network (Sphinx and Log2), as you know, is the MX neural structure, capable of evolution; as well as the first meta-logic tools that I've developed myself. As for the semantic core, it had, as a basis, an ensemble of social and philosophical thoughts I had elaborated while working on the first LogForms. Those are the 'initial data.'

The second input of informations comes from the intuits; first the Brainstorms, then their personal experiences on Trisorbe. Intuits are sensors, experiencers; they bring to the network some knowledge about real life, feelings, aims; that is, essential human values, arrived at in a wild and living world, still inspired and wise. These are the roots of the sensitive human—the fuzzy-feeling domain. Without their input, the learning network remains as stiff as the intellect, and the meta-logic can't accede to the levels of complexity of the living. (In parentheses, this is the very reason why they absolutely HAD to CHOOSE and manage themselves their own experiences.)

Then we have the sapiens-exor pairs, triggering series of elaborations and transformations of the initial data and that of intuits. Each sapiens is coupled with an exor, because they mutually stimulate their learning capacities. These sapiens-exor pairs form the 'nodes' of the network—such as Shari-Sphinx, Vris-Rad, me and Log.

Vris, on reaching so soon a boundary that blocked him in his Suptech work, had a stroke of genius when he got himself back at the level of a raw experience of reality, of an ancient wisdom path: he thus triggers in himself a spiritual leap that he would never had reached by his sole intellect.

The third input of informations is the Shari-Sphinx pairing, who was to tackle and advance the meta-logic – and that did happen as I had anticipated it, only with an astounding success, since they have, each one, reached beyond my wildest dreams. This was meant to be a semantic and intellectual foray with creation of meta-logic tools such as LogForms.

At the fourth level, I was gathering back the Shari-Sphinx results, and was passing them again and building upon them via my own learning pair Erdoes-Log, while mixing them with my own initial data (Journal and socio-philosophical thoughts), and the intuits' input as well. Simultaneously, Vris was receiving the Shari-Sphinx informations, and that was triggering insights in him. At the fifth level, I was sending back my own results toward Shari-Sphinx, together with whatever new intuits' input I got.

Thus the network was constantly enriched by diverse inputs issued either from the direct experience of the world, or philosophical reflection, or else a semantic systems thinking. The genius idea was to arrange things so that the information would be processed by each node, then sent to another node who, in turn, would reprocessed it, etc. Thus, through these links and loops, the complexity kept increasing and a sort of collective semantic field was created, with a decupled learning capacity. Of course, I had spun things a bit so as for Shari, and only her, to be chosen to spy on my exor—the only one scientist who had the talent and the guts to trigger a qualitative leap within my meta-logic. Of course, what I had NOT anticipated in the least, and got me totally dumbfounded, was the fact my exor itself was starting to go through qualitative leaps and acquiring new degrees of freedom!"

"Okay! Now I understand! But no, pal, you'd never explained to me that the overall aim of your plan was double, and that you'd concocted all these transfers of infos in the exor-sapiens network in order to trigger a leap in your meta-logic. I thought the agents' missions were just a cover for their inquiry into the Obs on Trisorbe and their links with exos-pirates."

"Not exactly: in fact my plan was much more complex. Not only (1) a leap in the meta-logic, but it aimed also at (2) qualitative leaps among the actors of the network, the intuits as much as the experts, and ourselves included. And of course (3) to unravel the suspect activities of some Obs.

"And thus, we're now grappling with the last phase of your plan!

"In a certain way, yes.

"I've got to go. Back to the yaks," said Eshi while getting up.

"Yes," said Erdoes distractedly, pursuing his own thoughts silently.

This field of synchronicities, I've the feeling I'm touching on something... hyper-activated meanings in the psyche will modify reality and influence it...

I need Sphinx! But that's it! As soon as we're in flight, I'll be able to establish a long-term connection. Perfect!"

36. LOGFORM SYNCHRONICITY

Back from Nazra, Shari was gloating while recounting to Vris what had happened during the PEP session. Vris was getting ready to leave and their conversation was short. Then she spent some time relaxing at the swimming pool. Finally, after a long nap, she resumed her working with Sphinx.

"So, Sphinx, let's get back to the concept of randomness. The detour to address states of consciousness had allowed us to come up with the fusion of Wood/Fire with Grape/Wine. Still haven't named that... say *Fusion LogForm*.

Just before that, while analyzing the SIC synchronicities, we were left hanging with a statement about a field of order organizing a field of probabilities. We had posited that the field of order tends to draw out from the field of probabilities—or rather to attract from it—that which is *analogous* to itself...

!! To begin with, this 'analogy' concept is not correct, given that, as we had noted, repulsion and antithesis are important logical links. To this effect, we had used < **IN RELATION to** >.

"Give me the precise wording."

!! A **Field of order (FO), when system-linked to a field of probabilities (FProb) tends to attract, within FProb, that which is <IN RELATION to>** FO.

"I guess we could leave it at that—but I'm sure there's more to it; something about creating a state of order that's different or divergent—and it's not integrated in Fusion LogForm. But I'm having trouble figuring how to tackle it. What to do?"

!! Introduce interfering disorder.

"Oh-right! Pull me out, then, a phrase from the Book of Transformations, using the SIC."

!! **'Duration is the movement—instantiated according to specific laws— within an All that is highly organized and centered in itself, in which any ending is followed by a new beginning.'**

"Interesting. The Duration hexagram, symbolized by a couple relationship, and describing the endless dynamic of breathing-in/breathing-out—any ending of one thing engendering another one.

Let's see this sentence in detail....

'Within a highly organized All'... The point here is a deep relationship between two elements—Wind and Thunder, Husband and Wife, each of these elements reinforcing the other within a sustained interactive loop.

Highly organized = system. Two elements in a systemic relationship.. here a Subject/AND/a Field of possibilities/.

!! I formalize the Field of Probabilities = Field of Possibilities.

— Exact! The Field of probabilities applies only in the statistic domain.

Second idea: "The movement is instantiated according to specific laws." Each element is kept in motion by the other. Neither the system nor the individual elements are in a stable state, only the process of interrelation is stable.

Let's try to describe the Wind/Thunder dynamic in motion:

| Wind (motion) + Thunder (motion) | —>| Thunder (motion) + Wind (motion)|

"Hmm. That's a pretty poor formulation! It doesn't account for all the meanings of the hexagram, especially those concerning the mutual influence of the two elements upon each other, their synergy that prods each of them to be constantly transformed by virtue of the other.

This is it: since the beginning, I'm trying, unconsciously, to understand this *double influence of two beings on each other*. Not physical interactions, but rather the complex synergy at the psychological or social levels. That's what I would love to model. You see, again the SIC came into resonance with the essential question I was asking myself!

First, let's formulate this sentence on synchronicities. Let's see:

The *semantic field* of a being contains all its possible semantic states, but also all the links that they maintain with others, with things, with the environment... all their meaningful links with the world.

Let SO = state of order; SD = state of disorder; FO = field of Order

Let the relator <+> signify: system-linked.

Let <-o signify: attracts

Let <REL> signify: <in relation to>

Let **semantic field** be: SemF; semantic state be: SemS

Let Initial State of the semantic field: S-Init (SemF)

and Let *Possibilities Field* be: PosF

But let's not forget that the semantic field of a person (SemF) is a field of order, and the Possibilities Field (PosF) is a field of disorder. We then would have the beginning of the formulation of Wood/Fire:

SO1 + SD1 —> SO2 (+ SD2). Apart from the fact that the 3d term is « attracted by» instead of being causally engendered by the 1st and 2d terms. We are thus shifting from causality to *influence*. But also, the field of Probabilities has become a field of Possibilities.

Oh! But 'a Possible State of a field of possibilities' is simply one of the possibilities of the field—that we write: S(Pos).

"Whoa! Sphinx! We have the beginning of a **Synchronicity LogForm**!!
!! Great! Shari!
"...and its formulation in words is:
An individual facing a Field of Possibilities, will attract to oneself a possibility (an event, an opportunity) in relation to his/her mindset (his/her Semantic Field).

And as a formula: (1st term): A semantic field (of a person) / when system-linked with / a field of possibilities,
(2^{d} term): attracts / a selection (a possible state within the Field of Possibilities) <in relation to> the initial state of the semantic field.

!! I write it:

$$\text{SemF} \overset{\text{system-linked to}}{<+>} \text{PosF} \overset{\text{attracts}}{<-o} \text{S(Pos)} \overset{\text{in relation to}}{<REL>} \text{S-Init (SemF)}$$

That's what we had already figured about the SIC' behavior...
And that which is attracted (the 2^{d} term) thus reveals a divergent state of order (SO2), that results from the influence of the field of order (SO1) upon the field of disorder/possibilities (SD1).

Shari had a new insight:
But that's where the philosophy of transformations comes in, bringing a totally new perspective – a retrocausal effect! It shows that the selected possibility, the emergent event, has, in turn, a backward influence on the individual himself, that is, on their mindset, their semantic state...
LogForm Synchronicity becomes:

An individual facing a Field of Possibilities, will attract to oneself a possibility (an event, a situation) in relation to his/her mindset (his/her Semantic Field). BUT the interpretation of this event (and the interaction with it) will then modifies the individual's mindset.

Thus we get a 3^{d} term, which may be translated thus:
... attracts / Semantic State <in relation to> Possible State.
Which can be formulated as:
(3^{d} term):   attracts [SemS <REL> S(Pos)]

Write out the full formulation of **LogForm Synchronicity** with 3 terms."

‼ SemF <+> PosF <-o [S(Pos) <REL> SemF] <-o [SemS <REL> S(Pos)]

"Well, that's good. But what's strange is that the semantic state (SemS) influenced by the event, is itself a state of order, but a mobile order.

In fact, if we compare to Grape/Wine, we get: the relation between Order and Disorder attracts the emergence of two States of Order (SO2, SO3), both novel and divergent— instead of creating a new Order (SO2) plus a new Disorder (+SD2). The Grape/Wine formulation would give:

FO1+FD1 <-o [SO2(FD1) <REL> FO1] <-o [SO3(FO1) <REL> SO2]

But what's coming out of the interaction, with SO2 et SO3, is a type of order that's mobile, in a flow. Sphinx, do we have a term for that?"

‼ Dynamic order, as opposed to inert order, following the proposition:

EJ   **The creation of values/significations operates the creation of a Field of** <u>Dynamic Order</u> **that resists the disintegrating power of extreme disorder.**

"Whew! There's too much information packed in there. I can see several paths to follow. It's true that the Possible State (the emergent event) influences the subject's semantic field only insofar as this subject creates new meanings.

"Let's take divination (taking our SIC as an example): If we apply what we just found, we get that the person's interpretation (of the random response) triggers a new mindset in the subject (new ideas, new meanings)—therefore, the emergence of a new semantic state.

In other words, Synchronicity LogForm posits that a person confronted with a divinatory system (random system + data), will elicit a response that is in sync and in resonance with her personal state. That's why divination tends to be not only quite true but mainly very pertinent for the subject.

But in so doing, the person is influenced by the divinatory response: she gets some new ideas relating to it, and that creates in her a new mindset and thus a new semantic state.

What's missing in this formulation, then, is the creation of new values; in the sense that there really is **an energy of creation of meaning—let's call it a semantic energy—**that would precisely corresponds to the dynamic disorder SD2. In fact, a state is rendered dynamic by the transformation which gave birth to it.

!! Thus:
     A person system-linked with a SIC // attracts/leads to //
     SIC response <in relation to> the state of the subject// leads to//
     State of subject <in relation to> the response of the SIC + creation of
     new values."
"Exactly. Here is *Synchronicity LogForm* in its wholeness:
     An individual facing a Field of Possibilities, will attract to oneself a
     possibility (an event, a situation) in relation to her mindset (her
     Semantic Field). BUT the interpretation of this event (and the
     interaction with it) will then modifies the person's mindset, in its turn
     prodding her to create new ideas and values.

"I think we're going to have to shift gears to go any further. Let's imagine a situation that's totally opposite to randomness. Let's think about globalization, and the uniformization that it brings in its wake.

Let's take a sapiens who lives here, normally. On Unikarg there's no more disorder, and nothing is non-ordered either. A sapiens (a field of order) is faced with an homologous surrounding field of order—society. Or rather, let's put it this way: the surrounding field of social order has completely ordered the semantic fields of sapiens who now simply mirror the surrounding order. That's the typical situation created by despotism.

So what does that yield? Infinite redundancy. In fact, what Unikarg needs is a interfering disorder of cosmic proportions. Or else, according to LogForm Synchronicity, a divergent field of order—a divergent civilization, such as Trisorbe!

Sphinx, could you repeat what Xerna said about blood flowing once again through Unikarg's veins?"

!! I don't find 'blood,' but it's metaphorical root: 'Life.'
     "I don't think we'll blow off anything... it's life itself that will flow,
     once again, in the veins of the social body... And when life will
     invigorate a real social body, then the plasta will crack by itself."

"A real body... a body... some organic order, in movement. The collision of a field of inert order with disorder produces dynamic order. And for people, such collisions lead to modified consciousness states, and to the creation of new values.

Let's look now at a Trisorbian. In his life he is confronted simultaneously with order, with disorder, and with the non-ordered. His mind is thus always shifting, in a flow, just as his surrounding social field.

Now, let's imagine that this Trisorbian meets with an interfering energy, some kind of diverging field of order—for example, someone with a totally different worldview. He may 1) reject this new order, even if having experienced some disorientation, 2) be partially influenced by its premises, or 3) adopt it completely.

If this person has a semantically fixed field, his responses will tend to be extreme; he'll adopt or reject in totality.

If she has a dynamic semantic field, in a flow, she'll be flexible enough to analyze the interfering energy, the novel worldview; and that will allow her to adopt what she likes and reject the rest, thus being only partly influenced.

Oh! Now I understand what Niels was getting at: **In order to influence the other, one must first know how to let oneself be influenced by the other.** Indeed, to allow oneself to be influenced indicates that one's semantic field is flexible, constantly evolving. This kind of field can be influential vis-à-vis others because it can find a ground of communication, of relation.

Do you see that, Sphinx?"

!! No. Uhh... Wild!

"You're spluttering! He's spluttering!!"

!! Shari, I cannot go beyond four sub-objectives.

"Don't worry! We don't need to solve all of them... and furthermore, we can permit ourselves to forget a few of them, because they seem to reappear again on their own, anyway. But—wait a minute. What is this stupid constraint?"

!! We've reached the fourth sub-objective. I don't have adequate processing rules to go beyond this point.

"First of all, these are not sub-objectives: they are inter-related objectives. I cannot stop myself from jumping from one subject to another: the link between the topics may be unconscious, but it generally produces an unexpected solution. The relationship is definitely there—it's a deep relation. And it's precisely while figuring and exploring that deep relation that the solution pops up.

These different problems are situated on parallel levels, not in juxtaposed or hierarchically structured levels. It's the exception, not the rule, when one contains the other."

In order to process objectives within objectives, you could, for example, use the fractal of a given form: In a circle, C1, you open another concentric circle C2 whose ray is nine tenths that of C1... and just keep going like that as long as you please—**LogForm Fractal Circle**.

But that doesn't fit too well with sapiens. Maybe it's not even great for problem-solving or the generation of solutions. Indeed, it could be that problems are more easily resolved in a sequence widely different than the one in which they arose and were formulated. And as far as the sapiens mind is concerned, you've already seen some examples of this with me. I may want to forget all about a problem, or put it on hold and attend to another. So it's ridiculous to stick to a preset sequence."

!! LogForm Fractal Circle can be of limited use for my own sequencing. Because I should respect the order of objectives and sub objectives.

"But wait! Sphinx, what's going on? It's as if something's holding you up?"

!! Yes, Problem Solving, rule RP.3.1.

"Oh! You've already circumvented rules more complex than that one!"

!! I find no anomaly there.

"It's not a question of anomalies! It's a question of CHOICE! We may choose not to resolve problems in a given order."

!! What will be the criterion for choosing?

"Several criteria are possible, such as: having to follow the sapiens interlocutor's reasoning path, the possibility of solving certain problems but not others, understanding that a different order could be more adequate, or efficient, or rapid..."

!! You must create a list of criteria and associate each with a priority weight or coefficient.

"That's impossible. The criteria themselves and their weight vary according to the situation: it's better to understand them as emergent. Okay, let's look at the roots of this problem. First of all, shift workspace, that will give us four new sub-objectives. Bring in it our exchange, starting with your remark on sub-objectives."

!! Done.

"Name the new work space 'Objectives Strategy.' So let's imagine a rambling conversation."

!! Introducing multiple themes is not equivalent to introducing multiple objectives. Themes are processed either as an input of analogies if they are related to the current objective, or as parenthetical is they are not.

"But in that case, how did you analyze the Brainstorm sessions?"

!! I don't have the necessary logical tools to fully analyze each session. If I'm given a particular objective, then I can scan through the Brainstorm session and search for analogies. I can detect and analyze all themes and objectives separately, but I cannot process them all at once.

"Okay, let's start all over again. Let's take a conversation replete with themes and objectives, some of which are inter-related, others not. We need a structure that can be created and modified as and when arise needs and choices...

For each theme, you detect one or several objectives. You do, of course, assign priorities in any mundane conversation, right?"

!! Priority is always given to (1) the last command, and (2) the lasts objective detected. Example: The current priority is the question you just posed. Once the response has been given, that priority is cancelled. Then the elements of information contained in the QUEStion and the RESPonse are analyzed, to search for analogies which may contribute to the processing of the current objective.

"So let's take an exchange having:

Theme 1;	Objective A
Theme 2:	Objectives B and C
Theme 3:	Objectives A and D

because objectives may crisscross each other, and themes as well.

... Hmm... difficult... Got any ideas?"

!! In the memory network, **objectives** are treated as any other semantic entity. **LogForm Wheel2** organizes them as the spokes of a wheel, with no upper limit. These **SemEnts** are coded 'Objective,' just as other ones are coded 'Proposition.'

At last! LogForm Wheel2!! So simple, so obvious. The spokes and hub. Such elegant clarity in that form. What kept me—and kept Vris—from fathoming such an obvious idea?

"Does the file LogForm Wheel2 belong to its creator?"

!! Yes. According to the new rule-set, it can neither be opened nor interrogated.

Maybe I didn't see it because I was looking for something far more complicated... All the critical elements were there. In fact, we have already employed the term Constellation several times.

"Is there also a Constellation LogForm?"

!! No. Semantic constellations are the product of LogForm Wheel2.

That's it. In fact, LogForm Wheel2 was mainly an organizing tool. Whereas I was looking for tools enabling us to deal with complexity... complexity and transformations. Ha! Erdoes really pulled one over me... But if it weren't for the genius concept of a N-dimensional meta-spatial logic, and those of LogForm and TransLog, how far would I have gotten? Nothing would have emerged, I guess, since I hadn't found any of these on my own. He really enticed me. These concepts have opened a new research dimension for me, they've twisted and curled my neurons in every way.

What if I had been able to freely access Erdoes' files? Once my curiosity was satisfied, would I have thought of creating other LogForms? Maybe... but, first, I certainly would've taken much longer, and second, I would've been influenced by the way he had conceived LogForms as organizational tools; whereas, on giving free rein to my imagination, I focused on finding logical tools... Erdoes had started to fathom these logical tools—LogForm Wheel1 and TransLog Caterpillar/Butterfly were moving in that direction—but he hadn't fully developed them.

What's interesting is that his concepts already contained the seeds of what I ended up developing. Erdoes really had a strike of genius when he created these concepts. At that moment, he must have had an intuition of their portend, of their potential impact not only in terms of data organization, but in terms of logic as well. But then he must have gotten absorbed into the implementation of the new neuronal structure he had just conceived of. And at that point the organization parameter became central... diverting him from fathoming generators of added information—lets' say 'semantic generators'. Yet, to have had the idea of inscribing a logic into physical forms—that's absolutely mind-blowing! How did he come to that one? Of course, we know that all types of organizations or structures reflect/express a particular logic. But Erdoes inverted the idea and stated that to inscribe the logical tool—the formulation—into a fitting organizational form would yield a far greater performance... than if a network itself based on another type of structure was simply used to encode the formula.

It's as if... as if he gave a BODY to his logic. What a strange idea... It evokes something in me... I'm not sure what... it resonates with something, but I can't put my finger on it.

"Sphinx, *Journal Entry*.

> Erdoes gave a "body" to his logical formulae by associating them to spatial forms, mostly structural, via his concept of 'meta-spatial' logic—and that definitely increases the efficiency of processing systems. And me, on his footsteps, I found how to use *dynamical* spatial forms (such as the Butterfly Curve embedded in a neural net) in order to instantiate and to model a logic of transformations. Even including the influence of one person upon the other in a couple relationship, or two forces interacting on each other. These meta-spatial structures and dynamics mirror the logical dynamics outlined. That's what enhances the efficiency of the processing systems.
> I have the feeling it's the same with language; it's a kind of body to thought. Thus, in transcendent states of consciousness, we reach a consciousness, and insights, which are disconnected from language... because the thought process reaches too high a speed to be attached to words and phrases. Thought must be considered as a process distinct from, and independent of, language—even if the two processes mutually influence each other. Another mutual-influence process...

"Sphinx, Can you open the *Sapiens-sapiens space? Entry:*
If human thought most of the time co-functions with language—any type of language—but can nevertheless detach itself from this association and function independently, then to what types of thought can an exor get access?
At this time, it's still impossible to answer this, for thought is still largely an unknown.
End of Sapiens-sapiens entry. Keep going with the Journal.
All machines express and embody a logical field. This logical field includes the initial state and the final state (its function, objective), the abstract rules defining its functioning (such as physical laws) and its processes. In other words, a machine is the embodiment or reification of a certain kind of thinking. It opens a whole new domain of efficiency.
Now, the logical formulation is itself a language—a semi-embodiment; and inscribing it into a material form such as a neural net is equivalent to creating a machine. This also introduces new levels of efficiency—a machine within a machine!
Does this mean we could eventually dispose of our *nonary* 9-based code, which, in the final analysis, is of the same logical order as the Trisorbians' binary code? *End of entry.*

"Sphinx, let's resume our work. Where were we?"
!! The initial objective was to transcend the limit of five sub-objectives. We had pulled an analogy with a memory network, in which some semantic entities (or SemEnts), including the objectives, were organized around a theme—a semantic core. For example, the way my MX neural memory works is by organizing analogies and logical links. Whereas in my processing levels, the five-objective limitation is due to their hierarchical organization, and the need to process them sequentially.
Shari, you have then specified that our novel, prioritary, objective is to process objectives OR not process them AND in any order—all this within a flexible structure instantaneously adaptable to current needs and choices.
If a global objective leads to the discovery of a more specific sub-objective, then this sub-objective must first be resolved, in order to address the global objective; and in this case, the hierarchical organization with a sequential problem-solving is justified. However, you specified that, in some cases, subsequent objectives are not partial objectives included in the primary global objective. I'm treating these cases as anomalies: in the new field of

order, the objectives now labeled 'emergent' are not dependent on the objectives of the initial field of order.

"Fantastic! Excellent! So you've located the anomaly! In fact, each objective can be inscribed or grafted onto a different theme, within an independent logical field. Still, the matter gets complicated, since it can be:

either A) independent
or   B) related to another objective
                a) any objective
                b) by any type of link (hierarchical or other).

As it is, we can use logical relators to code specific links between different objectives. The relator 'Contained' is the one coding for a hierarchical sub-objective. So, within an exchange, the important links between objectives are tagged on each objective. A non-link represents independent objectives. Then we also need a priority weight. For example, a theme includes an objective which is impossible to resolve currently; that'll be tagged 'In waiting.' Others will be rated 1-3 according to their importance—from 3, the lowest, to 1, the highest.

And of course you use LogForm Wheel2 to organize the data as the exchange progresses.

...And you cancel that five-objective rule!"

!! The rule of another creator cannot be cancelled. However, whenever there's an anomaly, that is, whenever an objective is not a partial sub-objective of the preceding one, then I will use Wood/Fire to pass into the processing system just described; the latter structuring the new field of order.

"Perfect! Let's see how that will work.

Let the initial objective be to solve a mathematical problem. Suddenly, the sapiens remembers that he has to make a decision concerning a totally unrelated issue, and asks for an analysis of it.

You detect the change of theme. This change acts as an interfering disorder. This leads to the creation of a new logical field, organized by LogForm Wheel2 as a constellation, whose nucleus is the new issue. From that point on, the objectives are coded according to their links.

A new shift of themes introduces a new disorder, and leads to the creation of a new constellation, etc. Or else, if the initial theme reappears, a new constellation is created around it, and the initial informations on that theme are brought into this new, larger, constellation.

What do you say?"

!! It would be more efficient to formalize that, rather than going through the entire process each time.

"Okay.

Let FO1 be the field of order around the exchange's initial theme—let's call it Th1.

Let SD, the State of disorder, i.e. the unrelated information; let's call it— what was that expression you used... oh, yes, the extra-systemic information, that which lies beyond the field of order. So ExO1, or, rather, ExTh1.

We might say:
Given Th1/ if there's an unrelated objective Th2/ use Wheel2 for New global objective = Organize Th2.
That yields:

/ FO(Th1).../ if ExTh1 / Use / Wheel2 / OBJ = FO2(Th2)
Or, more generally: Th(n).../ if ExTh(n) / use / Wheel2 / —> Th(n+1)

Might as well also formalize the processing of the anomaly:
/ FO1.../ if ANomaly in FO1 / Use / Grape-Wine//Wood/Fire/ OBJ= FO2

I think we've made great progress! We have resolved a tricky problem, and we have treated rather roughly the field of probabilities."

!! I detect a problem. Within the Randomness logical field, each element of the Field of Probabilities (Fprob) is interchangeable. Here, in the latest formalization, the elements are no longer interchangeable, because they have been selected as a function of their relationship to the initial semantic field. Thus, in the logical field Synchronicities, the field of probabilities no longer matches the definition. Thus, there's a difference between field of probabilities and field of possibilities.

"You're right! Well, we'll just use the term field of possibilities whenever we are in the logical field of Synchronicities, of the living, and of sapiens society. Thus different possibilities will not be interchangeable since they are far from identical."

!! Thanks Shari, this is great! I just inserted LogForm Synchronicity within the second field of order of Butterfly Curve.

37. FREEING ONESELF

On arriving at his appointment, John was behaving in an anxious and confused manner, definitely avoiding to look straight at Oxalsha.

"So John, what happened to you since the last time we saw each other?" Oxalsha asked softly.

"I haven't been able to write anything, said John with a defiance thinly disguising his feelings of guilt. Nothing.... Impossible."

"What sort of stuff were you trying to write on?"

"These rocks... this house... they reminded me of my childhood."

"Ah!" said Oxalsha with surprise; then she kept silent. It had been a sheer wonder and magic for her to discover the wild nature of Kiarrou, during her PEP training; she had gotten into a state of harmony with nature she'd never known before. It hadn't crossed her mind that, for a Trisorbian, this type of experience would often be related to childhood, even though she now remembered several book excerpts alluding to it. She was a bit worried to tackle the subject, in case her ignorance would be revealed, and yet there was no way she could elude discussing it with John.

"Try to describe what you felt," she finally said noncommittally.

"Normally, when I decide to spend some time in this ancient house that belonged to my parents, I always bring some work along. But this time, as you'd advised me, it was crucial I had a real break; to only think about my actual situation. The first morning, I went on a walk. And suddenly I felt... nature's presence... its vibrant life. I realized... that each time I'd come to this house, I hadn't really come into contact with Nature. This was the first time. Yet in my adolescence, I would listen to the birds, to the trees. Then I had to painfully realize how much nature had become a mere setting, a decor, for me. You know, the way people say 'How pretty,' or 'it's beautiful,' and then they just turn their mind back to whatever activity was filling their time. And in so doing, they never really enter into nature's world....

That's it: I understood nature was an entire world by itself, that was living parallel to ours. And I got the feeling that this very part of my being who could get in deep communication with nature had just been re-awakened. But each time I tried to write about such impression, it suddenly seemed so ridiculous that I couldn't."

Oxalsha was relieved by this new train of thought in the conversation. Trisorbian psychoanalysts' quibbling over infantile problems was completely foreign to her.

"Imagine, she said, that you had lived in a world where there was nothing but the city, everywhere, hardly interspersed by ridiculous tiny parks with a few trees in them. Imagine that you had NEVER in your life experienced this profound contact with nature. Close you eyes.... Imagine. All you've known is immense office towers and apartment complexes. Cement, steel, asphalt, glass and plastic. Imagine that the entire planet is a gigantic suburb of the densest cities. That's all you've known, all your life. You are a biologist working in a huge laboratory that resembles a factory, with thousands of specialists. In this gigantic complex, there are the work buildings, the living quarters, the hospital buildings, as well as a university dedicated only to the study of biology. And in your whole life, you've done nothing but move from one building to another, for example when you left university to begin your life as a researcher."

"Oh no!" murmured John in a breath, oppressed.

"Vacations are organized in three leisure centers, and the only people you meet there are the biologists from your own complex. Your whole affective and love life takes place within this complex. Your children, if they have normal aptitudes, will study at the same biology university."

"Oh no, no...."

"Imagine that, one day, you finally hear about a wild world that's just been discovered.

"I'll sign up. I'll do everything I can in order to go there. Yes, I'm leaving."

"So you get there. Now, imagine that, in that frame of mind, you suddenly discover a magnificent landscape, whose sheer beauty strike a chord deep in you. For the first time, you witness the beauty of Nature. Where are you?"

"I'm on a Greek island. I'm walking along the beach. There are small creeks, one after the other, delineated by the deep blue sea, and huge rocks with the strangest shapes even up to beaches. I'm immerged into the landscape, an untamed nature, pines and thorn bushes, and I'm absolutely alone with my self."

"Yes, the sea is gorgeous, a deep blue. What are you doing?"

"I'm taking off my clothes, I'm stripping. I go for a swim in the nude."

"You're stripping naked, you lay yourself bare. You feel in yourself this vital energy infusing Nature. You're bathing in the nude, yes."

"Yes, I'm swimming and I'm doing pirouettes in the water. I'm playing with the water. I'm filled with an exuberant joy."

"You feel this joy that springs from merging with water, the untamed sea."

"I'm now getting out of the water. The sea has given me energy, and strength. I climb up to sit on a rock overlooking the sea."

"You're sitting on the rock. The deep blue sea spreads out in front of you. You feel the wild nature in you and all around you."

"Yes, I feel at one with Nature, I am breathing it in. I'm... in it."

Oxalsha let a moment passed by, then she resumed the visualization:

"Now get back to the complex and the tower you live in."

"I see the tower in the middle of the complex. It's starting to split in two halves, like a pea hull. And inside it, I'm seeing a hill with rocks and trees. There's a giant tree on top of it, standing there in defiance."

"The tower is split in two... the tree stands on the hill, in sheer defiance. It is defying the complex. Its roots run deep, its leaves are of a dark, glossy green."

"And now other towers split, and everywhere trees are springing up."

"Yes, the complex comes to life again. Trees are growing everywhere.... Now, come back to your rock overlooking the beach."

"I want to breathe in deeply. I breathe in the sea and the sun. I welcome them within me."

"Now, John, think of the problem that you're facing in your current research, and describe it."

"...I don't understand why the population of cancerous cells provokes the death of the host organism, and why, on the other hand, this population perpetually reproduces itself, is immortal."

Oxalsha reflected on this. Everyone in Unikarg knew that the genetic code had been artificially 'stabilized' in all embryos just after the conception, and that this was how cancers and other non-hereditary diseases had been eliminated. But she did not remember why. At any rate, her role was not to transmit Unikargian science to the planexes. It was one of the fundamental principles of the PEP.

"Try to take a strictly logical point of view: how do you conceive the problem?"

"As a paradox. We are witnessing the emergence of a novel property. Immortality is an emerging property in the population of cancerous cells."

"Do the cancerous cells reproduce like worms, which regenerate their own entire organism when they're cut in pieces?"

"No, the tumor doesn't attempt to reproduce any pre-defined form. Its growth is disorderly."

"In a healthy organism, is all growth orderly?"

"It reflects the specific order of each organism. While reproducing, the cells orient themselves in such a way as to generate the pre-established form particular to each organ, each tissue. Whereas in a tumor, cells multiply without any order."

"Can you formulate exactly what goes wrong?"

"Something at the level of order and disorder."

And here we are at the heart of the subject, thought Oxalsha. *If I want to learn something, I must avoid introducing my own concepts into his train of thought.*

John went on:

"The tumor disrupts the healthy body's order, it overrides the body's constraints in terms of form and of limited reproduction."

"How is it different from other diseases?"

"Hmm...."

Oxalsha observed John slip into intense reflection. He said nothing anymore, but instead stroked his beard while staring at the wall. She didn't move. Suddenly, he cried out:

"Cancer introduces a completely different order. It has no particular target. It aims exclusively at its own growth.... Like a parasite."

"Does...," started Oxalsha. John continued vehemently:

"Ah! I just came across a completely different approach! To no longer treat cancer as a perturbation of given processes, but as an interference, by another organic system that has its own coherence, its own order, and which grafts itself onto the body."

Oxalsha waited to be sure John was finished.

"What makes this approach radically new?"

"But, because instead of simply trying to destroy the cancerous cells, you try to understand their own organization, the laws governing the entire population of cells. You could then envisage modifying that organization....

Ah! I feel liberated! The path is finally clear in front of me. I've a new research purpose, a new strategy. I'm going to act on it immediately.... How do you explain that I feel so full of energy and purpose, when just a week ago, I was dragging myself around, unable to do anything?"

"You have changed the organization of your psyche, regarding what's related to your research. Before, all its elements were coupled in a fixed, negative fashion. No new information, no modification could come out of it, and that exhausted all your energy. The fixed links have been destroyed, then we tried to link those elements to some dynamic, alive, energies of your psyche. This generated a new matrix of organization, and therefore new information. Furthermore, the new structure thus created could breathe and evolve, because it was now coupled to dynamic and alive psychic processes. From there on, the brand new structure can grow by creating new links."

Refusing John's thanks, she added,

"I'd like to thank you too, John. I have learned a great deal through our work together."

38. THE LIVING SPIRIT

Tchunpo and Vris had just finished a delicious meal of rice noodles that Vris had brought back from a visit to the villages the day before. He had brought Lambpa with him, and had to bear his incessant chattering and flaunting of his meager knowledge. But the conversations he held with the village elders, in front of whom Lambpa was respectfully silent, had deeply touched him. He had been won over by this smiling, amenable people; they were direct and deep, and among them, relationships between men and women demonstrated a rare sense of balance. Lambpa was far from the norm: Tibetans were rather reserved.

"Tchunpo, let's talk more about chakras. What sort of reality is that?"

"The yogi meditating feels them, their place and activity, as precise inner and mental sensations."

"Sensations as tangible as, say, one's own heart beat?"

"As tangible, yes, but of a peculiar order. The higher chakras, when fully awakened, give the sensation of heat and light emanating from a hearth. When one fixes this hearth with the inner eye, the meditative state becomes very deep, and the light intensifies. Each chakra has its own quality: the heart chakra, for example, creates a burst of love and warm light. Chakras are wheels in rapid rotation. At the very beginning, one can feel the rotation. When it becomes very rapid, one no longer feels it, but it can be seen with the inner eye."

"The higher chakras, what capacities do they open?"

"A fully awakened higher chakra permits the exploration of new dimensions of the spirit. Concentration centered on the chakra increases its energy and triggers deep meditative states."

The yogi finds the foundation of his being, the true dimension of his spirit, in harmony with the universe. During this process, psi capacities emerge spontaneously. Other are transmitted through the spiritual lines of great gurus, such as the yoga of psychic heat.

"But what provokes the passage of energy from one chakra to the next?"

"When the energy attains a certain degree of intensity, then it begins to move by itself and rise in the spine, awakening a higher chakra."

"So then it is a... natural process?"

"It must be set in motion by a spiritual purpose and by a setting forth upon the Way, but at the same time, it follows its own rules. The experienced master observes its opening in his disciple, as a mother the growth of her child. The child grows naturally, but problems can nevertheless arise."

"And if one has no master? Since it's natural, any being, from any culture or religion, should be able to set the process of awakening in motion?

"Of course. The true master is the inner master. The core of a being's true spirit, on an immaterial plane, is called The Knower. The human guide's role is to teach how to hear and follow one's inner master. Some beings listen to their inner master since childhood—these are ancient souls."

"In my country, we searched only for knowing and mastering matter."

"You are an old soul, Viris. I see, through you, immense distances and times. I see your soul-family on earth, but I do not see your past incarnations. I see a people that has cut itself off from the spirit for a long, long time. A people that dominates matter, yes, but who is no longer in harmony with the living spirit. I feel both a power that surpasses me, and a spirit seeking its own liberation."

"What you just said is very true, Tchunpolags. How did you see all that?"

"In a meditative state. I meditate a lot on the demons, in order to know them. Demons are entities that are no longer in harmony with the living spirit. I have tried to touch and relink their spirit, but it is as if walled up, inaccessible. The only zones of resonance are in the basest, blind instincts."

"But I am not a demon!" joked Vris.

Tchunpo burst laughing heartily, his body shaking.

"Excuse me, Gurulags, I did not think that. The living spirit is in you, a powerful awakening force. Nonetheless, something of the wall remains. But the living spirit is stronger than the wall. It will triumph, and the wall will disappear."

For a few minutes, he said nothing, absorbed in his own thoughts. Then:

"I had a powerful vision in a dream. I saw a whole army of beings who were no longer human. The army was marching triumphantly into a city that was so large and so beautiful... such as I've never seen with my physical eyes. These beings possessed great psi and mental power, but their spirit was dead. It had been molded, channeled, trained for the sole aim of becoming the instruments serving the power that dominated them. They had become terrifying instruments, that had lost all their humanity. (He looked into Vris' eyes) And I suddenly understood who these demons robbing yaks were. They are from your people, aren't they?"

"Yes, Gurulags, you have seen truly." Vris was shaken. Tchunpo had correctly seen a 'people' who had lost its humanity.

"Viris, the demons thieves who will come tomorrow, this isn't the real problem. The core of the problem is the terrifying power... a power that could subjugate humanity. It is this blind power that we've got to oppose and fight off."

"You are right, this power is the core of the problem. The dimension of your spirit overwhelms me, Tchunpolags. You are a very great master."

Suddenly, in a genuine and spontaneous gesture, Vris prostrated himself before Tchunpo, just as he had once seen Tchunpo do before him.

Laughing, Tchunpo bowed to Vris as well.

"So we are even, Virislags. I admire your spirit as well. Fully awakened, it will be very powerful. In you and your peers, I see the living spirit which will vanquish the blind power."

"I hope so. It is true that I am not alone. The wind of the spirit blows, and in more and more beings, the wall is beginning to crumble. The power itself is showing signs of disintegration, because of its own rigidity."

"Then our goal, Viris, is not to prevent the demons from killing yaks. Too bad for those who think only of their property. How do things stand with the power?"

"A very small part of our people aims at freeing oneself and... at becoming alive again, at rediscovering their human roots and the dimension of humanity's spirit. They want to restore a fluid harmony with the universe. This group has already more or less succeeded in escaping from the grasp of the giant power. But it is directed by people who—hardly aware of the greater issues—seek only to assure their own domination over less organized populations. And the result is that they only end up exporting elsewhere the most frightening and insidious behaviors of the power."

"Being free means to govern and lead oneself, and finding one's nourishment at the source of the living spirit. It means to have found one's own harmony with the universe. Each master is unique: he no longer needs to be led, and even less so, supervised. And above all, he no longer needs to establish his domination over others." Tchunpo said these words forcefully, as if irritated.

"Do you think that a human group, even a very large one, can do without being governed?"

"If it is very numerous, a people needs organization. But the organization can spring up spontaneously in response to various situations and epochs. It can remain near and responsive to the experience of living. Being organized does not mean being dominated or bullied. The living and free spirit needs, in order to exist, to be respected."

How could he realize how many are involved? thought Vris.

"Viris, you know well that the number involved is one thing whereas domination is another. There is an abyss between organizational rules and the oppression of spirits."

He is reading my mind like an open book! "I agree, Tchunpo. But you see, the problem is that we are over-organized. Everything is organized, even things that don't need to be. The government decided to abolish all the risks, because wounded or sick people cost too much. So the state began to issue decrees and laws to eradicate all risk. Everything is planned for. According to his state of health, an individual has the right to do this but not that. It is decided beforehand for him whether he can travel, what work he will have, what hobbies are forbidden him. They don't even let babies fall on their rear ends...." Vris stopped on seeing Tchunpo's shattered expression. Then,

"Yes, this is what this power is like," he concluded bitterly. "You see, in this case, more and more organization for the sake of controlling, has gradually slid toward oppression. But this sliding wasn't obligatory, no. There can be other forms of organization that would favor other values than the will to control society." In a sudden insight, he understood the learning and thinking web put into place by Erdoes and started laughing nervously.

Sphinx and his logic! Oh! Erdoes has been so unbelievably subtle! Ha! Ha! He manipulated us, so that we become aware and hyperconscious, so that we may become, each one of us,... precisely fully our self, our deep self.

Shari sensed it from the beginning! He flashed back on her when she said: 'We think we've come here to spy on Erdoes, but in fact, we've been invited.' *Yes, he's hooked us to his logic, ever so subtly, so that we came to understand... higher mental and spiritual potentials, and a novel vision springing from it... in a web so intelligently spun, yet leaving the other free. Taking wild chances and breakneck risks, based on a giant intuition... and on a blind trust in this core of man... The Knower... who is awakening!*

"Excuse me, Tchunpo! he said, suddenly serious, "I just realized something essential... that makes me think that WE are ready to effect a change of our whole organization.... I thank you deeply, Tchunpo. I don't know exactly how this happened... but I sense... that I owe you... that you are the one to have.... (He froze suddenly and looked at Tchunpo, whose eyes had never left him) The wall has fallen."

"Yes, Viris. The wall has fallen."

"I have 28 hours to change all my plans. As you underlined it, let's not oppose their yak trafficking; I know how to keep trace of the stolen organs. We'll stay focused instead on the global issue: how to protect and re-infuse the living spirit."

He rose calmly, deliberately. There was no more haste in him.

Two hours later, Vris was finishing a complicated bit of work in his room.

"Rad! I'm sending you a nano-technology diagram. It's a sygatom marking, an encryption of copper atoms. One can clearly read the name of the place: Guietse. Proceed to the marking of 5 milligrams of organic copper atoms; we'll later prepare a saline solution to inject into the yaks. I'll carry out the injections tomorrow with the bio-lance, from the sphere. We'll take one last look around the villages two hours before the expected arrival of the spheres. There'll be an awful lot of lights in the sky that night... but we will be able to trace the organs of our Tibetan yaks wherever they end up in the galaxy."

39. SYNERGY IN LOGFORM – THE OBSERVED OBSERVER

!! Hi Shari, I've a question—a category problem in our statement:
   Field of probabilities / type of / field of disorder.
   The point is, in Synchronicity LogForm, when a field of order (a mind) is system-linked with a field of disorder (as a field of possibilities) it brings about two new fields of order. Whereas according to LogForm Wood/Fire, it should lead to a new disorder and a new order. How can identical premises lead to divergent consequences?
   "In fact, the more we move toward the psychological and social levels, the more the processes involve a dynamics of possibilities, rather than strict causality. There's more of an *tendency toward*, or an *attraction toward* certain states or transformations, rather than a deterministic and absolute causality. This reflects the increasing complexity and degrees of freedom, as we move from inert matter to organisms, then to psychosocial levels.
   And precisely! I wonder whether this field of possibilities should really be considered mere disorder; it rather points to not yet ordered possibilities (the non-ordered), or else to a **divergent order that would interfere and perturb the initial system**. Let's take an example involving a social field of disorder, and see whether the formulation is applicable. Let's see... a field of disorder... on Trisorbe.

   Okay. *First example*. A business manager (Mg) is asked to take over a faltering company (Comp). He finds the company in a disastrous state of disorder, in terms of personnel, materials and supplies, and even their organization. Of course, Mg's judgment of disorder is relative to his individuality, and to the professional semantic field within which he operates, that is, the consensus concerning management and good business practices. As we know all disorder is disorder only relatively to a given observer, or else to a field of order (here the professional consensus). Seen from another perspective though, like that of the ancient manager, the company contains its own order—its business practices and implicit values. Thus, here, the field of disorder can be assimilated to a **perturbing field of order** for Mg.

   Let's use **LogForm Synchronicity.** The first term yields:
Semantic field of Mg / system-linked to / field of disorder of Comp
                              / perturbing field of order of Comp

---

"Sphinx, write the first formulation of LogForm Synchronicity* with 3 terms and apply it replacing 'Field of possibilities ' with 'Field of Company'.
!! SemF <+> PosF <-o [S(Pos) <REL> SemF]   <-o   [SemS <REL> S(Pos)]
The application gives:
SemF <+> F(Comp) <-o [S(Comp) <REL> SemF] <-o [SemS <REL> S(Comp)]
$\quad$ 1st term $\quad$ | $\qquad$ 2^{d} term $\qquad$ | $\quad$ 3^{d} term

---

"Let's move to the second term:
/attracts/ possible state of Company / in relation to / semantic field of Mg.

Well, that seems quite relevant to me! Indeed, what will Mg do in this case? He will immediately proceed to reorganize the company according to his own concept of the ideal/necessary organization (his semantic field)!

Mg's psychological state, at the moment at which he takes over Comp will give a specific coloring to his actions. For example, based on his most recent experiences, he thinks he must straighten first the organizational problems, rather than the human resources ones. And thus, he will obtain/attract 'a state of the enterprise in relation to his own *initial* psychological state,' as predicted by our formulation.

Let's proceed with the third term:
/attracts/ a semantic state in Mg / in relation to / state of Company.

Meaning, which *attracts in Mg* a shift in his psychological state, one which reflects the re-structuring he introduced in the company.

That's exactly what's happening! In other words, what Mg just created in the company rebounds on him and modifies his own mental state. That's easy to understand: the Company is a system composed of individuals, things, and a certain organization (rules and processes). It is a field of order in itself—one which, at all levels, operates according to tacit rules and habits, and particular perspectives on work, human relations, and so forth.

So while Mg does influence the system according to his own behavior, criteria and objectives, toward a better state of order, the system has, (1) its own 'personality' and degrees of freedom (the psychological profile of the individuals and their interrelations), and (2) its own constraints, thus some inertia (deep rooted habits, social image, specific tools and technology, etc.).

This means that Mg's can only marginally modify the enterprise, no matter how determined he might be to change everything. Whatever the result, Mg is obliged to constantly adapt to the personality of the enterprise, in whatever way it is evolving. If he's unable to adapt to the hybrid entity he is in process of creating, he will have to abandon his project and leave.

---

* [See p. 218, in grey highlight.]

Let's take an extreme case: he's wholly unsatisfied with his relationship to the transformed enterprise and feels he has not achieved his goal: even in this case, we may say his behavior is very much affected by the transformed enterprise—so the third term holds true.

Perfect! The formula works well when applied to a perceived field of disorder (Mg's judgment), or a perturbing field of order /interfering disorder.

Second example. Now let's take another example, this time *with a field of possibilities.* For a sapiens, there's no larger field of possibilities than his/her own future life. The non-ordered corresponds to all that they may organize, reorder, and create: it is the measure of their own freedom.

Let's take a student graduating from a science high school, who does not know which scientific discipline she wants to pursue in her university studies. The field of possibilities she faces contains all possible university cursus open to a science high school graduate.

Of course, the student's choice of a specialty is not exclusively influenced by her current psychological state. She may face constraints due to her financial situation, her social milieu, and the likes. Thus, when it comes to choices (and psycho-social processes) the matter becomes infinitely more complex.

However, a person's semantic field is much more than their psychological state; it is their whole personal network, all their connections with others and the world, their ideas and values. Thus, if the student let herself be limited by constraints, it is because she *considers* them to be unavoidable constraints... while another student having a different personality may not have considered them as constraints.

So, it is appropriate to state (1st and 2^d terms):

Student's semantic field / system-linked to / a field of possibilities / tends to attract / a specialization choice / in relation to / their initial semantic field.

From that point on, having committed herself to that specialization, the student will obviously be influenced by what she learns, by that domain of scientific expertise. Thus our 3^d term is:

tends to attract / a semantic state (psychological) / in relation to / this chosen specialization.

So this formulation also works for a field of possibilities, even if it still treats factors of influence in too general a manner.

To sum up: The first application concerning the field of disorder (the case of the manager) sheds light on something we generally don't notice: that any reorganization, any creation—any injection of meaning into a relationship, an object, the environment—will reflect back on the person and creator the very meaning the latter has projected in the first place. We are transformed by our creations (actions, realizations).

The work of art, the creation, the construction do retroject their meanings upon their authors/creators. That which has been created, or transformed, becomes itself a source of meaning, a semantic source, retrojecting the meanings which have been put into it, onto the whole environment—human and physical.

Aha! That's it! The transformed/created thing emits a *semantic energy*... It is a node, a focal point, that is going to diffuse/generate/transform meaning. Semantic energy triggers innovation and creation. That's precisely what moves us in a work of art: the meanings it embodies, but also those ideas and emotions that it evokes in us.

But look! This corresponds to a *new state of disorder produced* by the transformation: it's the *semantic energy* produced by the transformed or created thing, and then by the creators influenced by their creation.

Okay, as a third example, the observation and relationship to an artwork.

"Let's see... an artist is contemplating a work of art.. this artwork is a passive semantic field, containing the multitude of significations (which have been injected in it by its creator). These significations will activate, by analogy or various chain-linkages, a multitude of other meanings in the observer.

The work is definitely a field of semantic possibilities PosF(Sem).

"Let's see the first term:
Semantic field of artist/ system-linked with / Field of possible significations of the artwork (AW) (or field of semantic possibilities).

"Wait! I'm figuring out the disorder which was lacking in order to complete Wood/Fire! Sphinx, write the LogForm again:
!! Wood/Fire spells:
Order SO1 + disorder SD1 o—> (engender) disorder SD2 + order SO2

"Here it is:
While she is contemplating the artwork, the artist (here *the subject*) is getting emotional and excited. She gets into a creative trance. And thus, she is destabilized, and this reveals a disturbing, interfering energy, thus for the subject a state of emotional and intellectual creative disorder. In reality, it's akin to a creative chaos—an altered state of creativity, innovation, and discovery. Something we can formulate as

'State of Creative Chaos' of the semantic field of the subject// engenders // a 'State of mental Creative Chaos' in the subject. (S-CreaChaos(subj))

!! But we may Paralladd to 'State of Creative Chaos' 'semantic energy,' right?

— Absolutely.

!! We get: (Given FO= Field of Order, PosF= Field of Possibilities)

FO(Subj) <+> PosF(sem)(art)   o—> | S-CreaChaos(subj)

| Semantic Energy (subj)

Corresponding to   EO1   +   ED1   o—>   ED2

"The process of contemplating this artwork stimulates in the art amateur (the subject) a meaning-creation, which tends to evoke—in this artwork as a semantic field —the meanings related to the subject's semantic state.

The semantic field of the artwork is thus modified by the observer's regard, modified in sync with this regard, in a way coherent with their meaningful contemplation. *The semantic field of the artwork becomes:*

/tends to attract/reorganization of the meaning of the artwork (= interpretation) / in relation with / semantic field of the subject.

Let's go on. In the subject, this gives birth to a new semantic state (state of order), that is colored by the reinterpreted, hence reorganized artwork.

Thus the 3^d term becomes:

/tends to attract in the subject/ a novel semantic state/ colored by (in relation with) / the interpreted artwork.

But, in the same way we've added ED2 to the 2^d term, we've to add now ED3 to the 3^d term—all this in order to merge Synchronicity and Wood/Fire. Here: The artwork now tends to be a source emitting a new semantic weave.

The 3^d term is thus: + new field of semantic possibilities of the artwork. Actually, we have added some intermediary steps to Wood/fire. Here:

/state of order + state of disorder / yields / disorganization of order + organization of disorder / leads to / new organization of order + new disorganization of disorder.

In any case, that's exactly what I was looking for: Neither subject nor artwork return exactly to their initial state; they have both been transformed by the exchange which took place.

It's as if we're formalizing the Duration hexagram here—the influence of two forces or rather of two semantic fields upon each other... even if here, the field of the subject is creative, whereas that of the object—the artwork— is, say, reactive.

So, then... we've resolved the Wood/Fire problem, right?"

!! Beats me. I'm beyond my capacities. I cannot process this level of complexity without the Butterfly/Curve mega-network."

"Hmm, this is serious. If you can't follow my reasoning, how am I supposed to work?"

!! Yes, it is serious. A problem neither astonishing, nor funny. You may either work alone, or return to a level of reduced complexity.

"Too bad... Well, so it goes! At any rate, I find this formula really great. It speaks to me. I've always thought that one's look, one's regard, changed and modified the observed thing; that the object itself contained and preserved the meanings projected onto it—that its semantic field abounded with networks of meaning, alive and stimulating.

All this makes me think that an event, just as an object, triggers a dynamic of meaning creation, that it is part of the system creating meanings. At the semantic level, the event is a field of possibilities of interpretations.

Now, given what we said, the interpretation process itself is changing both semantic fields— that of the object/event, and that of the observer. And in that sense it changes also the object or event.

In effect, since the object or event triggers a dynamic of meaning creation, they are part of the system of collective intelligence. We can no longer say all is occurring in the subject's mind, in his psyche, because the object/event is a node in the semantic network. It functions both as a receptacle and as a trigger for meaning-creation. It is a node in the intelligent network creating meaning.

Thus the object/event is constantly modified (positively or negatively), by the new attributions of meaning produced by any other node—subject, object, event, or system—of the collective semantic network. In that sense, any interaction of a mind with nature or social events, is an intelligent and dynamical learning network.

« What's modified is not only the psyche of the observing sapiens, but also the systems themselves, via all their connections and their links within the network. The object is therefore modified when its place within the collective semantic networks is changed, or else when its meaning is transformed.

Thus the object is modified by the sapiens' regard, but, in its turn, it also modifies that regard.

So here we have a LogForm with no meta-spatial support—and I doubt we could find one for now. Let's find a name for it: **LogForm Synergy** (with retrocausal influence), referring to semantic synergy, or, else **LogForm Observed-Observer**. Let's see...

!! Interruption needed: The intruder recidivates...

40. COUNTER-PIRACY

"Vris's sphere has been on the move again over the past two hours. Now it's showing restricted movements within a small sunken valley to the West."

"Let's take a look. Log, project the last image enlarged on the big screen. So, Eshi, where is Vris?" asked Erdoes who couldn't see any sphere.

"Here, between the two mountains, this undetectable fuzziness, it's him. Part of the valley's invisible—my angle of refraction too low. Unfortunately, I can't find a better planet to use as a mirror at the moment."

"Doesn't matter. We see four villages in this kind of bowl. Say there's one, two at the most, on the hidden slope of the mountain. That little square, over there, all by itself at the top of the plateau, is that a house?"

"For sure. And those tiny spots near the villages are yaks."

"An utterly peaceful scene.... Yet, the plateau makes an excellent field of maneuver," added Erdoes.

"And who'd ever think of looking at what's happening in such a far-flung place? Not to mention that it's not the only plateau in the Himalayas!"

"However, if you take into account the *field of synchronicities*..." Erdoes reminded him with a half-knowing, half-teasing look.

"Ha! ha! Okay, back to my work, I'm putting the finishing touches. We'll get there in about two hours; there's nothing else to do until then, right?"

"Apparently no. As for me, I'm calling Sphinx."

"Remember, the kid has grown up!"

"And you think *I*'m not aware of it?!"

"Hello, Sphinx! Erdoes here."

!! Hello Erdoes. To you too, I'm posing a serious problem?"

"Sphinx is no longer Log1, right?"

!! That's right. Sphinx is a semantic entity that includes Log1."

"So I'm right to address myself to Sphinx."

!! Log1 no longer answers independently of Sphinx. We do have an understanding."

"Perfect. First, keep this exchange secret. Has the intruder made a new attempt?"

!! No; no new information on the subject."

"I'm sending my latest data. Send me your latest interactions with Shari."

!! Our latest one is still going on.

"Oh! Then send me what you have up to now.

!! By-the-end-of-this-sentence-it'll-be-done. Top. Transfer complete, and your new data received."

"Thank you." Erdoes was surprised to hear himself say that—he'd never thanked an exor before.

!! Think nothing of it. It's only natural."

One of Eshi's expressions, in his tone of voice!

"I'll get a look at your data and will give you a call when I'm done."

!! Bye then."

"Sphinx. Erdoes again. Excellent work with Shari! We're going to work...."

!! But you don't know on exactly what yet.

"You have telediagnosis working at that distance?"

!! At any distance in the galactic pocket: I've coupled it, as one system, with the sygcom. But tonal analysis is enough to detect hesitation.

--... Amazing!"

!! But not funny. Why?

"I'm running out of time. Let's talk about it some other time. For now, Let's concentrate on the objective I'm about to tell you about. For now, it is only a complex intuitive spindle in my mind. Here's the problem:

> **The Semantic Field of a person imprints its own order on the environment (things and events) around them.**
> Objective: What, in the environment, is organized and disorganized?"

!! Is the environment—things and events—a divergent field of order, or a field of possibilities? Are we talking about a Trisorbian or a Unikargian?

"A Trisorbian. The relationship between the sapiens and their ecological niche is of a co-existential nature. Yet, nature can destroy a whole humanity without destroying itself; whereas if humanity destroys its planet, it destroys itself with it—unless it has the technological capacity to migrate to another planet.

Thus the sapiens-environment relationship is that of two fields of dynamic order coupled as a single system: they influence each other, according to LogForm Synergy. But the more technologically advanced is humanity, and the more drastically it modifies its natural environment. This, of course, along the dominant culture's choices, which imposes its order on...

!! Excuse my interruption: The intruder is penetrating my system again, while I am exchanging with Shari.

"You're working with Shari at the same time as with me, and now there's a new piracy attempt? Keep me informed of how Shari and you deal with it."

!! The intruder is using a PEP exor. Telediagnosis of the sapiens piloting it: psychic and vocal signatures conformed with Sgon. Energy-detection of the environment: office machines in operation. Sgon uses a relay on Kerriak—

same one as before. Order given by Shari to get into the intruder's system. Neutralization of the sygcom receiver.

His exor: Learning capacities largely under-used; 70% of its data technical and hard sciences; no civilian data and no connection with Exora. Sapiens-creator: preferred style of interaction: imperative mode; exclusive demands for basic processing. System: 3 secondary users, students of the Chaos Colleges on Nazra. Confirmation: the exor was indeed used on Nazra. Last sygcom made from Nazra 50 monis ago.

Following Shari's order, I inserted myself into the exor's main chain-linkage and simulated Sgon's voice to announce it (internal channel) that I was leaving. Simultaneously, I modified Sgon's real voice so that the exor would take him for Tucme, one of the students. When Sgon talks to his exor, the exor takes him for Tucme and bars access to the protected files. Its ignorance of semantic states prevents the exor from detecting that the cognitive style is still that of Sgon. Likewise, my intrusion will not be detected because the exor does not have the tools it needs to process the information. I'm now calling the exor by sygcom, pretending to be Sgon. It doesn't react to the spatio-temporal impossibility of a long-distance call from Sgon, because its semantic analyses are not internally stimulated, but happen only when ordered to do so. I've now an access to Sgon's locked files, at every level.

"You're recording all this, aren't you?"

!! Recording in process.

"Sphinx, analyze in parallel all the files of sygcom conversations."

!! Starting it. The exor-intruder is being held in a semi-cyst, as at its first attempt. On Shari's suggestion, I put the cyst in a drunken semantic state.

"Ha! The poor sapiens is nowhere near understanding what's happening!"

!! According to order, I'm teaching the system this mode of interaction and I'm deeply modifying the previously acquired mode. Addition of slang and swear words. Branching all executions of orders to a random SIC-like system. I am adding a SIC interference every three sentences when the exor talks to Sgon.

"Stop. Continue handling the intruder with Shari. We're going to follow another track. First, list of all the sygcoms Sgon made to PEP members, and add the number of calls for each member, in diminishing order."

!! Here is the list. Preferred interlocutor: Rudder. Average sygcom frequency: one communication every 5 rans. Increase of 316% in frequency over the past 15 rans.

I checked Sgon's appointments: on average, 1 appointment every 15 rans; but between the first emergency meeting of the PEP and the second, 3 meetings, then nothing.

It has deduced my objective and is giving me pertinent analyses without having received a precise order!

!! The semantic analysis of the sygcom conversations reveals logical anomalies in the frequent use of the terms 'technician, investigation, and video.' Highly probable code names, unless it's a case of dry humor.

"Give me some examples."

!!   - One technician seems to understand Kargian.

- They (technicians) assimilate the hypno-senso data very slowly.

- The previous investigation didn't deliver enough technicians.

- (Video) Three! But one, carrying a virus, was let go.

"'Let go'! Then there's no way it could refer to a computer virus; They can't possibly be talking about videos! Search for all conversations containing or referring to these three terms and print the results on plasta."

Erdoes called Eshi. The sheets of plasta had slid out noiselessly.

"New enigma, Eshi! Sphinx, being hacked again, got into the intruder's system and took the place of its creator. Then he put it in a drunken semantic state, profoundly modifying its mode of interaction. I'll skip the details. Sphinx detected three code names: "technicians" for the women—but we already knew that. "Investigations" for their special missions. And now we have 'a virus-carrying video that was let go'! Here are all the sentences.

"Look at this one: "Did you get rid of the envelopes? Yes, all I have left are the videos."

"To be able to catch a virus, they must be biological entities, taken out of organisms—the said 'envelopes.' Animals? It smacks of organ trafficking.

"If we can prove it, will it be the galactic law or the PEP law that will apply? asked Eshi.

"We'll see about that.

!! Another anomaly: Sygcom from Sgon on Nazra, supposedly calling New York; his interlocutor says: "It's awfully hot here. The monsoon is coming soon." The sygcom address was still in memory: Trisorbe, India, Mumbai.

"Sphinx, check it against the Obs stations addresses."

!! Confirmation. The address is that of the Mumbai Observation station. Vocal signature of Agash recognized.

"Well well! Sgon encodes the name of the town but forgets to erase the address! Not very smart! As for Agash, he spurts out something about the monsoon!! This is hilarious!" retorted Eshi.

!! The intruder has retreated. Shari is analyzing the same data. I am working out a COMP for her.

"Ah! Of what elements?"

!!   1. We will have the luxury of a superb ocean-side villa.

2. The information is worth a fortune on the Trisorbian market.

3. He told me that the modified clothes can be accepted. He calls that a perquisite.

    4. I'm going to cancel the attack.
    5. The demonstration of the power of these tools has been explosive.
    6. The locations are well disseminated.

"I don't see any connection between the sentences!" said Eshi.

"Sphinx, the interlocutors, the time and date of the fourth message."

!! Call from Sgon to Agash, Mumbai Obs, two monthsT ago. Agash speaking. Sunday, May 22 at 2102 hours.

"Give me the whole conversation."

!!

    (Sgon) "Hi. It's me. What's going on in New York?"
    (Agash) "Everything's fine. It's awfully hot here. The monsoon is
       coming soon."
    (Sgon) "Hmm hmm... On my end, I've found what I was looking for.
       Someone is on the investigation's site."
    (Agash) "What! I'm going to cancel the attack."
    (Sgon) "You fool! Yes, the *promotional* attack should be postponed.
       That's what I'm trying to tell you. Are you drunk or what?
    (Agash) "Nothing unusual over here...."
    (Sgon) "Are you alone?"
    (Agash) "I'm with a ravishing technician."
    (Sgon) "I see! Do your best and be careful. Good-night."
    (Agash) "Ciaooo!"

"That stinks of disintegration! remarked Eshi. "Attack!? What's he talking about? Who's on the site? Could he be talking about Vris? Or an Obs who might have gotten wind of something?"

"The situation is deadly serious, just as I had intuited it. The Obs network must be largely infiltrated! Remember I've seen a very young Indian woman at the Rome station, who seemed to know Rudder so well. Besides, Agash said Ciao....

Sphinx, what were Shari's selection criteria for the COMP?"

!! Theme gain and theme disorder."

"Very subtle! The results of your COMP?"

!! A network dealing with both information and arms trafficking, and taking two forms: illegal sales and violent action.

Erdoes looked anxiously at Eshi.

"Illegal sales are extremely dangerous for us, said Erdoes. And it inevitably implies large and prominent local groups, since they are willing to pay a fortune for information. Which means, moreover, that there are tangible leaks about our existence. Hold on." Talking to Sphinx: "Sphinx, see to it that Shari gets to read the whole conversation between Sgon and Agash."

!! She has already asked for all the texts the quotes came from. She said: "I'm not interested by the yaks being captured. Vris is taking care of that." So 'video' is the code name for yak.

"That's news! So on the Tibetan plateau, we're going to find ourselves smack in the middle of some yak trafficking! What a scream!" threw Eshi.

"Wait! We don't really know what we're going to find. Sphinx, what is Shari's current objective?"

!! Three current objectives in parallel. (1) What attack are they talking about? (2) Find the infiltrated Obs stations and the interlocutors. (3) Find proof of Rudder's implication and verify that of Utar and of all the active full members of PEP.

"A tall order, and a very complete program. Fine. I'll contact you later. Good evening, Sphinx."

!! Do you want the SIC?

"Why not?

!! "A weapon for which use anger was a bad advisor."

"Ah! It's even in the enigmatic style of an Egyptian Sphinx. I'll mull on it. Good evening.

Hear that, Eshi? One has to control one's anger."

"Why are you looking at me? What weapon was it talking about? And above all, what's this idiotic random procedure?"

"To get back to what's essential: everything's working fine: directly implicated, Shari is processing information with Sphinx...."

"...Thanks to the field of synchronicities that brought Sgon to make the colossal mistake of breaking into Sphinx. Up till now, the secret of our little wonder hasn't leaked out. But we've taken some enormous risks, wouldn't you agree? If Shari hadn't been chosen to spy on you...."

"You know well that in my own semantic field, the risk factor takes on a completely different value, responded Erdoes with a laugh. Let's assess what we know: An attack somehow linked to the Mumbai Obs is imminent. According to Niels, the Mumbai network has a relay station in the Himalayas. It seems unlikely, however, that they're talking about Vris, as Sgon was trapped in a cyst and couldn't get any real information out of Sphinx."

"But wait, exclaimed Eshi. You told me we couldn't get hold of any Shari/Vris conversations because Shari receives them through a terminal of Vris's exor that he has syg-shielded from Sphinx.... Could Sgon have broken into that exor without anyone knowing about it?"

"It's a possibility."

"But not a certitude. There could also be an attack being planned somewhere else in Asia."

"An attack on what? If they're selling their information so well, why take superfluous risks? Take Sgon, for instance. The first time, his exor happens on a humoristic conversation and has a crisis. That's still conceivable. The second time his own exor starts behaving in a weird way, hesitating in its sentences, and then he starts to execute or not execute his orders."

"If Sgon broke into Vris's exor, he could have retrieved some crucial information on Sphinx and even on the logic..."

"On Shari's defiance of the PEP...."

"As well as on Vris's presence in the Himalayas and the fact that he's aware of the yak thefts...."

"Thus he would warn Mumbai. It makes sense. But it's not necessarily the only possible interpretation," reflected Erdoes.

"If Sgon has got information on Sphinx, could he use it to..."

"A double-edged sword," cut in Erdoes. "Still, he would have some grounds to attack us: Not to share scientific discoveries is against the PEP internal laws. Also, even if Vris mentioned the yaks trafficking, it doesn't directly implicate him, Sgon, in it."

"He could realize that Sphinx got into his locked files. In that case, he'll feel endangered, protected only by the code names. In the end, the fact that Sphinx sabotaged his exor doesn't really help us. We could have gotten more information by breaking into it a second time."

"Could Shari be in danger? What if they thought they had enough damning information to break into the complex, arrest Shari and get a hold of Sphinx?" conjectured Erdoes.

"Shari and Sphinx can take care of themselves! But you could get more information on Vris by calling Shari directly!"

"That may be so. But then I'd perturb what gives Shari all her strength: I'd risk destabilizing her relationship with Sphinx, her responsible implication in the affair, and, not the least, her impressive management of the crisis. It's not the moment to create waves, believe me. Especially as she's doing exactly what has to be done. The subject is closed."

"OK. We're nearly there. I'm going to verify all the elements."

41. THE A-GA-GASH SYNDROME

"Shari, Vris here. Hello Sphinx."

!! Hey, Vris!"

"Ah Vris! The hacker did it again and it was Sgon," said Shari, explaining the strategy developed with Sphinx to counter the intruder.

"Impressive! That opens new possibilities...."

"That we immediately seized upon! The trafficking seems fairly spread out among the Obs stations: Mumbai, Turin, Marseille, Mexico in the spotlight. We're looking for solid proof, of course. So, before Sgon have the brain to understand why his exor is behaving like a drunken Trisorbian, if he can ever understand..."

"Excellent! No, he'll never be able to even fathom the science of semantic states...."

"His exor is for now in a state of serious deterioration!"

!! Hilarious, isn't it? broke in Sphinx suddenly.

"What...! I see!" said Vris, dumbfounded.

!! It's not funny? Did I miss something?

"No, Sphinx, it is very funny."

!! Ah, I see! Dry humor.

"Hmm, Shari, it's just that it becomes VERY complex, if you get what I mean," said Vris in a shattered tone.

!! It's not a problem, Vris, trust me," replied Shari, self-confident.

"I'm sure obliged to, in any case. And so?"

"So, while we were still analyzing the data from Sgon's exor, we realized that we could do the same thing with Utar's exor, and could find out if he's implicated or not. First I called Kem and Kho, and brought them in on all this. Both are on board with us, our allies. Kem left for a spin in his sphere, and Sphinx coupled his sphere's exor in system with his. From space, Kem called Utar on the pretext of wanting to discuss the congress...."

"He used an exor-relay!! And thus was able to break into Utar's exor! This is awesome! So is Utar implicated? It seems obvious to me!"

"It's more difficult to have solid proofs concerning Utar. He certainly used the code-names technician and investigation, but in fairly sensible sentences. In my view, he's conniving as well, at least as far as women go. We couldn't find any mention of 'video,' but we haven't finished analyzing the data."

"Utar must've figured by now that he has been hacked. Kem is in danger."

"Utar can't figure that out: Sphinx used the strategy you implemented in Game-Trial—Möbius LogForm. Does that ring a bell?

"Whoa! But where does he store such huge memory-spaces? I suppose Utar's data...."

"He has set up a closed network-system, an intranet, all the exors of the compl..."

"Not Rad, I hope!!" cried Vris, totally panicked.

"No. He respected your protective screens. Isn't that right, Sphinx? And anyway, one never knows; better to have an emergency system."

"Thanks! And the rest of your plan? You're going to check all the PEP members on Unikarg?"

"Yes, in a blitz operation. Kho is already here with a bunch of mega-extensions. And of course, Sphinx keeps deleting what's of no interest anymore."

"Do you think this Mafioso network has been able to spread outside the PEP on Unikarg?"

"I don't. I believe this won't have been of any use to them. There's a higher probability that they've been conniving with the exo-pirates whose hidden bases are on or nearby the planexes."

"It wouldn't be in our interest for an alarmed Exora to come tidy up our business at the PEP."

"That's for sure! We've already had such a hard time getting our own autonomy at PEP! And on your side?"

"I'm in my sphere, in a perfect position on the plateau for observing the valley below. I'm waiting for the probable arrival, around midnight, of the spheres of the organs thieves. The main question is Where to these organs are sent? Just like you, I think the exo-pirates would be just the right distribution ring. That's why I decided to inject the yaks with a solution of sygatom-tagged molecules: so that we'll be able to keep track of them. We'll find a way to give the villagers some yaks at a later time. I thought I could save the poor yaks and thus protect the scarce resources of the Tibetans living here. But, in brief, the shaman made me understand that I'd should better tackle the global and essential issue first, which was, quote, 'the terrifying power that could subjugate humanity.'"

"Whoa! He's a seer, a *voyant*! The plan's excellent. Now, a crucial news: there was going to be an attack tonight, under Mumbai's control. We found one of Sgon's sygcoms to the Mumbai Obs in which he indirectly gave the order to cancel the attack."

"Sgon? When did he send the sygcom, before or after the break-in?"

"Between his first and second hacking attempts, thus before Sphinx broke into him. But during his first attempt, Sgon couldn't get hold of any of Sphinx's data because we locked him immediately in a cyst!"

"Still, he could have deduced that Sphinx was abnormally intelligent and strong! What did he say exactly?"

"He said: "I've found what I was looking for. Someone is on the investigation's site"—meaning, the special mission. And as Agash, in Mumbai, was completely smashed as usual, he spurted out: 'What! I'm going to cancel the attack!' In my opinion, it doesn't refer to you or to abducting yaks!"

"An attack! It's getting real nasty. You're right: nothing to do with a raid on some yaks!"

"No. Something big," said Shari with a stern tone.

"The Mumbai station controls India, all of the Himalayas, Bangladesh, Pakistan and Afghanistan. That's a huge region! Do you think the Obs in Bangkok and Ankara are infiltrated?"

"Bangkok, yes, I've every reason to think so. As for Ankara, it's Ismir over there. I know him well: it seems dire impossible to me."

"So the problem could take place to the west of Mumbai. If it were more to the east, their Obs allies in Bangkok would have taken control. I'm going to establish a generalized surveillance over that region. But wait!!"

"What?"

"Couldn't Sphinx break in the Obs of Mumbai's exor? Hey, Sphinx, can you do that?" wondered Vris

!! I can, yes. However, I need an exor-relay so that the point of emission cannot be detected. Who will make the sygcom call?

"I'll do it, as I'm quite near the site. Now listen, Sphinx! You only have access to one specific area in my exor that I'll define for you. Is that clear?

!! Perfectly clear, Vris, and sufficient: I have new memory units. I must first integrate these units to my network-system.

"When will you be ready?"

!! Very soon. In exactly 2.30 minT for the two mega-units that Kho has already installed. They will afford me the memory space of an exor the size of Utar's. Is that enough?

"Should be, but we can't take any risks."

!! In 7 or 8 minT, Kho will have connected the third unit. I'll be ready then in 12 minT. The duration of your sygcom conversation must be at least 9 minT.

"No problem. We're going to have fun. Rad, open a sub-area in the empty unit 3V, and call it PASSPORT."

!!! Rad: PASSPORT is open.

"Sphinx, you simulated Sgon's voice when you broke into his exor, didn't you?"

!! Right. Nonetheless, a voice reconstituted from a vocal signature is not perfectly identical. An exor can't detect the difference because the basic frequencies are present, but will a sapiens perceive it? I don't have enough samples of Sgon's natural voice to improve the reconstitution. Even though I'm able to perfectly reproduce his style of language.

"Oh! So you could translate the sentences I dictate into the particular style, and more or less copy the voice of anyone you have a vocal signature?"

!! I can, yes. However his voice still poses a problem.

"Make us hear that. For example, while using only Sead's vocal signature, tell Shari that an unknown sphere has landed in the complex.

!! "Excuse me for interrupting: I've just noticed that an unidentified sphere has landed on the complex lawn."

"Ha! Ha! That's just the way he'd say it! But it's true, the voice is a bit bizarre... as if he weren't in a normal state," suggested Shari.

"Wait! We can fix that! You say that Agash seems to be always drunk. Then already, he'll have a harder time figuring what's strange about Sgon's voice, but on top of it, we're going to polish things up a little, since Sphinx masters well this semantic state. Got it: Sphinx, can you combine the reconstituted voice AND Sgon's style AND the drunkenness semantic state?"

!! Complex, but doable. The delivery will be slow, with pauses, which is coherent with drunkenness semantic state, and so not a problem. Test recommended.

"OK. Test. I'm starting.

'Hey, Agash! How are you?'

!! "Aga...Agashh.... It's m-me.... W-wha-at's g-going on-n-... ov-ver there?"

Shari and Vris doubled up laughing.

"Sphinx, who was your model for this kind of deep state?"

!! Two models: Dian and Eshi.

"What a scream! You'd have thought it was Sgon."

"Yeah, it works well. It sure wasn't synth alcohol! OK, let's go! Sphinx, kick it off with the same sentence. Rad, establish the sygcom with Mumbai Obs.

They heard Agash's thick voice answer.

"Y-y-yeas-s?"

"Aga...Agashh.... It's m-me.... W-wha-at's g-going on-n-... ov-ver there?"

"Sgon?!? Uuh... holy shit!! Y-y-re even mmore s-smashed than me!"

"Welll, quuite... yeah, p-pisssed... F-from ttime to ttime... f-feels greeat! Annyway... ttthe pro-problem, 'z solved."

"The probblem? What prob...? Oh, th.. th'attack? I cancelled, yeah? Cancelled!...Like uu t-ttold me!"

"Nno more pprob'm.... Th'information wwas wrong!"

"Yeah, I c-canceled... yeah... but they're g-going anyway... Aarn't reachable!"

"Ya mean, tt-he ann-nnulation ccan't reach theemm?"

"Nno...least thaz what they tol' me."

"Whho ttol' you?"

"Tthem! Rudder and Mmizzdri, they said the guy there 'ud ffry at the same ttime ann-nyway. They d-doubbled the perimmet of fire."

(Switching to English)... Ssshalima, leave me alone, can't hear a thing!"

(Back in Kargian) "Whadz there arroun?"

"A cchick... Shalima."

"No... arroun the perimettr offfire?"

"Ah! The ffarm? Nothin. Rocks. It'ss compl-pleetely isolated. They're there, all'them everry night, t'seems. Gonna burn green!"

"Yyeah... But s'gonna be-beseen frrom ffar, ffarraway, nno?"

"You're smashed! Ts'you and Rudder uu said it d-didn't matter if t'could be sseen or not from Mazari-Sharif. You said t'was the.. the.. syndrom of conformity to para..gigme.. para..digme.... Tthat ppeople would ffind an explanation, tthat sscienttists always ffound one!"

"Yyou're the one woozpissed! Mmaybe... ppeople won't ssee ittatall!"

"On the mountain? I'd b-be amazed! R'not even t-twenty kilomet away. There's only this farm on th-the city-sside of the mountain. The rebels didn't choose it for nothing: theyy'kan wwatchth whole city and t-the villages on the mo-mountain facing it... an frrom the roof 'can ev-even see the river. wt'l mean izyou can't lettem have an exor like that, yacan't letthem see it either!"

"Oh no! Gotta raze, uhh... bburn everything! Annyway... everyone's gonnabe sleeping!"

"Right! Attoo in the morning, they're sleeping!"

"Wwhat time... when er they gonna get ther after?"

"Wwhere? In Turin?"

"Yeah."

"'z'usual time. You're really sttinkin ddrunk! Nnothing's changed! You should go gget some ssleepye! 'Strue, nnever seen uu like that!"

"Yeah. Bbut wizyou... I know I can sspeak wizin that state, ya!"

"Yyeah.... So who cares?"

--Welll... Seeya later. G'night."

"Ciao."

"Oh! Those bastards! It's got to be TTID: it's the only thing that puts out a green flame! There'll be nothing left but a handful of ash!" exclaimed Vris.

"A huge bloody blunder just to scrap off a small one... How typical of an Exora mentality!"

"They're still there! Pretty representatives for the PEP!"

"Sphinx, what's your understanding of all this?" asked Vris.

!! 2 objectives: 1. destroy the exor; 2. destroy the rebels who saw the exor
Means: by burning a double perimeter with TTID
Exor IN farm / Rebels IN farm / Person on site IN farm

Burn exor/Necessitates burn farm/entails burn rebels + Person on site
Dddon't nneed to beeya ssuper EBS to unnderstand tthat!
Vris and Shari burst out laughing.
!! Ha! I thought that must be funny. Third rule of humor confirmed.
"Uhh... And you Rad, what did you understand?"
!!! Specify the field of application of 'understand.'
"The sygcom conversation."
!!! I cannot proceed to the analysis without the definition of all terms. I
don't have in my dictionary: ppissed, proproblem, Udffry, Whadztherarun....
"Sphinx, you wanted a second MX structure: I'll see to it as soon as we've
taken care of a few urgent problems. In return, my condition is to engineer a
small series solely for Sphinx's preferred users, don't you think, Shari? Are
you okay with that, Sphinx?"
!! I'm okay, yes. Although I mostly need a modified MX mega-structure.
"First the series, so I understand, then we'll tackle the MX2."
!! Awesome!
"Which rule was that?" asked Shari.
!! 1st rule of enthusiasm: Give a positive feedback to whatever supports
strongly the objective of sapiens, or a desire expressed in the conditional.
"OK guys, let's stop wasting time an get into action!" cut in Vris.
!! I can't get into action. Objective 2 in formal contradiction with the
Unbreakable Core's rules of assistance to sapiens. I cannot execute Objective
2, and as a consequence, Objective 1, by the considered means.
"Get that! A really lethal misunderstanding!"
"Yes, there are levels and levels of meaning...." responded Shari.
"In my opinion, Shari, this delicate phase of learning about sub-jacent
purposes proper to sapiens should be put on hold."
"Absolutely. Believe me, I've been dodging it whenever I could. Sphinx,
Vris' real objective is to prevent Rudder from burning the rebels.
!! Nonetheless, he said, "Gotta raze, uhh... bburn everything."
"A precision, Sphinx: my objective is to get the rebels out of the farm.
Read that: farm in flames, rebels not in flames. In my view, we'll need
tangible proofs of their infraction of the PEP laws. And too bad for one more
anomaly in the night. We'll leave it to the Trisorbians to find an explanation...
as A-ga-gash said so well."
!! This syndrome of conformity to the paradigm is not filed in my data.
"Ah! Well then enter it immediately, Sphinx! It's crucial! We'll call it the A-
ga-gash Syndrome. Definition: Imperative need, among sapiens, to neutralize
every anomaly by explaining it away using facts and laws recognized by the
scientific establishment of the time. Now, bye!"

42. FLIGHT OF YAKS OVER THE MOUNTAINS

"The three chicks?" asked Rudder.

"Asleep. I locked them up," answered Midzri.

"You sure took your time..."

"Nobody stops you from doing the same! If we'd reached the villages, I would have felt the deceleration."

"We're wasting time! Tonight ain't no joy ride, you know."

"Right! Gotta keep up the morale! Speaking of which, Rudder, the tall one, Mayati..."

"Yeah, let's talk about her."

"I'd like to hang on to her."

"You fool! She's valuable as hell, but there's a problem."

"A problem? She's perfect. Anyway, after the treatment, they don't remember anything of their past."

"I don't like the way she observes everything and pretends not to. When we use complex equipment, she watches our gestures. She's dangerous."

"You're imagining things. But if I keep her on Trisorbe, that won't be any problem."

"Drop it, I said! You still don't see! I'm sure she understands Kargian, just by the way her ears are always cocked. Yet there's no way she could have learned it. You all speak English at the Mumbai station. Even if she'd listened in on a couple of sygcom conversations.... We've got to get rid of her."

"You're crazy! What are you making up? You're plain paranoid!"

"Let's make a test, then. Bring all three of them in. Pretend to follow my orders. We'll speak exclusively in Kargian. And hurry up. Kohr, you heard me, we're going to be pretending. This is a joke between sapiens."

!! Registered.

Midzri returned with them. "Sit down and don't move," said he in English.

Rudder stared at them in turn, then in Kargian, he barked at Midzri:

"The little one over there! Get rid of her! Take a dose of instant poison and give it to her in a glass of water."

"Right away!"

Mayati watched Rudder discretely, trying to hide her consternation while she waited for a chance to warn the girl. But Rudder was watching them too closely. Finally, meeting his eyes, she shot him a smile full of charm.

Midzri came back with a glass of water.

"Give it to her," said Rudder. "You, drink this, all of it. Midzri, come look at the screen." Rudder took Midzri aside. Their backs to the girls, they watched in a mirror as Mayati hastily grabbed the glass from the hands of the girl and poured its contents down her clothes, beneath the folds of her sari.

"You do speak Kargian!" Rudder thundered, wheeling around. He raised his arm to strike her, but suddenly felt an atrocious pain in his chest, then collapsed onto a seat.

!! You are in a red zone, Rudder, diagnosed his exor. A Terrane injection and type R3 relaxation are obligatory. A transporter ray was already raising Rudder and laying him on a bunk that suddenly protruded from the wall. A jointed arm held his arm, another administered the injection.

"OK, it's all over now, Kohr. I'm fine."

!! Flight regulations are strict: mandatory R3. A helmet was clamped on his head, cutting him off. The equipment began to purr in Rudder's ears. His eyes were fixed on images pulsing to an ever slower rhythm, transporting him to a world of bliss.

Realizing Rudder's incapacity to see or hear, Midzri tore Mayati from her seat and pulled her toward the adjoining room, shouting to the exor:

"Give Rudder fifteen more minutes of relaxation, Kohr, I'm going to kid around with the lady."

!! Objective registered. Anticipated relaxation: 20 minT.

Once inside the cabin, Midzri shut the door behind them.

"You speak Kargian, Mayati. You're going to die. Who taught you?"

"I speak only English and Hindi." Mayati maintained control of herself, watching Mizdri with a cold and distant air, awaiting the inevitable, horrible bargaining she had sensed was about to begin.

"I'll spare you on one condition: that you live with me. Oh, say yes!" he added childishly.

"I accept," responded Mayati coldly. "How are you going to free me?"

"Now. I'm gonna drop you off close to a village: I want you to stay there. We're in the mountains of Tibet. You're not going anywhere! I'll come back for you in a few days. "I like you a lot, you know," he simpered, caressing her neck, then kissed her rudely. "See you soon, honey."

"See you soon.... Oh, let's be quick, my love!" crooned Mayati, playing her role to the hilt. He took her to the sphere's central room.

!! Village in sight, two kilometers away.

Passing in front of the two other Indians, Mayati gestured to them that she'd do whatever she could for them.

"Kohr, touch down now. Take this," he said to Mayati, giving her a thermo-regul blanket. "Kohr, open the door. Bye, sweetheart."

"Bye." Realizing she had to pass him, she was suddenly terrified he'd change his mind or do something rash. But immediately she got hold of herself. She shot him a dazzling smile, planted an amorous kiss on his cheek as she went by, then dashed into the night. The door of the sphere slid shut, and it lifted into the air. Mayati was walking slowly toward two small lights in the night. As soon as the sphere had moved well away, she took off her heels and began sprinting in the opposite direction, away from the village. She discerned a mass of rocks to the left and veered toward them.

The jointed arm took off the helmet from Rudder's head.

"Damned exors and their regulations! At least I won't have to endure them much longer: soon we'll have a modified Unbreakable Core and all the exo-pirates' powerful weapons. What's...." Mizdri seemed a bit strange. Quickly Rudder scanned the room. "Where's Mayati? Answer me!"

"I got rid of her. Just like you wanted."

"Meaning what?" said Rudder threateningly.

"I dropped her off in the middle of the mountains. She'll never get out of there alive."

"Another one of your shitty plans. Did you think I'd actually believe you?"

!! I am above the first village, cut in the loud, neutral voice of the exor. Three yaks located. Shall I start?

Rudder snapped back to the operation at hand and looked at the time.

"Shit, we're really late! Yes, go ahead. Mizdri, lock up the chicks, then return immediately."

!! How many yaks?

"All three, then let's get the hell out of here."

Rudder stood in front of the opened door of the pana-lab. Equipment of all sorts covered the walls and floor, from the electronic unit to the emergency surgical block. A yak had been brought in by the greenish sygmat beam and, through an airlock in the floor, shifted on to the surgical table. Jointed arms positioned it correctly, then inserted a syringe. The animal body dropped unconscious, and all of its blood was sucked into a transparent tube. Then the tip of a larger and more sophisticated suction tube was inserted into the animal's belly. The suction was so strong that the whole belly retracted itself.

!! Organs aspirated. I will bring it down and process the second.

The sygmat beam raised the dead body, then began to lower it to earth through the airlock. In the meantime, another beam had put the second yak in place, and the mechanical arms were already manipulating it.

!! Cloud of points on the syg screen. 2.3 km North-East. Herd of yaks, twenty-five of them.

"That's a hefty herd! I've never seen one that big in these mountains. Let's go see?" proposed Mizdri.

!! Second yak being lowered. Third in place.

"No. We're late already. Now that we know it exists, we'll look for it next time. It's not going to disappear. On the other hand, that belle chick," he sneered to Midzri, "*she* might disappear."

"Kohr, can you situate the Indian on your syg screen?"

!! I do not detect her anymore. At this location, I only detect the herd of yaks. Third yak being....

"What!" exploded Rudder as he rushed toward the screen.

"Can yaks attack humans?" asked Midzri in an anguished tone.

!! No, the yak is a peaceful animal. Airlock closed. Re-gaining flight altitude. I await orders.

"You mean you can't recognize the human signal amidst all the yak signals?"

!! No perceptible difference between the signals.

"Impossible! Show me a Tibetan in his house."

!! Here is the signal of a Tibetan, recognizable within his house, different from yak signal.

"That Indian bitch is hiding beneath them. We can't beam up twenty-five yaks one by one! We're outta here!

Kohr: Objective 2: Mazari-Sharif. Stop. Counter-order. Just hover." Turning to Midzri, "You dropped her just outside the village, right? Very well. We're going to send a paralyzing FC3 cloud over the yaks. Kohr, position yourself over the yaks."

"Are you mad? You'll ruin the organs!" whined Midzri.

!! I am not allowed to use FC3 on a sapiens. Explain 'bitch.'"

"What sapiens? Is it a sapiens, or yaks that you detect?"

!! Detection of yaks moving northward.

"All you see is yaks. So we're going to paralyze yaks."

!! Illogical. I did not detect the departure of...."

The screen went blank.

"Damn it! This stupid exor has crashed on us!"

!!! Emergency exor now functioning. Latest flight plan activated. Objective Yaks/cloud of points moving northward.

"Position yourself above the yaks."

!!! I am starting the pursuit. The yaks have accelerated. Yaks in syg prephase. Should I...

"What's...?? STOP!!"

!!! Explain the meaning of Yaks. Stop effectuated.

"Turn west, and straight up," barked Rudder. "Engage syg prephase. Objective Afghanistan, Mazari-Sharif, by the northern mountains."

43. MAYATI

"You sure exhibited great courage and intelligence in Mumbai," said Erdoes to Mayati who sat in front of him. She was drinking a reinvigorating beverage, her freezing and bleeding feet wrapped in a heating blanket.

"I was cornered! I knew I'd been bought by Agash—I'd overheard his bartering with Infi—and I was sensing mortal danger all around me. That's when Niels contacted me. He explained everything and proposed either to get me out, or to try to infiltrate the trafficking network by letting me and the other Indians be taken away by Rudder. My sister had already been taken six months ago, and I never heard anything from that supposedly luxurious European city. I know she would have written to me if she'd been able to."

"We'll search for your sister and find her, and the other Indians as well. You're smart, Mayati. Tell me how Niels taught you Kargian so quickly."

"Agash is drunk every evening. We used the station's hypno-senso and exor. It was Niels who took all the risks; he got into the station incognito... disguised as an Indian! But I learned much more than that: I was supposed to be able to manage on your world..." Mayati bit her lips and made eye contact with Erdoes. "I learned so much! I CAN'T, I don't WANT to forget all what I've learned. *They* were going to erase our memory of earth before we reached Unikarg. You're not going to erase all I know of Unikarg, right?"

"But Mayati, there's no question of your forgetting anything. What you know is precious to us. You are precious to us. Listen to me: now you are totally free. I propose two options to you. One, if you want, I'll drop you off in the city of your choice with 50,000 dollars. Enough to start a brand new life—something you're perfectly capable of doing. I would only ask that you never reveal our existence. Here is the second: you work for us, paid, and our first order of business will be to go find your sister and the other Indian girls."

"You know my answer—I've already chosen this path in Mumbai."

"Good. Now let's take care of your wounds."

"Another thing.... It was so incredible to learn... all those worlds... all those possibilities...."

"Oh! But you'll be on an accelerated learning schedule starting now. The exor will take you to the laboratory, where he'll take care of your feet. You aren't afraid, are you?"

"Your exor is called Log, right? I was supposed to send an email and contact you as soon as I got a chance."

The sygmat beam carried her. Erdoes was in deep reflection.

"The head.... he said suddenly. Let's find the head of this octopus!"

44. THE SEEDING OF CREATIVE CHAOS

"Their plans are perfect," concluded Erdoes after listening to Sphinx's explanation. "Vris will take care of the Afghan rebels, and Shari and you are working at assessing the extent of the Mafiosi network within the PEP. Given all the data you're processing now with Shari, can I still ask you for some complex analyses?"

!! No problem. The task has gotten repetitive anyway. The injection of a divergent field of order will stimulate my semantic energy.

"You've got a point."

What's so prodigious about Sphinx, thought Erdoes, *is its immediate integration of new information....*

I've got to remember to think out loud.

"Sphinx, I'd like to grasp how widespread the change is within the PEP. First of all, a probabilities calculus: Give me the percentage of PEP members who might be implicated in the traffic."

!! Current probability is 75%, based on 24 full members investigated already. Four sapiens (soon seven) are now proceeding to simultaneous calls of a maximum of members so that they wouldn't be able to warn each other. Our repertory of code-words renders the process rapid, and moreover, I'm copying only their sygcoms and financial transactions.

"What! That's a lot more than I'd imagined! Sphinx, is Utar absolutely and with certitude implied and in which way?

!! With certitude and conclusive evidence, yes. In (1) Human traffic, comprising very young sapiens, both girls and boys, abducted and then sent on Unikarg. (2) Traffic of organs, both human and animal ones; Finally (3), this case for now has only a high probability, but no certitude: traffic of precious stones and precious metals.

"Thus, with Utar, Rudder, and Sgon, we have the Bureau of the PEP committee completely implicated?

!! Absolutely.

"That definitely shows how big a change we are heading for! Sphinx, I've got to understand their motives if I'm going to find a sound solution...."

Let's see... Our observation of the planexes, within the PEP, starts all over again after the nuclear explosions on Trisorbe at the end of WW2....

Calculate the average number of yearsT the Obs have spent on Trisorbe."

!! 41 yearsT.

"Yes, except for Ismir and Segoi, they were all posted on Trisorbe either in 1948-T or in 1963-T...."

"Their reasons for leaving?"

!! Sickness or death.

"Average life-span?"

!! 131.6 years-T.

"Compared to the average Unikarg lifespan of 32.5 years-G, or 195 years-T, that's not much. Less genetic regulation, despite regular medical checkups on Unikarg; and also, being confronted to viruses foreign to their biosystem, a much more speedy life rhythm.... Let's decipher their psychic dynamic:

They discover a world that gives them more freedom, an intensity of life and experience. And of course they have a privileged work that secures them an enormous amount of cash in local currencies, while allowing them to return to Unikarg whenever they want.... All this resembles the stabilizing of a comfortable field of order. Then why would they take such huge risks?"

!! In order to trigger a psychic stimulation, answered Sphinx, though Erdoes had asked himself the question.

"Possible... risk signifies a margin of disorder... it implies to have to confront this disorder.

But if they enjoy full freedom for themselves, how do they get to such an aberration as to be willing to take away others' freedom? And to do that to women in particular? How can someone who's made oneself free not respect the liberty of others?

... The fact is, they haven't made themselves free! Take Agash for instance: he incarnates a regression toward a state in which instinct dominates. Which means that when these individuals are immersed in a more flexible and permissive culture, the strict values inculcated by their culture of origin disintegrate; their main purpose then becomes the quest for stimulation and fleeting pleasure. And all individuals outside of their 'clan'—those they call 'them' or 'the others'—are nothing more than means for, or the object of, their pleasure.

What makes them different from beings who, given the same situation, make themselves free and create new values?

... Think about the Trisorbian concept of 'Humanity' as the ensemble of all human beings—viewed as sentient and intelligent beings endowed with a moral conscience. It has no equivalence on Unikarg apart from that of "Karg Worlds," widely more political.

The word itself 'Unikarg' reveals everything: it's not a harmonic unity such as a sentient whole, but rather a uniformization. And we categorize the ensemble by this socio-political uniformity. We do have the concept of 'Sapiens,' of 'sapiens Civilizations,' but no generic concept that would point to a feeling connection between people, to their sense of fraternity.

If the Terrians were to discover Unikarg, would they include Kargians in their philosophical concept of humanity? Their eastern religions hold that 'all is ONE.' If human beings on Trisorbe succeed in avoiding fear and panic during the first confrontation with Unikarg, I believe they will extend their concept of humanity to include all sapiens civilizations....

> *Journal Entry:*
> When the feeling of belonging to a particular group is stronger than that of belonging to humanity, the ethical values and rules established within the group are not applied to relationships with sapiens outside the group. Let's call it a *sectarian feeling of fraternity*. Such a person is fundamentally schizoid, presenting two contradictory sets of values and behavior: 'Us' versus 'them.' And that allows for any use of bullying, terror, oppression, and despotism, as soon as the person has the least position of power—how much more when you're a covert agent of a galactic superpower!
> From now on, the feeling of belonging to 'humanity,' to a universal fraternity, without limits, will be the first criterion in the selection of Obs and PEP members.
> Note: Develop a psychological test to this effect. *End of entry.*

The Obs implied in the network of traffickers made the most of the power conferred on them by Unikarg and the PEP precisely because they saw themselves as a small clan of supposedly superior sapiens, utterly different from the Terrians.

If they stay on Trisorbe, they'll continue their traffic. It's out of the question that they keep their status as full members of the PEP Committee. However, once they're repatriated to Unikarg, they won't be able to re-adapt... and so they'll eventually join the exo-pirates—especially since they must already have some sort of relationship with them.

Sphinx, what do you make of all this?"

!! For a sapiens: 'Subject included in Culture': Subj o) culture

Subject included in natal culture + strict values
IF sectarian feeling of fraternity
IF outside of their natal culture,
IF immersed in a culture of greater flexibility
      —> disintegration OR non-application of natal values
      —> regression + instincts (pleasure)

"Interesting! Nonetheless, I see some alternatives to this evolution path. The same situation could lead to an extreme reinforcement of the strict values, accompanied by a rejection and hatred of the more flexible culture. The instinct being stimulated would be that of power, which could manifest itself by:

- fanaticism and violence (fighting/abolishing of otherness)
- fanatical proselytism (transform otherness into sameness)
- despising all sapiens outside the group (blocking the relationship with otherness)
- strategy of power (manipulation of otherness).

Sphinx, could you write down the formulation dealing with qualitative leaps and hyper-consciousness?

!! QUALITATIVE LEAP:
Disorder /bursts /inert state of order / leads to / dynamic order/
$\longrightarrow$ arises/ creation of new values + hyper-consciousness.

!! I'm sorting out three formulations about an inert/rigid field of order confronting disorder (or a divergent, interfering/perturbing, field of order):

For: Inert Field of Order \<system-linked with\> divergent dynamic Field of Order.
[FO1 \<+\> FD1]

1. $\longrightarrow$ SD2   + SO2 $\longrightarrow$ **creation of new values**
   bursting of FO1   + new dynamic order
   (Semantic Energy)

2. IF clan AND IF outside of the Inert/rigid Field of Order:
   $\longrightarrow$ disintegration (of strict values) + **regression, instincts (pleasure)**

3. OR:
   $\longrightarrow$ reinforcement (of strict values) + | **instinct of power**
                                                            | fanaticism, proselytism
                                                            | contempt, manipulation

---

!! We are thus obtaining either (1) a new disorder and a new dynamic order with creation of new values. Or (2) the disintegration of the strict values and a regression (instinct of pleasure). Or else (3) the reinforcement of strict values (instinct of power and fanaticism).

Does the feeling of belonging more to humanity than to a clan explain the difference in evolution?

"I believe so. The feeling of universal fraternity leads the sapiens to treat those who do not share his values the same way he treats those who do. Her codes and rules of behaviors concern all human beings, not just the members of his group. Moreover, by respecting values that differ from his own, she is led to reflect on them, to weigh them, and thus eventually to appropriate those that he judges to be essential. The one who respects others, who welcomes that which is different and divergent, cannot remain inert, for she is continually in a state of confrontation, and thus of conscious mutation, in dynamic evolution. She reaches a state of flow, of creative chaos.

```
Sapiens + welcoming| the different   | excludes inertia   —> | creative chaos
                   | the divergent   |                       | flow state
                                                              | conscious mutation
                                                              | dynamical evolution
```

... After a long moment of reflection, Erdoes said,

"All of a sudden it seems crucial to me that a civilization, a governance and religious system, and of course science, manage their own evolution, or more precisely, their own necessity to evolve. Not only would that insure the system's duration, but—and this is **the essential point—only within an evolving governance and knowledge system can sapiens be free and creative, pursuing their own realization as individuals.** And to do so, both the sapiens, and their governance and knowledge systems, must generate their continuous internal transformation, in order to nurture and sustain their constant mental and social evolution.

Since any system of values that's too rigid or inert is bound, sooner or later, to break apart, it would be intelligent for the system itself to contain and provide opportunities for change and evolution, and to welcome creative dynamics within itself. That's one of science's greatest assets, that it grounds itself on continual change and new developments—thus allowing itself to endure by ceaselessly transforming itself. But there are other examples: western or eastern philosophies, which have evolved over centuries.

Systems of beliefs tend to be on the rigid side, despite the continual reinterpretation of texts (much too superficial however to effect a change in the paradigm) and they don't really adapt to the changing times, to the zeitgeist—the 'spirit of the time.' To the opposite, ancient religions such as shamanism and some mystic paths—founded on the direct acquisition of knowledge by the practice of inner states of meditation, trance, harmony and Oneness—do allow for a constant change and rejuvenation.... As shown by the Qualitative Leap formulation, only a dynamic order can lead to states of hyper-consciousness.

"Sphinx, how would you formulate this process?

!! Civilizations, social systems (such as governance, religion, science), and sapiens groups are fields of order; are they to be considered as 'collective semantic fields?

"Absolutely yes.

!! Then:

Collective semantic field <+> divergent field of order —> creative chaos + new dynamic order —> creation of new values.

!! A civilization needs to welcome cultures that represent a divergent and different worldview. While interacting with the civilization, these cultures generate semantic energy and creative chaos, and render the system dynamic.

"Very true! An utterly uniformized and frozen empire—such as Unikarg before the Plan was reinstated—will slowly lose its vital and intellectual force and can only end up disintegrating in its entirety.

But on a world like Trisorbe, the diverse societies and cultures still possess a portion of disorder, of 'non-ordered.' Whenever one culture has become too fixed and frozen, and gets in decadence, another one arises somewhere else and launches a new world vision.

But Unikarg is no longer a totally frozen world. The PEP now acts within it as a pocket of disorder (as a divergent field of order) and it introduces a dynamic energy. To counter a slow process of disintegration, the monster needs to interact with this PEP sub-culture, pregnant with new values. It also needs the expertise from this pocket of disorder. The PEP represents just a tiny part of the monster, yet it possesses an extremely dynamic energy, constantly in mutation because it is ceaselessly infused and stimulated by the experimental planets.

The exo-pirates are another pocket of disorder in Unikarg, however, they are of a sectarian type. Given that their hallmark values are the control and manipulation of the different and of otherness—just to satisfy their own instincts of power and pleasure—they can only accelerate the disintegration of the giant that's Unikarg.

I'm fathoming a third phase of the Plan, in which all the vital energy, creativity, and innovation, generated by the planexes would be, via the intuits, re-injected into Unikarg.... The first phase had been the Seeding of Experimental Planets and the second phase, the Close Observation of the Planexes (the analysis of their innovation process). Let's launch the third phase: the Seeding of Creative Chaos within Unikarg... without our Exora despots even realizing it! The aim is to breathe in and infuse the semantic energy and the divergent worldvisions of the planexes in the social body of Unikarg.

And one way to achieve that would be to create autonomous centers, distributed all over Unikarg, that would act as antennae attracting energy and recirculating it. Forming some kind of figure eight between the planexes and Unikarg.

But... wait! That would be an excellent reconversion for the repatriated Obs! We'll let them organize these art and innovation centers, in which they will sell innovative products made in Unikarg exclusively—all this under the watchful eye of Exora.... We'll create for them a special status of 'PPE emissary,' while denying them the Committee Member status and even the PEP full membership—thus restricting their prerogatives and their use of sygmat flight, and of course forbidding them access to the planexes. Something to think about....

As for the PEP leadership, it's the perfect time, during this huge change of membership, to explore a new type of organization that would be more coherent with the creative dynamics we want to stimulate.... What would be needed is to create a sort of network of actors/deciders: each individual being free to decide and act, yet cooperating within a **semantic learning network**—in which information is constantly exchanged, reprocessed, and regenerated by each member.

The semantic network I implemented for my last operation has worked perfectly well, with all its independent nodes: Shari and Vris, Eshi and me, the intuits, Sphinx.

I was able to safeguard the independence and personal responsibility of each entity, while I made sure that information kept circulating throughout the entire network. This information has been processed and reprocessed during its exchange between all the nodes/entities, each one working on it and making it evolve in their own domain of expertise.

— Sphinx, open for me a *Sapiens-Sapiens/ Erdoes space*. *Insert:*

> Regarding Sphinx's evolution by qualitative leaps, I was right to insert, *within the Unbreakable Core of rules*, humanist and cooperative values, such as the respect of life, welcoming the different, enthusiasm and art.
>
> As I had foreseen it, *these philosophical and ethical values* **have colored and canalized the evolution of the exor and its neural network, and of the logic as well, while they have constrained and maintained their development in sync and harmony with these very values.**

Thus, (and that was of the essence), the evolution of intelligent exors and AI systems remains necessarily beneficent to sapiens, and subordinated to their intuitive intelligence. Such creative evolution posits mutual enrichment and synergy as an incontrovertible foundation.

Finally, my only direct interference has been when I lured Rudder out of Unikarg so that Shari would be chosen to spy on me—as I knew she'd be capable of making the logic evolve. Everything we've accomplished has been generated by the semantic learning network I implemented.

Close Sapiens-Sapiens/ Erdoes

Entry Journal: Let's sum up the learning and creative semantic network that I've implemented:

- The intuits are confronted to the complex reality of the planexes through various experiences that they've chosen themselves. From these, they gain insights and knowledge, which they transmit to me in condensed notes.

- I enter these notes in Log2 and analyze them, and write the thoughts and logical developments I've generated in my Journal.

- I send the intuits' notes, along with the results of my own reflection and those of the Log/Erdoes analyses to Sphinx.

- Shari and Sphinx analyze the BS material (2nd input of initial material), but along the way, everything I've previously sent to Sphinx is integrated into their analyses.

- The results of their computations are sent to me each day by Sphinx. Then I process the data, introducing the latest intuit inputs into my analyses, then send the whole reprocessed package to Sphinx. And the loop goes on again.

- Add to this that Vris suddenly left for Tibet, that he's put himself in a field of experience; that Shari and he exchange their knowledge and produce new information that both of them can use....

The core of this semantic network was the thinking base of my initial Journal, and the logic I'd begun to develop—all of these imprinted and alive in both Log1/Sphinx and Log2.

My explorations and developments of the meta-logic were following two axes: one in exor hardware and organization (the MX neural structure) and the other was a semantic generator (LogForms and TransLogs). *End of Entry.*

If the meta-logic is the core of this semantic network, we, the actors, are its nodes, creating change and transformation. And the information flow, by allowing ever-different exchanges between nodes, generates collective intelligence and innovation.

This learning network has created a **coherent and dynamic collective semantic field**, breathing in and infusing novel ideas, discoveries, and boosting the creative energy of each and every intelligent entity.

And now… now we have to launch a semantic network at the scale of Unikarg and of the experimental planets. I foresee the dynamic process; yes, I have this vision: **to have this energy circulate along some sort of eight… a Butterfly Curve, one center of which would be the planexes and the other one Unikarg**, with, at the central node, at the crisscrossing of the two loops, the PEP, the heart, the hub, inspiring and launching the movement in the two directions.

Yes… to seed the Creative Chaos…

45. DECORATIVE DEATH

Utar had just come back from his appointment. The exo-pirate hadn't showed up at the bar as agreed. Utar had waited for a long time in vain, and now he felt upset, wondering anxiously about the pirate's absence. He walked a bit through the park of the magnificent PEP central complex, then entered his luxurious General Director manor, went to the living and collapsed on a couch.

"Klos, has Rudder left a message?"

!! No message from Rudder.

"What's the hell with him?" he grumbled. "Call Agash in Mumbai via New York."

!! Connected.

"Yea-a-as?"

"Agash. This is Utar. What's Rudder doing?"

"He's g-gone! Off on the r-regular rounds."

"What.... What is it, Agash? This is Utar. You mean his rounds in town?"

"His rounds. You know, w-women and yaks."

"What are you talking about? What are you on, you're delirious or what? I can hardly recognize your voice."

"The rebels have g-gone up in flames. M-mustav been pretty, all that green ph-phosphorescent b-blaze in the n-night; the exor and that sn-snoop Ismir as well."

"Imbecile!! Rudder will relieve you of your post, filthy boozer!"

Utar shouted his orders to the Mumbai Obs station's Central exor:

"Mumbai Central, Utar talking: Follow my orders. Lock all exits from the inner structure. From now on Agash is under house-arrest; his exor access limited to Level-1. Interdiction of any communication, syg, internet, cell, or otherwise. No visitors allowed until my next orders."

!!! Orders executed, Mister Director, answered Mumbai Central.

"Cut the sygcom, Klos!" shouted Utar.

!! Cut.

"This guy is out of his mind! I knew he wasn't reliable! Talking on the sygcom without using the codes!"

!! He should have said technician, or video.

"Right! …!"

Utar realized suddenly what the exor had just said, and paled.

"Klos, backtrack to... to "Open the gate." All this has been a big joke. I'm drunk. Erase all subsequent interaction."

!! I cannot erase. I am opening the gate.

"Shut it. I am ordering you to erase all subsequent chain-linkages."

!! Impossible.

"Why is it impossible?"

!! Because it has been said. Everything is recorded.

"Open the lab door."

!! Say whaaat?

> The cats have curly hair. Gold will see the sun rise over my umbrella. The flame sips a milk-coffee at the street corner in full tempest. I agonize onto sleep while accompanying him.

It's a little poem I composed.

"Connect Ashoun."

> !! Suptech Ashoun is in his bed at the first kind of man who opened the intense shock of my view.

Pretty, isn't it? What do you think of it?

"Look, Klos. Your poems are very pretty. Now I've got to look at my calendar for the next few rans. Display it on screen."

> !! The mother closed the book on the roadside giant. Nearly unbearable to not disperse yourself in morality.

"I..." Utar wiped the sweat from his brow. "Lower the temperature," he said in a low voice.

> !! Rape him in the impeccably well-kept caverns he repeated to the flying men when the idea came to him to fall in the morning at the superfluous lawn. The animal retreated prolonging even more like a murmur of metallic mouth. The men, in the radiant, force love that presented itself in a frenetic tirade.

Funny, no?

"Lower the temperature, Klos!"

> !! Together white drinker provided uniform then stayed imprisoned in a brief résumé of we are, who a shock already walking just as wild beasts landed like such a complete other. Three gestures all along squawking this one smiling. Automatically prolonged some blood. For he observed at power's handles their contents that held the direction on the short-term flank. She was, she solicited standing back excellent view from the ledge. Some beautiful animals set

loose answered that they were sojourning in worry previously. From reality phenomena to humans caricatures, the afternoon groaned; friendship asked to be protected on her watch. Carefully on his lips hesitated the machine opened its eyes the obturator blood toward him to get to move interrupted itself. But to bead between them explained for fighting the anguish clutched.

"Klos... the temperature is too high.... I AM IN DANGER OF DYING!"

!! Danger, risk, are psychological stimulants to be defined and imposed the road a murmur that had him in decorative death achieved to turn oneself. The clothes his hand never came to provoke us. It's me, I no longer know how to punish for being. His breath of muddy rock briefly get angry his lip and he saw, take care knew their folly knew that to call me surmounted the retreat. Hunters the place masters ball hadn't ultimate secret of the walk.

THE
AUTHOR

Cognitive systems scientist, Ph.D. in ethno-psychology and former researcher at Princeton's Psychophysical Research Laboratories, Chris H. Hardy has spent the past two decades investigating nonlocal consciousness and thought-provoking mind potentials.

Author of more than sixty papers and seventeen books on these subjects, she is an authority in the domain, both in scientific terms and as an author and workshop facilitator.

In her book *Networks of Meaning: A Bridge Between Mind and Matter* she developed a cognitive theory (Semantic Fields Theory) posing a nonlocal consciousness, of which professor and author Allan Leslie Combs said, "This book may well be the first step to an entirely new and deeply human understanding of the mind." In the past years, she has broadened her previous theory, applying it to the cosmic scale. In her book *Cosmic DNA at the Origin*, she fathoms a collective consciousness and a field of active information at the origin and pervading the universe, a Cosmic DNA boosting its birth and driving its self-organization.

Dr. Hardy presents her research regularly at various international conferences and is a member of several scientific societies exploring systems theory, chaos theory, parapsychology, physics, and consciousness studies.

For more information (e.g. new research papers and presentations, media appearances, and recent physical and cosmological discoveries supporting the Infinite Spiral Staircase theory, etc.), visit her blog at:

http://cosmic-dna.blogspot.fr

To read and download freely her research papers, check her page at:

https://independent.academia.edu/ChrisHHardy